How to be a Tarot Detective

How to be a Tarot Detective

Revised Edition

Rev. Vikki Anderson

Copyright © 2015 by Rev. Vikki Anderson.

ISBN:	Hardcover	978-1-5035-2913-7
	Softcover	978-1-5035-2912-0
	eBook	978-1-5035-2911-3

All rights reserved. No part of this book may be reproduced or transmitted in any form or by any means, electronic or mechanical, including photocopying, recording, or by any information storage and retrieval system, without permission in writing from the copyright owner.

Illustrations from the Rider-Waite Tarot Deck® reproduced by permission of U.S. Games Systems, Inc., Stamford, CT 06902 USA. Copyright ©1971 by U.S. Games Systems, Inc. Further reproduction prohibited. The Rider-Waite Tarot Deck® is a registered trademark of U.S. Games Systems, Inc.

Any people depicted in stock imagery provided by Thinkstock are models, and such images are being used for illustrative purposes only.
Certain stock imagery © Thinkstock.

Print information available on the last page.

Rev. date: 03/12/2015

To order additional copies of this book, contact:
Xlibris
1-888-795-4274
www.Xlibris.com
Orders@Xlibris.com
546374

DEDICATION

THIS BOOK IS dedicated to my mother, Agnes Rose Delaney Ciervo, whom I never understood as a child, but later emulated as an adult.

She unconditionally loved her husband, Sam; her children, Vikki, Sam and Rose, and her grandchildren Cailin, Keri, Clare and Emily and her grandsons Quinn and Clark. Mom most especially loved her great grandson, Brayden and although she will not be around to watch him grow up or meet her new great granddaughter, McKayla, we know she is looking down on them, protecting and guiding them to a positive, bright future. Just as Mom was always present and supportive through life, she continues to be present since her passing. She will always be a part of us and we will *always* keep her alive in our hearts.

We love you, Mom. We will all be with you one day, so keep the light on for us and get the macaroni, sauce, and meatballs ready for dinner. I am especially looking forward to having my birthday "ice box cake" again.

We miss you.

SPECIAL ACKNOWLEDGEMENTS

I WANT TO EXTEND a very special thank you to my brother, Sam Ciervo, who did the final review of this book. I was able to take advantage of his 32 years' experience as an English teacher in the NJ private and public school systems to make this book what I always wanted it to be. My brother has always a God-send to me by helping me with many chores and projects around the house as well as with his good advice, but now he is helping me beyond my dreams. Thank you, Sam, for being the best brother in the world! You will always be my favorite brother.

Sam Ciervo is a retired high school English teacher who is the proud father of Clare and Emily Ciervo and the husband of Joanne. He currently resides in Montclair, NJ.

I would like to send a big hug and thank you to my very good friend, Patricia Scillia, who helped with the preliminary editing of this book. We are spiritual sisters; she has helped me finish this book faster than I could have on my own. As she said, "A fresh set of eyes is what you need," and indeed I did. You have been such a blessing in my life, Patricia! Thank you so much for your enlightenment, hard work and beautiful spirit. Peace be with you always. Blessed be.

PATRICIA SCILLIA, M.Ed., L.P.C., is a teacher, counselor, a photographer of natural scenic settings and a designer of 'one-of a-kind" jewelry creations. She has received national recognition for her published photograph, "The Promise". Her art is exhibited in art shows, psychic and metaphysical fairs, bookstores and local spas and salons. Ms. Scillia also received local recognition for her photograph, "In Bloom". She teaches and counsels adults in transition and is a member of Salute to Women in the Arts and a Graduate and Advisory Board Member of "Using the Arts in Prevention" Program at Rutgers University.

<u>Cover Artwork by SK Art and Design</u>.

I would like to add a great big thank you to my cousin, Steve Kaminsky, who designed the cover for me and was very patient as I kept rearranging the order of the cards. Steve is an extremely talented graphic designer. He may be contacted at <u>sek2344@aol.com</u> if anyone is interested in a great Graphic Design Artist.

ACKNOWLEDGEMENTS

THANK YOU TO Linda Marks, my dearest friend, who has been relentlessly pestering me to finish this book since the original version came out in 2001. You were right; all I had to do was sit down and edit a little each and every day. Thank you so much for your continued nudging and friendship. It still is a bigger job than you could ever imagine. I don't want to tell you when I am editing my Feng Shui book because all this fuss will start all over again!

I must mention my good friend, Robert Vecchio, former owner of Practical Magick 2, who helped me with the interpretations of candle magick. Blessings to you, Robert, in your new adventures in life. To make an appointment for a reading with Robert, email him at pmagick2@gmail.com.

Thank you to www.blessedbegarden.com. They were kind enough to share some of their crystal descriptions with me to add to my own. Blessed Be Garden is a Metaphysical Store established 10/31/13. Formed by two practicing witches, Andrea & Krista welcome the opportunity to earn your trust. It offers the convenience of one stop shopping with a variety of Pagan, Wiccan, and Witchcraft, Occult, Metaphysical and spiritual supplies. Send Andrea and Krista an email for more additional information about their services at info@blessedbegarden.com.

And last but not least, a thank you to all of my students, clients, family and friends who have been encouraging me to finish this book. It is not easy to write a teaching text, everything has to be just right, and now I think I finally got it! Thanks for your undying support and love. I hope you enjoy it and learn how to read the tarot easily and accurately.

TABLE OF CONTENTS

Dedication v

Special Acknowledgements..vi

Acknowledgements...ix

Foreword...1

Introduction...4

Learning The Tarot..6

Background...12

General Information 16

Major Arcana Cards And Roman Numerals............21

Do Whatever Feels Right...23

The Major Arcana: Spiritual Secrets.......................28

Numerology...29

Karmic Lessons Through Tarot And Numerology.....30

The Minor Arcana: Mundane Secrets 31

The Four Suits 34

Court Cards..40

Dos And Don'ts 45

Notes From A Tarot Sage 46

Crystals..59

Healing Crystal Meanings 60

Color Interpretations...76

Preparing The Cards..84

Interpreting The Cards..85

The Four Overviews...85

Questions To Ask...90

Symbology 95

Timing Of Events 114

Totally Tarot Timing Method 115

Traditional Timing Methods.................................. 115

Major Arcana Interpretations 118
Minor Arcana Interpretations...................................... 175
    Wands 176
    Pentacles...217
    Swords...248
    Cups 279

Reading The Cards 310
Court Cards 319
Types Of Spreads 322
    Celtic Cross Spread 322
    Celtic Cross Diagram 324
    Astrology Spread 325
    Astrology Spread Diagram......................................329
    Year-Ahead Spread...330
    Year-Ahead Spread Diagram...................................332
    Your Own Spread...333
    Simple Cross Spread And Diagram..........................334
    Name Spread..335
    One Card Spread..336
    Yes/No Ace Spread 336
    Yes/No Spread With Aces 338
    Yes/No Spread Reversed - Upright............................338
    Yes/No Reverse-Upright Spread...............................339
    Yes/No Spread Major And Minor Arcana 339
    Birthday Spread..341
    Three Card Spread 341
    Past, Present And Future Spread..............................343

Daily Cards... 344
Quick Reference Section The Major Arcana.................... 346
The Minor Arcana 353
    Wands – Fire 354
    Pentacles – Earth 357
    Swords - Air 360
    Cups - Water 364

Astrological House Interpretations	368
Astrological Sun Signs	369
Planets	375
Positive And Negative Signs	380
Glossary	381
Last Thoughts	388
Author's Biography	391
References	395

FOREWORD

THE FIRST VERSION of this book which is out of print was entitled, "Totally Tarot: How to Be a Tarot Detective." It was dedicated to the spreading of love and light to the people who were ready to receive the knowledge contained within. This book was written to give everyone *more* spiritual and karmic lesson knowledge. With these tools, Readers can do more accurate and detailed readings. This book combines the first book for those who have never read it and another part of this book includes new insights and information that was not included in the original.

Sacred Tarot (not tarot or oracle cards that children play as party games) is not a game. It is a method and modality of finding out about family, friends, career paths, health issues, opportunities, guidance, direction, your life and the future. It is a way to find answers to those questions in life when you are unsure about your path and the choices that have to be made which are important to whoever is involved in making a decision.

Tarot can be taught one way and interpreted another way by each Reader. It is not magic and your understanding of the truth of the cards certainly changes with use. Remember the old saying, "Your understanding of the truth changes, but the truth always remains the same." Your interpretations become more in-depth, more accurate and then evolve into other spiritual interpretations or added insight that you get each and every time you use the cards. This is why I had to write a revised version of this book. I have gotten much more insight on the cards and wanted to share the additional information I have received throughout the years. I have always taught the cards with a bent towards astrology and numerology so that you will get multi-dimensional meanings from the reading because three separate modalities are involved. I think this is the only way to use the tarot.

The intricacies are crucial. It is very important to read everything you can get your hands on. It is very important to talk to others who read tarot and see if they will give you some guidance as well. You will eventually be guided by your own guardian angels or spirit guides (or whomever you believe in and contact) to tell the person for whom you are doing the reading (who is referred to as the Querent, Significator or Sitter) everything that they are supposed to know. However, we must filter the information. All of us get the information differently and we need to find our comfort zone in explaining this information to the best of our ability in the most positive way possible. Some students say they do not feel as if they are getting spiritual insight or connections to the spiritual realm (or Astral Plane or Akashic Hall of Records); this is probably true if you are a beginner. Remember, you may not know where the words you are saying come from. You may start out reading the practiced and learned meaning of the card and then go off on a tangent about something completely different. Where did that information come from? Most likely, it is information that was supposed to be shared with your Querent. If you have the intent of sharing this sacred knowledge for the Querent's best interest, then nothing you tell the Sitter is incorrect and will be for his or her best interest. It will all have a special meaning to them even if, at times, you may not understand it. Just trust that they will understand the knowledge you have imparted to them and let it go at that.

How to Be a Tarot Detective started out as notes that I used in weekly tarot classes at various libraries, adult education courses, private and group lessons and at lectures for groups and organizations. I had always wanted to write a book, and my students would laugh and say, "You have enough handouts to make a book! Why not put them together and make one?" They were right. So, I organized a book of notes and came up with my first tarot book entitled, "Totally Tarot: How to Be a Tarot Detective," which was published in 2001. It was published by a wonderful but small publishing house in Florida and was not marketed well so I did not sell a great deal of them. That first book is out of print and I had recently found two last copies on Amazon.com at a price of $548 each! Now I am sorry that I gave boxes of them away to friends and metaphysical groups years ago. I could have been rich in my retirement years by now!

I always had my book available at lectures and expositions and I also did a few book signings, but at the end of the day, I think my students were the only ones who benefitted from the guided knowledge. With that in mind, I combined the first book with this updated and revised edition because I was not sure if anyone who purchased this book would have enough background on the way I taught tarot to have this new book make sense. This second book is called, "How to be a Tarot Detective," Revised Edition. I have revised the meanings of the cards somewhat throughout the years and karmic lessons were part of the whole picture. So in essence, you are reading my first and second books for the price of one. What a bargain!

This is a beginner and intermediate workbook detailing all of the necessary steps to make reading the tarot a reliable and helpful tool in guiding your decisions and life path. But now, many years later, it has morphed into the second part of the journey including new updated information on what the cards mean and how to gain insight into your every day karmic lessons as well as your life-long spiritual karmic lessons by using numerology and figuring out your birth path number. I have added a separate meaning for* teenagers section as well as a brief affirmation or meditation with each card. I'm sure you will find it meaningful in your quest to be a terrific tarot Reader.

I frequently do lectures on Karmic Lessons through Tarot and Numerology; this information is also included in this book. Once someone knows their karmic lessons, everything in their life makes sense. People confess to me, "Oh, that's why I always have problems with money," or "I knew there must have been some karmic issue with relationships because they never work for me, but now I know why." There are so many revelations towards handling karmic lessons that people actually make better choices in their future because they know that if they do not handle the issues in this life time, it will be thrust upon them again in the next and the next life, etc., until they successfully handle the issue. Handle your issues now so you will be free of the "negative or emotional" experiences you constantly attract and have to deal with on a daily basis. Release, relax and send love and light to everyone as well as the universe. Then, let go.

Purchase a Rider-Waite deck so you can follow along with each of the seventy-eight cards and their explanations more easily. It is the original Rider-Waite deck which has card of The Magician on the outer box. There are four Rider-Waite decks and some have different coloring in them which may throw off your reading if you are not familiar with this deck. You may always buy additional decks later on to enhance your readings. I personally use all of the decks now and can still use a great deal of my interpretations in this book to make the cards' images come alive. But as a beginner or an advanced Reader in the old, traditional way of reading the cards, please take a little time to learn the Totally Tarot Method. It is easier and makes more sense than the older method. It is also the best way to get the most extraordinary reading you will ever give to others or yourself.

INTRODUCTION

I HAVE FOUND TAROT to be a useful tool in aiding people in conflict and in general who are looking for answers to life's issues and concerns. In the forty-two years that I have been reading and teaching tarot as well as many other metaphysical modalities, I have only had one person who regularly came to me each year around his birthday simply to get an update on his life for the upcoming year. This is quite rare; he just wanted to know what positive opportunities he should expect. Usually people who contact me are attracted to my energy because I am an outstanding listener and very good in handling emotional issues. People who are in crisis are also attracted to my energy as well as those who want me to help them make their decisions. This is something I would never do since decisions lead to your path and your future, so a competent and ethical tarot Reader would give options and choices to any question you may have but then ultimately you must decide on your next course of action.

If people were not in crisis, there would be no need for tarot guidance or direction. Do not get me wrong, there are people who just want to know what is coming up and what decisions have to be made because they want to take control of their lives or handle the responsibilities dropped in their laps. But more than not, there are people who need to know when they are getting married, if they should stay married, if they should have an affair, if they should stay in an affair, have more children, have any children, should they leave their job, or dump the married man they had been dating for five years, behind a husband's back (Yes, this also happens to women as well). These may seem like ridiculous questions to seek advice about, but to the person (Sitter, Querent, or Significator) seeking the advice and help, these issues are important. They would not be seeking advice if they considered it to be an easy road ahead.

When people are desperate, they seek answers from those who can help them get through the obstacles and challenges or at the very least, provide some insight into the situation which could lead them into making better decisions. They need the hope and positive alternatives Tarot Readers provide. Some need to be referred to a healthcare professional, whether for therapy or medication. Tarot must not be used as a substitute for medical attention. Some clients had started to come to me on a weekly basis, and when I asked why they were coming for advice so frequently, they said, they had left their therapist or psychiatrist. When I questioned them further about why they took such action, they usually said something like, "When I go to therapy, my therapist asks me what I think. If I knew what I thought, I wouldn't need therapy. When I come here, you give me options and choices for my future. I feel more in control and more secure." This is when you would tell them that tarot is not a substitute for therapy, but perhaps an adjunct to their medical care. Then you have others who come for readings so that they do not have to go to a doctor. For instance, one might ask if their health is okay. Or someone might ask if his or her high blood pressure will level out over the next few weeks or months. An ethical and seasoned tarot Reader would also suggest that they consult a healthcare professional, if they thought it is needed, and disclose the additional advice the client may need from the card pulled in the reading.

I do feel that many people just need someone to listen to their problems and be assured that everything will be all right. I also think that because they are emotionally involved or invested in a particular situation, it is hard for them to make a logical decision. As an unbiased Reader, you can give insight and an unemotional or logical approach to resolving their problems or challenges. Remember, every situation has a solution. Perhaps you just haven't discovered it yet.

Knowing the energy of the cards and the energy of the person is very important. As a tarot Reader or consultant, I help them make many decisions to move their lives forward in a very positive way. It also helps to know astrology since I always ask my client or student for their astrological sign. Once I find out the information I was seeking, I know how to speak to them so that they will easily understand the information I present them. There was only one time that I asked someone for her sun sign and the client would not give it to me. In that instance, I felt she was a negative or feminine sign and treated her as such. (I found out later that she was a Virgo . . . need I say more?). If you do not know astrology, I would suggest treating a person who would not give you his or her sun sign for whatever reason as a wounded child or someone with a broken heart. Speak clearly, concisely and compassionately to them and your message will be received and quickly understood.

You may check out the Sun Sign Descriptions in the back of the book so you can familiarize yourself with some of the signs and learn how to talk to these clients. Otherwise, Linda Goodman's *Sun Signs* is the perfect book on astrological descriptions to help you familiarize yourself with each of the twelve sun signs on the ecliptic.

LEARNING THE TAROT

STUDYING TAROT HAS always been a fun and relaxing pastime for me. As I read the many books available on the subject throughout the years, it was always a mystery to me that all the tarot books had different meanings for the cards. The "student" had to compile information from various sources to eventually devise a "general" meaning of her own choosing for each card. There was just too much information available on the subject and too many conflicting books and nearly over one thousand decks to choose from! Each deck has its own book of meanings, so you really have to pick one or two decks and become an expert on them. As I had previously said, this book will be using the Rider-Waite deck. You certainly may buy any other deck you choose; however, I am not sure all of the meanings for this deck would be practical for any other deck.

Also, some people buy tarot decks because they are drawn to them whether they are spiritual, Native American, medicine, animal, witch, fantasy, fairy, Halloween, or a million other topics for the particular deck. Be careful not to collect too many as they will wind up in a drawer and you will do nothing with them. The information in these decks is very deep and it would overwhelm you if you thought you would learn all of the decks purchased.

With practice and patience, one learns to pick up on the overall vibrations of the cards. Each reading is a totally different experience, even if you place the exact same cards in a year ahead spread for two totally different people! I doubt this would ever happen; however, if it did, you would feel different vibrations. You would also receive different messages. Even if the messages do not make much sense at the time, I usually share the messages I receive. It usually means something quite important to the client. If it does not mean anything to them at the time, tell them to just think about it. More often than not, the client or student would call within a week or so and tell you why that information was important to them. Trust your intuition. If you are unsure about the message, you can always say something like, "I am getting (whatever the information is . . .). Does this mean anything to you?" If they say yes, all is good. If they say no, then you can say, "Well, let's go through all the other cards and see if it will make additional sense."

People have asked, "Where do the messages come from?" What an interesting yet poignant question. In my readings, my messages come from my guardian angel with whom I have been in contact and working with since I was fourteen years old. Others may tune into the Universe or Spirit Guides, God and Goddess, The Source, The One, The All, Spirit, The Angels, The Alpha and Omega, Universal Energy, the Akashic Hall of Records or whatever name(s) you put to the Creator of the Universe. Everyone attracts the information they need to give to the one who is asking for guidance. With time, practice, patience and study, you will not question where your insight is coming from.

I was asked by a student, "How do I know I am not getting the information from evil forces?" This too is a great question. First of all, I asked her if she considered herself to be evil. She replied, "Definitely not." So I responded, "Then why would you feel that your information would be coming from an evil source? Why would you be attracting something so negative if you are positive? Opposites repel." It was the Old Catholic guilt showing up again. She said, "The Bible says . . ." I stopped her right there.

I consider myself very spiritual and to be a liberated Catholic. I do believe that the Bible is the greatest piece of literature and history in the entire world. By studying the history of religion and the Bible, one realizes that so much was changed, left out, and what we know today in its many versions of the Bible, has changed so much from the original for control of the masses, for political reasons and just because the "powers that be" at the time deemed it necessary to change. The Bible deleted at least forty-eight gospels and psalms to make all Christians conform to a specific doctrine. It was mind blowing to find out that there were over two thousand different versions of the Christian faith in the first two and a half centuries of Christianity.

Did you know at the Council of Nicaea in 325 AD in present day Turkey was made up of bishops who made it their job to decide what was going to be in the canon and what was not going to be put into this newly revised Bible? They deleted many gospels and only left those of Mark, Matthew, Luke and John because it conformed with what they wanted to convey to their flocks. Also left out of the Bible was the Dead Sea Scrolls which are the doctrines of the Gnostics or Essemes, a metaphysical and spiritual group of followers; Jesus Christ was a member of this spiritual community of worshippers. Their gospels were left out of the Bible because their beliefs were that God and Goddess was within and that in reality we did not need priests to absolve us of our sins or bless us. God and Goddess and Jesus dwelled in everyone's heart. You can see why this information or theology did not go over well with the clergy of the time.

This council also decided what was righteous and what was considered a sin. As previously said, forty-eight gospels were deleted from the Catholic Bible including the Gospel of Mary Magdalene and The Gospel of Thomas. Biblical scholars now believe that Mary Magdalene was Jesus' wife and not a prostitute as was reported in the early Church; I believe they changed her status in the 1960s to reflect that. Women were not considered important in the days of old and to have Mary Magdalene's gospels in the Bible was unthinkable. A woman who can think? What would be next, a woman who could be a disciple? Just something to think about, especially when you consider that the Church has had its own agenda and never let their congregations know what was going on behind closed doors. Of course, this still continues today.

I am not here to debate Catholicism, the Christian religion or infer that I do not believe in Christianity; I do consider myself a

Liberated Catholic or some people say, a Recovering Catholic. I know the process of being a Catholic, but do not abide by many of the rigid rules concerning our rights regarding conception and limiting gay rights to name a few; however currently, Pope Francis, is making great strides in many positive directions and I am forever hopeful that Christianity will blossom on some level.

I do want people to realize that one of the reasons that the Bible condemns witchcraft (now I'm a witch too according to many because I teach tarot!) is because people from the olden times had little money, if any, and many were going to see astrologers and Tarot Readers instead of the Church for advice and guidance. The Church decided they were not getting their fair share of money from its congregation at weekly mass because it was spent on psychics. When it was discovered where the money was being spent, it was now "the work of the devil" to go to these types of fortune tellers. Of course, if the Church said that going to see astrologers, psychics or Tarot Readers was the work of the devil, good Christians would return to the Church and never see the fortune tellers again. They would think that it must be true because the Church deemed it so.

I always believed that "Jesus had a great idea and then man created religion!" I think the Golden Rule applies to many faiths and should be the standard for moral behavior. That is the end of my spiel on religion as tarot is neither a religion nor a philosophy. It is a belief system that helps you make positive choices and lets you understand what is going on in your life and how you may want to change the challenges that you face each and every day. It is a tool to guide and help you choose the proper direction or path for your life. So, when someone asks if tarot is the work of the devil, now you know what to say. (Or you can say, "Yes it is and if you don't stop bothering me . . . just kidding).

Since the 1970s, with the new millennium energy fast approaching, I decided that I would not interpret the cards in a negative fashion, but would use the reversed position for timing purposes only. I not only note them, but usually find that the reserved cards show the areas of concern that surround the Querent. The more reversed cards you have in a spread, the more areas of life would be negatively affected. It also shows how many more months it will take to get you through the "hard times" you are experiencing. For instance, if you have eight reversed cards in a year-ahead spread, those eight cards tell me that it will take at least another eight months to get over your challenges unless you call upon your free will and be proactive in areas of life that need attention. Every time you make a positive choice, are proactive, or decide something, you actually take one month's negative energy away from you. So, prioritize your issues and create a plan to make a major decision once a week or once a month, etc. When you do, you will be very surprised at how fast things will be resolved and serenity, organization, and stability will be restored to your life.

You must be proactive in determining your future. Once this is done, the timing becomes more reasonable and positive energy will attach to you in no time. If you procrastinate, you will be in the same negative energy field during those eight months which will continue to bring you more responsibility, obligations, concerns, issues, worries and obstacles. If you do nothing, then the positive energy will be bounced off of the negative energy stuck to you and move on to someone else. You want to be a positive energy magnet, so be positive and make good choices for a satisfying future.

In a year-ahead spread, I also use reversed cards to denote that the actual meaning of that particular card would not come to pass until seven to twelve months after the date of the reading. I also use it as the second half of the timeframe. If you are doing a reading for one month and get a reversed card, it indicates that your issue will be resolved in the second half of the time span which would be the third or fourth week. Of course, if you start in the middle of the month, you must figure out the next four weeks from the date of the reading and then the first two weeks are represented by upright cards and the third or fourth week are represented by the reversed cards. If you were asking for a particular day, an upright card would mean from midnight to noon and a reversed card would indicate noon until midnight. If you are asking for a week, an upright card would be the first 3.5 days of the week, and a reversed card would be the remainder of the week. You get the idea, don't you?

Remember, a year-ahead reading is from the date of the reading to the next year on that particular date and not until the end of the current year. It is also useful to know what obstacles are ahead of you. Then the Querent can create realistic solutions to the issues facing him or her and they can be handled in a very intelligent, analytical and logical manner because you know what the outcome should be.

Every time you do a new reading, you are to let go of the last reading and concentrate on the new reading with a new future date. For instance, if you do a reading today, this reading is good until next year on the same date. I have one client who continually refers back to each and every reading I have ever done for her. She continually refers to her notes, and even though I try to explain that we had done at least six readings after those readings and they are no longer valid, she still brings up past readings. Just stick to your guns. If you tell them that the new reading supersedes that last reading, you have done your job. There is nothing else you can do.

When Readers refer to the past, it is meant from yesterday or the day before the reading back a year, sometimes it can be a longer period, but it refers to at least a year.

For those who would like to learn tarot in a quick and easy manner, here are some suggestions: read the cards through the interpretation of colors, backgrounds, and symbolism. In that way, it is easy to remember any card without memorizing its textbook meaning. In fact, I would suggest that you look at the little insert booklet in the pack of Rider-Waite cards. You may get some insight into the cards from those meanings as well. Remember to use all types of resources to make your readings come alive. Eventually, the meanings will just come to you after practicing with them, but for now, the associations from this book will work out well.

For instance, billowing or fluffy clouds mean that "situations" are brewing behind you, or unexpected secrets are going on behind your back which you do not currently see. Storm or streaking clouds indicates that you are in the middle of an argument, fight or confrontation right now. Level or smooth ground means you are stable, centered, grounded and balanced while rocky ground means you may trip, fall, stumble, be unbalanced, and have unsure footing. Standing in water means there is too much emotion, compassion, empathy, sympathy, sensitivity, emotions or sentimentality surrounding the Querent or situation. Putting any body part in the water connotes you are adding to your own emotional problems. By learning this symbolism and associations with colors, you can put so many clues together *LIKE A DETECTIVE* that one would have a detailed and informative meaning for each card without ever having to refer to any other outside source.

How to be a Tarot Detective

(I actually teach a certified tarot course in only twenty hours and it nearly took me ten years of various classes, teachers and lectures to be proficient in reading for others! Everyone was afraid to give away their knowledge back then, but I like to share what I have learned. It has helped me so much and I am sure it will help you too.)

Thank you for purchasing this book; I know you will feel as if you are one of the best detectives in the world once you start finding the clues I have set forth in this book for you to learn, study and practice.

Happy Tarot.

BACKGROUND

ALTHOUGH THERE HAVE been many theories, tarot is an ancient form of divination of unknown origin. The cards' first appearances have been linked to Atlantis (a highly advanced scientific civilization that was said to have used tarot as well as astronomy and astrology to help define the future as well as many other scientific experiments and accomplishments); Egypt (where the Pharaohs' priests would go into the pyramids and throw branches toward the walls depicting the twenty-two Minor Arcana cards. Wherever the branches landed represented the advice they would give to the Pharaoh); Europe (where people used the cards as a way of planning their future and finding hope when Christianity became overly oppressive and restrictive) and The British Isles (where it was said a King in the sixteenth century had asked a famed artist of the day to design a playing deck for his amusement). Today, there are well over a thousand decks encompassing all cultures of the world; each culture seems to have had used tarot or oracle cards as a form of guidance in determining their futures. Almost every civilization I have ever studied seemed to have had their own set of tarot cards with the archetypes and symbology that was accepted within their culture at their particular period in history. More tarot decks are being created each day!

I was playing around with a fairy deck and wrote most of the accompanying book, but then noticed there were many similar decks already published on fairies, so did not continue. Then I wanted to do a Star Trek deck, but there were too many obstacles and hoops to jump through and they already had playing cards with Star Trek images on them; however, I have devised a great plan where I divided the four suits into the various Captains and their crew. Kirk (fire), Picard (earth), Cisco (water) and Jayneway (air). One day I hope to find someone to help me with this deck, but for now, I have it safely stored on my computer and in my mind and copyrighted with this book's publication.

My point is that tarot cards can be created by anyone. This book is written for the Rider-Waite deck and has never been tried out on any other deck other than the Rider-Waite cards. There are four different versions and it works well for all of them except the Universal Rider-Waite where the colors are transposed in many of the cards especially showing green for water, and different colors for the sky.

When a proficient tarot counselor does a reading, events involving important decisions, health, living conditions, loved ones, career changes, promotions, spiritual matters, and emotional growth can be addressed. Any information that is needed can be determined, explained, and logically defined with positive outcomes and choices. I always encourage clients to bring a list of approximately a half-dozen questions with them in case the year-ahead spread does not answer all of their concerns. Many times it is very hard for a person to think of questions "on the spot." It also wastes valuable time for both the Reader and client as the clock is ticking away for them to be thinking of their next question. You will be surprised at how hard it is for some to even think of questions. (I remember when I first started tarot, it seemed as if I had a million questions, but as time went on these questions diminished, and I can honestly say now that there are very few things that I still need to know. This will also happen to you.) Sometimes, only one or two questions remain unanswered after a year-ahead reading as the topics of concern were already addressed.

Many readings can go on for hours, so it is wise to charge an hourly fee or at least limit your readings to an hour. You can also do a twenty minute or half hour readings or whatever you feel comfortable with. Make it very clear to your client what your fee policy is before doing a reading, so there are no surprises for either of you. In the past, I taped all sessions on cassettes, but with the improved electronics these days, I now allow my clients or students to tape a session with their digital recorder.

I encourage my clients and students to keep listening to the reading throughout the year and gain guidance and a positive outlook from it. It is also for your own protection so someone cannot say that you told him or her something that did not come from your mouth. If it is or is not on the recording, you did or did not say it and that is the end of the story. This certainly is up to you, but when you feel comfortable with your readings, you may want to consider adding a taped session where you can make a digital recording or CD for your client. There are also free conference call phone numbers that you can find on the internet where your client can call in on the 800 number and you can both talk on the conference call. You can also make a recording of the conversation and then send it to your client. By taping the reading, your client can then relax and pay more attention to your predictions and insights rather than trying to scribble down illegible notes that he or she will never be able to read after your conversation. Of course, you can always use Skype to do readings from anywhere in the world. "Where there's a will, there's a way" as the saying goes. You may also use the free conference call sites that allow you to call into a specific number and you may record the calls and have your Querent phone back to listen to the recording from time to time. I am not sure how long the recording is on the site, but if they listen to it a few times, they should remember a great deal of it.

If you are unsure of your skill, practice on family and friends. Everyone wants to know his or her future. You can refer to my book since you are a student and keep a journal of what you said and note if that prediction comes true or not. Everyone you know and their friends will be available for your readings. I used to get free lunches for many years when I worked in corporate because I did a half hour tarot reading at lunch for many of my friends and co-workers. It was never an equal exchange since lunch was usually under five dollars, but it gave me exposure and I had made many permanent clients from those days. My daughter told me that she charged a dollar a minute in college which paid for many of her textbooks throughout her many degrees. A dollar a minute is what a beginner should charge, so you can do a fifteen minute reading for fifteen dollars, twenty for twenty dollars, etc. You paid for books and classes; your time is worth money, so you should be paid for your knowledge just like any other training for a job or vocation.

Please stop now if you are talking about it being spiritual work and that should be given away for free . . . let us talk about religion again. Even though you can go to mass for free, there are always collection plates or building funds, etc. There is always an exchange of energy. Did you receive all of your classes, lectures and workshops for free or did you have to pay to attend them?

Spiritual work is like any other work where you use your knowledge and intelligence to get to a conclusion or goal. You are helping people, just like a doctor or therapist does, and we know they get paid well, so why shouldn't you? As my accountant Barbara continuously says to me (when I hated taking money for my services), "When you go to the dentist or doctor, do they feel sorry for you and tell you the visit is free? There is nothing wrong with receiving fair compensation for a performed service." She also asked me to ask my mortgage company if they would let me skip a payment without penalty because I did not charge my clients for the month and asked them to do the same. What do you think the result would be? It helped me realize that Tarot Readers do provide a valuable service to the public, one that should be compensated like any other profession or service. No one realizes that readings can be exhausting and draining. Just because we are in the spiritual field does not mean that we should not be able to make a living from our work or allow people to take advantage of our gifts. Now, it is your turn to get back some of your investment of the time and money you spent on classes, buying tarot books, attending seminars, workshops and practicing your new craft. All that accumulated knowledge is worth money, so use your knowledge well.

Human beings are blessed with free will and are able to change the future in any way they wish. Simply put, tarot is a chance to glimpse into the future and see all the wonderful possibilities that will be there for you as well as some of the difficult challenges. (I sometimes call free will a curse since many of us know what we are supposed to do, but second guess ourselves continuously, thus making more wrong or negative decisions than needed). It allows you to decide which opportunities or challenges you will act upon and which ones you will let play out to their conclusion. It also shows the probable outcome of your choices so if you do not like the outcome, you must be proactive about your life and make positive changes to get the desired results.

Tarot is a way to accomplish goals and objectives in the most positive manner possible. It also teaches us to choose a better path on our spiritual journey and to reunite with the God and Goddess, our ultimate goal. When the proper choices are made, we will be filled with peace, harmony, abundance and love. We will be able to live the life God and Goddess had intended for us.

(By using the words "God and Goddess", I am referring to the Creator of the Universe, depending upon your belief system. He/she can also be called The Source, The One, The All, The Alpha and Omega, Universal Energies, Spirit Guides, Guardian Angels, or any one of your particular deities or belief systems. I happen to believe in God and Goddess as the undying balance and infinite source of the universe, and two parts of the same Spirit, so I will use that term throughout this book. (If you happen to be an atheist or agnostic, universal energy or the universal vibrations may be substituted or choose something that you feel comfortable with).

GENERAL INFORMATION

TAROT DOES NOT have to be mysterious, nor does it require years of study and practice unless you plan to give advice as your full time career or in a spiritual counseling capacity. Practice is definitely a confidence builder and gives more insight into a reading, so ask friends to help by letting you "practice" reading the cards for them as I had mentioned earlier. You will be surprised at how many new friends you will attract as soon as they know you need volunteers to practice this ancient art of divination. Everyone has questions! Be sure to tell them you are a beginner and doing this for practice and fun. You may also refer to this book if you have any doubts about what a card means in a spread. These answers will always be correct; however, many times different meanings will come to you as you use the cards on a regular basis, so just go with the flow and say whatever comes to *your* mind. Apparently, this is what is meant to be told to your client, family member or friend and you should trust in the guidance you are receiving. Remember though to speak with tact and compassion because some of the information you receive may not always be positive.

Many people who come for a reading take this advice as gospel and unless you are proficient in reading the cards, you may unknowingly cause someone anxiety or distress. Also, if you do readings in a more professional manner, check with your state's ordinances to see if you must write down on your website or business cards that your work is "For entertainment purposes only." This is to protect the Reader from lawsuits, but will also protect the Querent from taking this too seriously unless they are on a spiritual path and know the power of the cards. Most people use it for fun, such as entertainment at private and corporate parties, so if this is the case, keep it light. When it is a one-on-one consultation, you can then go into detail and explain the positive and challenging energies working around the client.

Giving this sacred advice and guidance is not to be taken lightly, nor should it be used for your own personal gain. You should use it to receive insight into a situation or relationship that may be helpful to the Querent (or yourself – and yes, you can read the cards for yourself. I will tell you how in a few paragraphs). You are a facilitator or conduit of the cards' energy and a higher power whether it is your higher consciousness, the Akashic Hall of Records, a spirit guide or Guardian Angel or your connection to the wisdom and knowledge of a higher plane of existence. The Querent must know that if he or she chooses to do nothing with the information you have given them, it is okay. It is their choice. They do not have to change their lives; they do not have to learn the lessons of this lifetime, nor progress on the right path. It is always their choice. You may guide or suggest paths that they could take, but ethical practitioners never use scare tactics or instill fear to push people in any direction. You should give your clients several appropriate options but may never tell them what to do. Only a licensed therapist or psychiatrist can do that. Even though it may be obvious to your clients and you, you are not a licensed mental health care professional. You may even have to recommend that some of your clients get that type of professional help for a short period of time, but all in all, you are a tarot Reader.

I remember having several clients who left their therapists and wanted to have a reading on a weekly basis. I would never encourage that since some people need a health care professional to guide them through traumatic stress syndrome, unresolved parental issues, siblings or a partner concerns, etc., and although tarot can give wonderful insight into any situation, sometimes therapists or psychiatrists, who can prescribe medication, work much, much better because of their skilled medical knowledge. When I asked why they wanted to stop going to therapy and come to me on a weekly basis, they answered, "Because the therapist always asks us what we think. If we knew what we thought, we would not have to go to therapy. You give us answers and options to our issues and make us feel as if we are in control of our lives." These are interesting comments to think about; however, I still say that medicine, holistic approaches and spiritual modalities have their place in our lives and many times, they should be combined to see the whole picture and a perfect result.

Charlatans always say that there is a curse upon you, your family, etc. and usually prey upon the elderly. When you hear about the large sums of money that can rid you of "this curse", then you can be sure that this charlatan is or will be cheating you very soon. Be wary of these Readers - they are con artists and give the legitimate metaphysical community a bad reputation! These are the people who have little stores on major highways with the words PSYCHIC outside of their shop. They tell you that you need many readings, even once a week! Most should have a reading once or twice a year, if needed, but a once a year checkup is really all that you need. I recommend having readings around the Solar Eclipses each year – the only day you can purposefully change your life – and then if needed, they may call with additional questions at any time throughout the year if a new issue pops up. Or another popular time to have a reading is in January so people can figure out what the year ahead holds for them; however, the most popular time is around one's birthday. Then the reading would be from this current year's birthday until next year's birthday. What would be better than knowing what your birthday year holds for you? This also combines with numerology and which personal year would be coming up for you from your current birthday until next year's birthday. You can combine the several modalities to get a very accurate reading for your next year.

Otherwise, just to be clear, no one will burn candles for you or pray for you – at an extremely high cost, I might add, other than you. If you really need to pay anywhere from $300-$500 for candles, go to a dollar store and you will be able to buy enough candles for the rest of your life. Or go to your church and light some candles where the money would go to do good in the community or for the poor.

Do not fall victim to these people who are getting rich by perpetuating fear, doubts, worries, procrastination and indecision to those who may be going through a very rough time. Stay away from these people! You are getting faulty information, losing your money and nothing they do is changing your life for the better. In fact, with the scare tactics they use, you will be attracting more negativity and challenges because you will always be in a state of anxiety and fear. You can only attract similar energies; so do you really need more negativity in your life? The only one who feels better is the person taking your money and laughing all the way to the bank! And it's not you!

The Reader helps clients understand and be able to cope with their circumstances by giving them practical alternatives to their current or future obstacles and challenges. If you feel worse when you leave a reading, something is wrong. Either you are a very negative person and did not understand the information that was shared with you or you have been getting advice from a charlatan. Their purpose is to make you feel anxious and fearful so that you can buy all their bags of tricks and continually come back for many more readings until your money runs out. Then, they ask you to borrow from family and friends so they can help you. So the never ending cycle will not get any better, but will leave you with a few pennies left in your piggy bank.

If you, as an ethical Reader, help clients understand and cope with their circumstances or give them tools to deal with unpleasant situations ahead, they are using tarot for the highest good of all involved while guiding your clients or yourself to a more productive, positive and happy life. In turn, you will feel a sense of accomplishment and inner harmony because you have made an important difference in that person's life and in the world by making a negative person or situation just a little more positive. You may be the only one a particular person trusts or comes to for advice, so make your reading, guidance, and suggestions appropriately optimistic and for their highest good. I am not saying that you should not tell them the truth about something that is coming up in their future; however, if it is negative, give them the alternatives they need to master the issue. All the cards have a resolution inside of them.

It is easy once you learn the actual meanings of the cards and how to resolve any issue(s) that come up within the year reading.

Also, be a good listener. People who seek Tarot Readers sometimes just need someone to listen to their issues and want someone to tell them that everything is going to be all right. Be the person that your client needs. Be a responsible and compassionate Reader.

I continually get comments from my clients on how much I have helped them or how honest I was with them so they could make appropriate choices. They also comment about, "How did you know about . . ." They shuffle the cards and hand them to me, so their energy is in the cards, which shows me the mundane or spiritual issues that need to be dealt with at this time. It is not magic; it is energy being transferred from the client into the cards so that the Reader can assist with the areas of life that may be overwhelming or confusing. Sometimes situations come out in the cards because it is a confirmation of what your client is feeling or going through. In this way, the universe is telling your client to deal with the situation(s) before it gets worse. Conversely, it also tells one when good opportunities or better times are coming so that the client will know when the hardships will be over and they can plan accordingly. Again, it is that light at the end of the tunnel that everyone looks for and in this instance, YOU are that light and you are brightly shining for them.

I feel it is also important to have a deck for *your readings for others* and one deck *for yourself alone.* No one should touch it to change your vibrational energy on them and you should always use it when you have a question that you are answering for yourself. It can be the pocket, mini or another full sized deck, but one deck needs to be yours alone. This deck is specifically for your guidance into your own personal journey and should be treated as your sacred tarot divination tool.

As I mentioned above, many people think that they cannot read the tarot for themselves. This is not true. I have taught people how to read for themselves easily and their readings were accurate. First of all, if you pretend you are doing a reading for a family member, friend or client, your readings will be more descriptive. We tend to look at a card for ourselves and say, "Yeah, ok, I need to be more grounded," or "I have to prioritize my issues," etc. However, if you were reading for someone else, you would go into the: "who, what, where, why and when of the cards" but for some reason when we read for ourselves, we skip much of the important information. Tape your reading for yourself as if you were going to send it to someone else and then listen to it a few days later. You will be surprised at the result. Later, you will be able to do your own reading without pretending it is for someone else. Never rush your own reading. Take your time and look at all the clues in the card like a detective for yourself like you would for anyone else.

MAJOR ARCANA CARDS AND ROMAN NUMERALS

MAJOR ARCANA CARDS are from 0, The Fool, through XXI, The World. It may sound silly, but I have had a few students throughout the years who did not know how to figure out or read Roman Numerals. In fact, I had one older gentleman in one of my adult education classes years ago who left the class because he said, "If I knew I had to learn Roman Numerals, I never would have taken this class!" If you do not know your Roman Numerals, you should practice reading them since the cards are labeled in that system. However, in all of the Major Arcana cards, if you have a number at the top of the card, you will see that many of the suit in the card. For example, if you pull the three of swords, there will be three swords in the card.

Roman Numerals	Current Number System
0	0
I	1
II	2
III	3
IV	4
V	5
VI	6
VII	7
VIII	8

IX	9
X	10
XI	11
XII	12
XIII	13
XIV	14
XV	15
XVI	16
XVII	17
XVIII	18
XIX	19
XX	20
XXI	21
XXII	22

The Fool is the first Major Arcana Card numbered zero. For numerology purposes, I have added it to the end of the Major Arcana because there is no zero in numerology. It is usually the first card in all instances other than when using numerology.

XXI is the highest Roman numeral used in the Rider-Waite Deck for the Major Arcana; however, because zero is not a number, we use XXII as the last card in the Major Arcana which is The Fool. You have probably already learned something new. Try to write the numbers above until you feel comfortable that you know what the numbers mean without thinking about it. If you would like to play around with the numbers, here they are listed for you.

I = 1, V = 5, X = 10, L = 50, C = 100 and M = 1000. Our year is now MMXV. M + M + X + V = 1000 + 1000 + 10 + 5 = 2015. If you notice above, the Roman Numerals only use the "I" to represent 1, 2, or 3. For instance, look at XIV (14). The I or one just before a larger number means that you must minus or subtract it from that larger number. You subtracted 1 from the V (5) = 4. X + IV = XIV or 14. Try another number. How do you get XIX (19)? The X (10) is listed first, then you must minus the I (1) from the next X (10) which = 9; X (10) + IX (9) = XIX (19).

If you look at the end of movies, you will see the year they were released written in Roman numerals most of the time and now you know how to read them.

Another thing to do if this is really an issue for you is to write the actual numbers on the card with a black Sharpie pen and then there will be no issue. Meanwhile, you will associate the number with the Roman numeral and you will be learning how to read them without even knowing it.

However, you may use one deck with notes written on them with Sharpie markers to learn them easier and then get another deck to use for your clients. You would not want them to think you are a beginner now, would you?

DO WHATEVER FEELS RIGHT

I HAVE BEEN INTERESTED in tarot since I was fourteen, reading many different books as well as trying different decks to see which ones resonated with me. My first one was the Egyptian Deck which not only had hideous pictures on them, but in fact, was an evil deck *for me*. I remember sleeping with the entire deck under my pillow (as was the practice way back in the good old days of covered wagons and cowboys), and dreaming of someone ripping open my stomach with a sword and pulling out all of my guts night after night. Finally, my husband said, "Do you think it could be those cards?" Well, indeed it was, so I started looking for another deck to use which would be more user friendly and allow me to sleep in peace. My search was over when I discovered the Rider-Waite deck.

Unfortunately before Rider-Waite, I never felt comfortable with any of the ones I found and inadvertently collected over two hundred of them. Later when I realized I would not be able to use all of these collected decks, I donated them to charitable events or to students who could not afford to buy any of the decks they wanted to study. I donated some to a new age shop to sell with the profits going to a local animal shelter and now I am concentrating on Oracle cards, Chinese tarot cards, and Crystal Cards and Feng Shui cards. I have not gotten as far as I would have liked with reading these cards, but it is my firm belief that you can only be an expert in three decks in your lifetime. One deck will always be your favorite and it would always be the one with which you are very comfortable and knowledgeable. There is just too much information in each deck, and I believe there is not enough time to master many more than a few in your lifetime.

I studied with many teachers who all had their own way of teaching the cards, but again I did not feel a connection with the teacher or the deck they were using. After finding one special teacher who shared her knowledge openly, (unlike many in this field) I was then open to the wonderful world of tarot. It started to all make sense to me. She encouraged us to use intuitive insight and bring that into each reading. Since I had always had a connection with my angel, this seemed like exactly what I needed to make these cards an important part of my life. This teacher taught classes with the utmost ethics and morals which were passed onto her students. She also wanted us to be aware that the Querent was probably in a depressed or saddened state of mind and advised us to carefully choose our words. We could be the one who gave that person the ray of sunshine or the hope that they needed which would carry them through the next month or year of difficult times. Conversely, by saying the wrong thing, you could also make that person feel as if there were no hope and make them think that it would be a waste of time to try to change things because life would not get any better. Using optimistic and hopeful words is always the best medicine.

I find that most people who come for a reading are in a very confused and depressed state of mind; many have even given up on their circumstances. Some are considering suicide. Others think they are the only ones in the world with a particular problem with no clear path or choice ahead of them. It is almost comical to say that most readings are alike, but they are. They are about money, finding a job, romance, marriage and family issues, cheating, and deciding where to live. Of course, many want to know when they are going to meet the love of their life. Then, the area that always surprises me is that so many are involved in affairs with married "friends" and many times are married themselves, so in all fairness, how positive is a reading going to be? I try to be objective and help them with their issues, but I also try to pepper the reading with some common sense and moral behavior even though I am always careful "not to judge" others.

So, it is very important that you treat the Querent (the person for whom you are doing the reading) with extreme compassion, empathy, understanding, and kindness and give them many positive options for their conflicts and challenges that await them. Let them leave your home or office with a very positive and optimistic attitude. Your goal is to make them feel much better about themselves and their situation than before they came to you for guidance. In this respect, it is something like therapy or counseling by a healthcare professional; however, you are not a healthcare professional and your client must be aware of the difference. If you feel that your client needs professional help, it is important that you mention it. You could say something like, "Perhaps you should make an appointment with a counselor or therapist even if it's only for a few sessions. Sometimes you need the guidance of a health care professional to give you another side of the story." Then you leave the decision up to them.

My interpretation of the Rider-Waite deck will follow throughout the next few chapters. The interpretations are mostly mine; however, there is a short paragraph from the Quick and Easy Tarot by U.S. Games Systems for the same deck so you could see the difference. This is not the interpretation from the regular deck, but a simple and easy explanation to make my point. Many people like my interpretations and symbology better because it is so much easier than the traditional way of learning the tarot. Others had dismissed my method, but when I did readings for them at psychic fairs or if we bartered our services, they had actually said on so many occasions that the reading I did for them was the best reading they had ever had! So, I interpret the cards the way I think one should and let the Significator make their own judgment about the merit of my reading.

The particular method of interpretation that I use is called, "*The Totally Tarot Method.*" There have been some students who actually never finished my 18 hour course nor became certified in this method who were teaching it to others. If you are not certified in "The Totally Tarot Method," then you may not teach it to others. I do not want beginners showing other people how to read the cards when they do not fully understand the nuances of my method themselves. You must be certified to teach this method to anyone else.

HOW TO BE A TAROT DETECTIVE

Many students have asked if my interpretations relate to other decks. It does not seem to relate to other decks from the intermittent tests I have done. It does work with the Radiant Rider-Waite deck, but not with the Universal Deck since many of the colors are changed in this version of the deck. For those who are interested, the original deck that I use is the one with the Magician on the tarot box. I have found this deck to be the most spiritual, metaphysical, symbolic and informative of the three that I use and by far, the easiest to teach and learn. So please follow the meanings of the Rider-Waite deck with me and I would encourage you to test out the cards on friends and family to see which results you get. You may use the Ace Spread for yes or no questions or you may only pull one card and give them a full description of its meaning. Note the results of the reading and then try to go back to the person you have read and see how accurate you were with your predictions. You will also obtain additional added insight into the cards and readings the more you use them, so start practicing!

You will be surprised at how quickly you will learn to give accurate readings for family and friends. Be prepared, for once you know how to give accurate tarot readings, you will become a very popular person indeed. You will most likely be invited to many parties and gatherings for your knowledge of tarot and entertainment abilities and not necessarily as an honored guest. This had happened to me over and over again in the beginning. I was asked to attend parties to be the entertainment and was not getting paid. Others were having fun by getting a free reading and I was working. I did not stop this as quickly as I should have since I thought I was helping out friends; however, it is a tough line to walk between trying to please others and setting boundaries, but boundaries need to be set. You can do this if you are a beginner and say you will read for an hour or so, but then you will join the party and have some fun too. Always be wary of someone wanting to be your friend and then telling you how negative his or her life is. The ultimate goal is for you to do a free reading. You can do this, of course, but do not be taken advantage of. Give them a card and say, "You are always welcome to call me and set up an appointment."

My example is that I had a Feng Shui colleague who was moving to the South. She had wanted to get rid of a lot of her Feng Shui books and trinkets. Some of her stuff was useful and some was junk. However, when I arrived at her home, she asked if I could give her a reading in exchange for the merchandise, but of course, she said, I could say no if I wanted to. How was I to say no? So, I gave her an hour plus reading which calculated to nearly $200 worth of my time. We both packed up a few large bags of stuff and once it was in my car, away I went. I thought it was very nice of her, but I had many of the books she had gifted me and much of the other stuff were trinkets that I could not really use, but it was a gracious gesture.

After she moved, she frequently contacted me by email from her new home, but every time she contacted me, it was about if the new guy she just met was the right man for her, or was he the one she would marry or was the one she would have a positive relationship with, etc. After about the sixth time, I told her I would answer her question, but that she should set up an appointment in the future for more answers to her questions. She was indignant and said there must have been some misunderstanding. I replied, "No, there was no misunderstanding. You asked me about six different men and I gave you the answers for free. The only time you contacted me was when you wanted an answer to questions about your relationships and I told you if you wanted further tarot predictions done that you should make an appointment." So, you know I never heard from her again. People will use your good nature to get what they want. Start off with definitive boundaries and you will be fine.

At the beginning, you can practice, practice, practice, but as time goes on, you must charge a fee for your expertise. You paid for your classes, book and deck, crystals and box, didn't you? So you deserve to get back the investment you had made. I recommend a dollar a minute for beginners. Let others know that this is work for you and you should get reimbursed for the amount of energy you are putting out into the universe. Also, you do not want to be constantly drained and tired, so you may tell a small fib and tell others that you do not have your cards with you if they ask for a reading.

You need reciprocal energy. Your time, talent and energy can be given to others in exchange for money, which is considered energy. Of course, you can barter services, which is perfectly fine. Do make sure that the services you give are equivalent to the ones you are getting. For instance, if you are charging sixty dollars an hour for a reading, do not exchange it for someone to come to your house and let out your dog if they only charge twenty-five dollars an hour. You should get two visits.

Compensation can be anything; that was the only barter example I could think of at the moment.

THE MAJOR ARCANA: SPIRITUAL SECRETS

THERE ARE TWENTY-TWO (22) Major Arcana cards. These are the cards guided by God and Goddess, Spirit Guides, Guardian Angels, Spirit, the One, the Source, the All, the Alpha and Omega, universal energy or whomever you (or your client) believe in. You may say that God is sending good luck, help, or money, etc., but if the client is an atheist, agnostic or pagan, let us say, God does not mean anything to them. Always ask your client whom you should use to reference the spiritual cards. We also use the Major Arcana cards for karmic lessons that are prevalent throughout your life. There are either two or three lessons that you will be exposed to over and over again in this lifetime until you understand why you are attracting the same issues and negative energy with continued negative results.

The way to recognize a Major Arcana card is that they all have a word or words on the bottom of it giving us a brief description. Some examples are The Fool, The Magician, The High Priestess, The Empress, and The Emperor, etc. The more of these cards (from 0-21) you have in a spread, the more God and Goddess, the Source, the One, the All, Guardian Angels, Spirit Guide, Spirit or Universal Energies, will guide you to choose the correct opportunities presented to you to get your life back on the proper path. If you are a chronic procrastinator, the Major Arcana will push you onto a new path and create many little earthquakes or detours along the way until you get on the right road. It is as if the Universe is saying that you have had an extremely challenging year and knows that it would be in your best interest to make some of the decisions for you. You may have been too overwhelmed or upset to make any further decisions on your own, so the opportunities will be presented to you without further thought on your part. Of course, it is still up to you whether or not to accept those gifts or opportunities that will be brought to your attention.

The more Major Arcana cards in a spread, the harder the person's circumstances were the prior year; however, the easier it will be for them during the upcoming year.

Do not confuse the court cards (Aces, Kings, Queens, Knights, and Pages) with Major Arcana Cards even though they do have written words at the bottom of the card as well. These cards have words that say "of Wands, of Pentacles, of Swords or of Cups." For example, The Page of Wands, The Knight of Pentacles, The Queen of Swords and the King of Cups are not Major Arcana Cards. Major Arcana cards do not say "of" any particular suit. The only card that confuses people is the Wheel of Fortune, but it does not say the Wheel of Wands, Pentacles, Swords or Cups, now does it?

NUMEROLOGY

I F YOU ARE interested in numerology, it is very interesting that the Major Arcana cards represent the karmic lesson(s) you are destined to learn in this lifetime. It is very simple to figure out which cards are your life's lessons. Write down your birthday numerically, like in the example below or use the simplified version that I previously used.

06	Birth Month
14	Birth Day
1951	Birth Year
1971	**Total**

The total of your addition is equivalent to a specific year that usually has important significance to you. Sometimes it may take you awhile to figure it out; however, it could be a wedding, birth of a child, graduation, engagement, signing up for or getting out of the military, some type of accident that left a lasting impression, or a hundred other things that have meaning especially to you. Think about it. (See below for more explanation on how to do this.) Then you take that year (1971 or whatever year you came up with) and add them together to equal a single digit number.

For instance, 1 + 9 + 7 + 1 = 18. Numerology only deals with numbers one through 9, so you have to add the two digit answer together to come up with a single digit: 1 + 8 = 9. What Major Arcana Cards equals 9? Well, there is the Hermit that is an IX and The Moon that is XVIII. Remember the number eighteen I got as an answer above? Well, 1 + 8 = 9. Add any of the numbers from 1 to 22 together to equal your original number and learn your karmic lessons.

The earlier numbers from one through four have three karmic lessons in this lifetime. The numbers from five to nine only have two. Is it better to have more or less? Who knows? We all progress at our own speed and maybe some people need more lessons to learn in this lifetime, while perhaps only two major lessons is enough for someone else's lifetime. For this purpose, be sure you count The Fool as #22. In many decks, The Fool is the last number card in the Major Arcana, but in this deck it is first, or Number 0. What are the lessons you must learn in this lifetime? Look at the cards, study them, and try to fit them into your life. Most people are amazed at the accuracy of their karmic lesson cards and usually laugh when they are chosen, since the lessons were obviously not yet learned.

KARMIC LESSONS THROUGH TAROT AND NUMEROLOGY

1	2	3	4	5	6	7	8	9
10	11	12	13	14	15	16	17	18
19	20	21	22	-	-	-	-	-

- Add your birth date together. Month, day and total year.
- Example: June 14, 1951: Add 6 + 1 + 4 + 1 + 9 + 5 + 1 = 27
- If your answer is a two digit number, add those together until you get one digit.
  27 = 2 + 7 = 9. You are a "9". Notice where the Xs are shown below to reflect the birth date.

- Find the number on the top row of the table above that corresponds to your answer and look down the column. Those numbers are your karmic lessons.

1. The Magician	12. The Hanged Man
2. The High Priestess	13. Death
3. The Empress	14. Temperance
4. The Emperor	15. The Devil
5. The Hierophant	16. The Tower
6. The Lovers	17. The Star
7. The Chariot	18. The Moon (1 + 8 = 9) X
8. Strength	19. The Sun
9. The Hermit X	20. Judgement
10. The Wheel of Fortune	21. The World
11. Justice	22. The Fool

Fire Signs:	Aries, Leo and Sagittarius	Your tarot suit is Wands
Earth Signs:	Taurus, Virgo and Capricorn	Your tarot suit is Pentacles
Air Signs:	Gemini, Libra and Aquarius	Your tarot suit is Swords
Water Signs:	Cancer, Scorpio and Pisces	Your tarot suit is Cups

Find your number and suit and that card is your Minor Arcana "everyday mundane" karmic lessons you must deal with.

So the #9 card above, turns out to be The IX of Swords if the person is an air sign (Gemini).

What's your everyday or mundane karmic lesson?

THE MINOR ARCANA: MUNDANE SECRETS

THERE ARE FIFTY-SIX (56) Minor Arcana cards and out of those, there are sixteen (16) Court Cards. The four suits that are represented in the Minor Arcana are Wands representing fire signs,

Pentacles representing earth signs, Swords representing air signs and Cups representing water signs.

These cards represent particular areas of life such as Wands represent your career, health and education. Pentacles represent issues such as your money, possessions and financial security. Swords represent conflicts, problems and responsibilities. And lastly, Cups represent love and happiness, in general. These cards unlike the Major Arcana relate only to your everyday or mundane life, obligations, concerns and worries.

So if you discover your birth path number and your element, you will be able to have a mundane karmic lesson as well to add to your Major Arcana karmic lessons. Find the sun sign that is your astrological sign below and see which suit represents it.

Wands would represent	Aries, Leo and Sagittarius	(FIRE)
Pentacles would represent	Taurus, Virgo and Capricorn	(EARTH)
Swords would represent	Gemini, Libra and Aquarius	(AIR)
Cups would represent	Cancer, Scorpio and Pisces	(WATER)

So, let us say that you find out that you are a water sign, so you can be Cancer, Scorpio or Pisces, and you discover because you are one of these sun signs, your Minor Arcana suit is Cups. Then you have to add your birth date together and come up with a number. All numbers in numerology can only be broken down to one through nine. You would look at the Cup suit and find "your number" of Cups. Look up the meaning of this card and this would most likely be the issue you are working on in your lifetime on an everyday level. As already stated, add your birth date together. A simple example is the month, day and year. 11+ 11 + 1953 or $1 + 1 + 1 + 1 + 1 + 9 + 5 + 3 = 22$ (you may only use one number in numerology, so $2 + 2 = 4$). So your Minor Arcana card is the 4 of Cups/water.

Use the chart below to find your particular Major Arcana karmic lessons. They will make sense to you as soon as you find out what they are.

The Mundane or everyday meanings of numerology are listed below:

1. (Aces) New beginnings, starting fresh, new life.

2. Couples year or continuing to make your new beginnings prosperous and abundant.
3. Year dealings with children, love triangles or three partners as well as creativity.
4. Year dealings with foundation issues, responsibilities or obligations.
5. Fun and artistic year.
6. Service to others year. This is also called the Christ number because you are selfless and helpful to everyone. You join many charities or organizations which help humanity.
7. Faith year. This is also a year for you to be alone and figure out what you want out of life.
8. Money year, good or bad. If your 7 year was great, your 8 year will not be as abundant; however, if your 7 year was financially lean, you will be able to do well in business, gain more money through investments, the lottery or inheritance. Money issues will go your way.
9. Endings. Get rid of the old to make way for the new; this is a very spiritual or metaphysical year. This is a garage sale of your life. Get rid of everything you do not like, need or want.

In the following pages, I describe the General Explanation of the cards, Court Cards, the Four Minor Suits, Dos and Don'ts, Preparing the Cards, Interpreting the Cards, Crystals, Color Interpretations, etc. and many other interesting topics. These interpretations have worked well for my students, clients and me for over forty-three years; however I always encourage others to seek a variety of sources. Take what feels right for you and incorporate meanings from other teachers or books and disregard the ones you do not like. This book is a wonderful place to start your journey of learning the tarot. You cannot learn the tarot overnight. However, I promise that if you read or study one or two cards per day, the meanings of the cards will resonate with you and they will be so easy to remember as you go through my book. Pick a card of the day and study it, look at it and see what sense it makes to you. Practice will make perfect readings.

Remember, whatever you choose to believe is right for you and your interpretations. If everyone believed the same or reads tarot cards exactly the same – there would be no need for so many Readers, would there?

How to be a Tarot Detective

We all gain information differently and our belief systems are usually varied, so readings are excitingly diverse as well.

THE FOUR SUITS

WANDS

WHAT DOES IT mean when I say The Page of Wands would indicate the start of an issue relating to the suit? This would mean that you (or the person for whom you are doing the reading) will begin a new venture in career, health or education.

The Knight of Wands would indicate that you are now in your job (let us use the job or career for the Wands for demonstration purposes). So now that you have the new job that the Page has foretold, you now are half way through the experience, which means that you are now learning the job, its policies and your responsibilities within that job. This could be things such as: whom to call in an emergency, what your company's products are, the chain of command, how much empowerment or authority you have and may even learn all about other employees and/or management. You are learning the job.

The time you are at the level of the Queen of Wands, you have pretty much handled all of the work and are a real pro at your responsibilities, so much so that you may find the job a bit boring because everything is very tedious or routine. It is a good job and you are making money, but you have your eye on possibly something more exciting or perhaps a position in a different field, although at this time you rarely do anything to change your position because you do not want to rock the boat.

Once you have reached the King of Wands' level, you are the boss, running the company, have now become the owner of your own business or are one of the main principles. You are the king of your castle now. This card usually comes later in life when you have been in the experienced position for many years and may be near retirement. Many times this card does signify retirement. It is someone who is holding onto a job for the paycheck, the benefits and the security, but is tired of this job and needs to let it go to see where the universe will take him next.

The Ace of Wands is a gift or blessing from God and Goddess in your career, job, health or formal education (which also includes lectures, seminars, workshops, certification courses and training on the job). Everything in these areas will work out for the Querent's best interest.

Let us continue with this concept, so that you will understand the progression of the Pages through Kings in each suit.

PENTACLES

The Page of Pentacles would indicate a new money venture through a new job, inheritance, IRS mistake, lottery or perhaps a promotion or being given additional responsibilities for more money. In any event, more money will be coming into your life.

The Knight of Pentacles now has the money and is deciding what to do with it. Should he invest it or talk to a financial consultant? Should he take all of his money from bank accounts and transfer it to CDs? It is a planning stage where the Querent is trying to figure out what is the best way to handle financial issues to make the money grow in the shortest amount of time.

Next, comes the Queen of Pentacles who is worried about decisions that have been made and if they were the correct ones? The Queen is looking in the wrong direction, is not strong enough at this time to make the right decisions even though she is smart, logical and analytical. She keeps worrying about her money, so negative money issues will continue to be attached to her. The Queen needs to stop procrastinating, make the hard decisions and move forward even though she has little self confidence left in herself. If she makes a mistake, she can always fix it in the future. Not making a decision is not a decision; it is called procrastination which will cause more problems down the road.

Now we have The King who is rich and has worked his whole life; he is enjoying the fruits of his labor as well as his financial security. He is confident that he can provide for his family even through retirement if that is his wish and has money to lend or give family members and close friends, if needed. Security is assured. Hard work brings the financial abundance and prosperity that was always dreamed about throughout his life. His dream has come true.

The Ace of Pentacles is a gift or blessing from God and Goddess in money, financial security, prosperity and abundance. This is a great time to play the lottery. If you do not win when this card is pulled within that year's time, do not waste your money in the future because this is the luckiest you will ever be. The Ace of Pentacles assures that money issues will be resolved and that there will be financial abundance to get you through any of your hardships, obstacles and issues.

SWORDS

The Page of Swords is a crafty fellow. This card represents new problems, challenges, concerns, issues, obligations, responsibilities and worries. He is trying to deal with them, but keeps looking towards the past while trying to keep his balance in the present and it just does not work. He has the success of all his goals and objectives coming true in the future, but in tarot, if you do not see it, you do not get it. If he continues to look into the past, he will never get to a positive future. The clouds show that this is the worst his issue(s) will be, but he still needs to pay attention to the future.

The Knight of Swords is also going in the wrong direction and is a bit of a scattered person who may also be ADD, ADHD or OCD. This is someone who does many things at once, but then goes onto new projects before the old ones are completed. He has many unfinished projects and situations around him, but just keeps charging ahead trying to handle everything that he can. It is overwhelming and fruitless. He needs to turn around and go towards the future and prioritize his projects and life so that everything will run smoothly from now on. If he does not, it will be a very long time before this person can find his way to a positive future. This is also a health warning card, so he may even find himself under the weather a great deal until he rests and nurtures himself.

The Queen of Swords is someone who is a kind and loving person and a bit of a sucker. You will see that word throughout this book because it is quicker to say that than "too loving, too caring, too giving, too kind, too generous, too honest and trustworthy and does everything for everyone else and nothing for herself." This is someone who really cannot say no to anyone and winds up doing everything for others and gets exhausted mentally, physically and emotionally because her projects, dreams, goals and objectives have to be put on the back burner. This person needs to set limits and boundaries and stop being everyone's friend. It is time to use that sword to deal with everything that needs to be handled and be secure in the knowledge that she is on a protected and stable foundation to continue her role in the world as a Queen.

The King of Swords then is someone who is balancing negativity and trying to keep peace with everyone. He is still very compassionate and emotional (although men always try to hide emotions) and is secure in the knowledge that he is handling all situations well. He is satisfied with everything he has done to get to the conclusion that has happened.

The Ace of Swords is then the resolution of your conflicts, problems, responsibilities, obligations, concerns, worries, issues, obstacles and anxieties about your problems. This is another blessing from God and Goddess.

CUPS

The Page of Cups is an easy card to read and a lovely one at that. The Page of Cups is the beginning of a new romance so you will meet a new romantic significant other in the upcoming year or whichever time frame you had used. I use a romantic significant other or romantic partner because it has been an embarrassment for me to tell someone that they will meet a man or a woman at the end of the year and they would insist that they would not. This was well before the Gay community was out of the closet so to speak and I never thought in those terms because I never knew anyone who was gay. Now many of my friends and a few family members are openly Gay, so I try to be particularly sensitive to this issue of gender. So if you use "romantic partner", you will not have to suffer the embarrassments I did so many years ago.

This is a new partner, a new romance, someone who makes you feel wonderful and someone you can trust. This is one of the two most trustworthy and honest people you will ever meet. It is the perfect match. However, what if the person you are reading for is married or engaged? It seems there may be a hard choice that the married or engaged person has to make between the new love and the old one. It can also mean that one in the couple is not looking for someone else per se, but would not mind having a fling with a new acquaintance for a short time and then be faithful again to his or her spouse or partner.

The Knight of Cups is the other wonderful romantic card although the only problem with the Knights is that they always wear armor because they were hurt in the past. They always seem to be protecting themselves and you will note that the horse, on which the Knight is riding, is moving to the future very, very slowly. If one or both partners are impatient of the progress of the relationship, one of them has to speak up or perhaps one of them would simply leave to find a more satisfying relationship. Someone is happy with the slow moving relationship and usually the other one is annoyed that it is moving too slowly. Communication is the key to this card so that both of you can get on the same page as to the expected timing of events. For timing, this card could mean the beginning of discussions about living together or becoming exclusive.

The Queen of Cups is one of the worst suckers in the whole deck. She is facing the past and holds the only cup that has a cover. She needs to keep love alive within her relationship and family. The Queen would do anything to keep her romance going even if it means not fulfilling her life or her goals and dreams. She is slipping off of the secure and stable cement throne into the water which means that she is causing her own emotional problems and will drown in emotion and sorrow. If she does not look to the future and try to figure out what is going wrong in her life and/or with her relationship, she will be stuck in this negative energy for a very long time. For timing, this is usually an engagement card.

The time the King comes along, there is a marriage proposal or you have agreed to live together. This is the end of the journey from meeting someone, then getting to know them, getting engaged and then married. In this day and age, living together is considered a marriage since there was no such concept as living together in 1908 when the deck was designed and published.

The Ace of Cups, the best card in the whole deck, means love, happiness, prosperity, and joy, inner peace, guidance, strength, wisdom, self-confidence, self-esteem and everything that is needed to make you happy. This card also brings other blessings such as children or perhaps the house of your dreams, or overcoming love issues and concerns (perhaps not being able to conceive a child). This card is a blessing from Above in making everything in romance go in the best direction for all involved. There are the most blessings in this card, so if you leave your future to God and Goddess, you will find more peace, love and acceptance in all things than if you tried to handle things yourself. Faith is the key to happiness with this card.

SUMMARY:

WANDS represent your job, career, health and anything you do for the most part during the day such as volunteering, being a mother or housewife, and being retired. If you volunteer, that is your job. If you are a student, that is your job. These represent astrological fire signs which are Aries, Leo and Sagittarius.

Think of Wands as wood – and think how easy it is for wood to burn. Wands represent fire as well as the season SPRING.

PENTACLES represent finances, possessions, how you save, how you spend and what you think about money and how one relates to it. It also stands for how you feel about financial security, if you are generous or cheap, if you are a saver or spender and how you regard money in your lifetime. Pentacles represent earth signs which are Taurus, Virgo or Capricorn.

Pentacles look like coins or money. Remember Pentacles as coins or money which can buy land or earth as well as the season of SUMMER.

SWORDS stand for conflicts, obstacles, confusion, arguments, fights, restrictions, limitations, responsibilities, obligations, concerns and issues. It is also how you deal with conflicts and issues and if you let others handle them for you. It also represents if you are the type of person who lets others fight your battles for you or can you stick up for yourself? Swords represent air signs which are Gemini, Libra and Aquarius.

Swords can be flung in the air or used in the air as a weapon and they represent the season of AUTUMN.

CUPS relate to love, happiness, prosperity, and joy, inner peace, guidance, strength, wisdom, self-confidence, self-esteem and everything you need to make you happy. This is the emotional and sensitive suit and, in my opinion, the best of all the suits because many of them bring you so much love, happiness and joy. These represent water signs which are Cancer, Scorpio and Pisces.

Cups may be filled with water or liquid and represent the season of WINTER.

COURT CARDS

COURT CARDS ARE represented by Pages, Knights, Queens and Kings that also tell of the timing of events. So the additional insight is given to the two through five birth path person, so not only do you have a regular mundane Minor Arcana card as I described above, but you also have another card explaining in more detail about yourself and the trials and tribulations you face on a daily basis.

I will be using the gender of the card, for example, The Page, Knight, King will be male and the Queen will be female. This energy can be attached to either the male or female Querent. It is connected to your client in some way and can be used as his or her energy. Just because a card is feminine or masculine does not mean that it would not pertain to the person you are doing the reading for if he or she is the opposite gender than the card.

PAGES

Here is an analogy that I use with a pie (or event) explaining the Court Cards:

THE PAGE indicates the start of something new. It also indicates from a new beginning to one quarter (¼) of the adventure (or pie, if you will) is over with or done. So someone ate one quarter of the pie and now it is gone.

The Page of Wands, for example, shows that he would be starting a new job, new health direction or starting a new school, attending workshops, lectures, classes or training. For instance, in the Page of Wands, he would be starting a new job, deal with new positive issues or conclusions with health concerns and perhaps starting a new school, semester or new advanced degree program.

The Page of Pentacles would foretell that there will be a new opportunity coming to the Querent which will be bringing in more money and securing financial security by a new job, inheritance, lottery or some other method.

The Page of Swords indicates new issues, obstacles, responsibilities, arguments, fights, problems, conflicts and obligations that will come into his life. This Page can handle anything that comes his way and knows that this is as bad as it is going to get, and understands that the future is more promising and positive.

The Page of Cups always indicates that there will be a new love interest. It signifies new happiness and joy, inner peace, guidance, strength, wisdom and knowledge and everything to make him happy. If married, it may indicate that someone else would be coming into his life, such as a secret love affair, or someone that he might fall in love with and change his married (or living together) arrangement. It occasionally can mean the birth of a child, such as a grandchild, which would undoubtedly be a boy.

KNIGHTS

THE KNIGHT continues the quest from the quarter leftover from the Page and continues his mission until it is now half way completed. It indicates that half (½) of the pie or adventure would be done or the pie would be eaten. There is only a half of the pie left.

The Knight of Wands indicates the newness of the job, health issue or school has now become the energy to learn more about your career, health or school. He is learning procedures and policies of his company and/or school. If it is talking about a health concern, at this point, he would be getting another opinion and trying to follow through with what the doctor had suggested as a health regiment.

The Knight of Pentacles shows that money is starting to flow into his life or the ability to have the money is coming into his life and he must decide what to do with it and how to make it grow. He may wish to speak with a financial planner, accountant or revamp his investments in some way. A consultation with a professional is always recommended. However, if he is good with money and has set goals for its future growth that also may be a viable direction to take. This is a continuation of the new money that originally came into your life with the Page of Pentacles.

The Knight of Swords indicates that he is running around frantically not knowing exactly what he has to do and in which direction he should go. However, he is getting things done and handling all of his concerns and conflicts even though his actions are unpredictable and erratic in attaining these goals and objectives. This energy puts him under a great deal of stress; however, much of the stress comes from himself! This is also a health warning card saying that if he does not calm down, chill, rest, take time for himself or relax, he will get ill with colds, the flu, bronchitis, pneumonia and any immune system issue there could be.

The Knight of Cups portrays a romantic partner. It says that this person will offer him love but he has been hurt before as indicated by the knight wearing armor. He is protecting his heart. This also indicates that the potential partner has also been hurt as well so you will both move ahead very slowly and carefully so that neither one of you makes another mistake in love.

QUEENS

THE QUEEN indicates that the event is nearly completed. She picks up at the half mark with the Knight and continues until the mission or project, dream or goal is three-quarters (¾) completed. Now there is only one quarter of the pie left and that is the job of the King.

The Queen of Wands is someone who is not that happy with her job, health situation or education. She has seen it all and is ready for a change. It is someone who is looking towards the future in these three areas: career, health and education. She is also looking out for new ventures, new journeys, new beginnings, new careers and a bright, new future.

The Queen of Pentacles is someone who is concerned with her financial security and is always anxious or worried about her financial situation. She is wondering how to make her money grow, move forward, and get more return on her money! She wants to have more financial security and stability. However, worrying about it does not make it grow; it actually makes more negativity and fear attached to her money, so her finances get worse. If she is positive about her finances and its future, she should be fine.

The Queen of Swords represents someone who has always been too giving, too caring, too loving, too kind, too generous and too honest. She does everything for everyone else and no one ever does anything back to her in return. But it suggests that she overcome her issues and concerns by standing up for herself and stop being the sucker that everyone uses and takes for granted. She must say no, set limits and boundaries and be sure to keep some of the time for her own self cultivation rather than donating all of her extra time to helping others.

The Queen of Cups indicates someone who is completely and inexplicably in love with love and whomever she is currently dating, living with or married to, etc. She will soon be drowning in emotion and sensitivity. One foot is on the rocks below which causes her pain and the other is in the water causing emotional issues as she is sliding off of the stable cement throne into the water. This woman is her own worst enemy and does not realize that she is enabling men in her life to treat her badly. She is, however, the problem because she really does not want to hear or see the truth about her partner.

KINGS

THE KING indicates that the event is completed or finally finished. He takes over at the three-quarter mark from the Queen and continues until there is no pie left on the table and everything that had to be accomplished is now done. The pie has been eaten up!

The King of Wands indicates that The King is ready to continue to the last phase of his life. It can be retirement, a change of job (because the one he has now is boring, and he is just holding onto it for the security, the paycheck and benefits). He does not like his job any longer and wants to move onto his next job, or new beginning in the next adventure of his life.

The King of Pentacles is someone who has made it in life and has all the financial security and abundance he has always wanted. He is surrounded by financial security, well being, fruitfulness and prosperity. The way this person gets money may not always be the most ethical, but he is a very prosperous man and will hold onto his wealth regardless of any circumstances around him.

The King of Swords has summoned all of his courage and has handled and dealt with all the problems, obligations, concerns, worries, issues, obstacles, and responsibilities, etc., that needed to be taken care of. He can handle anything that comes his way and now those issues are done.

The King of Cups has always been associated with the highest form of love there is; however, I have a different perspective. There is a King sitting on a cement throne in the middle of the ocean. How long do you think he will float? I find that except for timing, this card ends love relationships or possibly may resolve some love issues, but for the general reading, it usually indicates the end of a romance where at least one of the partners wants to get out of the relationship. The emotional partner drowns the logical partner and someone in the relationship is looking for balance in his or her life and wants to get away from the loved one.

ACES

The ACES always bring additional blessings to the person who is getting the reading (the Significator, Sitter or Client).

The Ace of Wands is a gift from God and Goddess in protecting and blessing your career, health and higher education (including lectures, workshops, certification programs, and training).

The Ace of Pentacles is a gift from God and Goddess in protecting and blessing your financial security, prosperity and abundance.

The Ace of Swords is a gift from God and Goddess in protecting and blessing you in resolving all of your problems, obligations, concerns, fears, doubts, worries, issues, obstacles, and responsibilities, etc. It also helps in making you more decisive and alleviates the procrastination that has been holding you back from attaining your goals.

The Ace of Cups is a gift from God and Goddess in protecting and blessing you in all the love, happiness, prosperity, and joy, inner peace, guidance, strength, wisdom, self-confidence, self-esteem and everything else you need to make you happy. (This is undoubtedly the best and luckiest card in the whole deck).

DOS AND DON'TS

IT IS IMPORTANT to try various spreads in order to see which ones work best for you. If you find you have more accuracy with one particular spread, stay with that one while you slowly experiment with others. Your aim is to be the most accurate and ethical Reader you can be and practice is the key to that accuracy.

You may wish to write in a journal at first to see which spreads were the most accurate. You can do this by writing down the summary of the year ahead spread o the answers to family or friends' questions and then see if they came true. I am sure that your Querent will be happy to give you lots of questions to answer, so you will have a lot of yes/no or regular year ahead spreads to experiment with.

Keeping a journal about the cards you pick for yourself and your impression of them is always helpful as well. If you write out what you really feel about the cards you pull for yourself and their actual meanings (when you look them up), you will get a truthful reading. I also tell new students to tape readings that are intended for yourself as if you were doing it for someone else and pretend you were going to mail it. Listen to it a few days later and you will be amazed at the information you received about your future and choices. Many people suggest that you cannot do an accurate reading for yourself. I wholeheartedly disagree.

After you have figured out your accuracy rate, you can then decide for yourself if you would like to continue giving this type of intuitive insight or just read from this book (or others that you are using) for the interpretation. If you feel confident it is knowledge the person should know, by all means offer it in a compassionate and loving way. The insightful information may also aid you in interpreting certain cards during the reading or give you a totally different meaning that you were supposed to share with the Querent.

You probably will not receive a lot of extra or added insight into it at first because you may not realize that it is information from Above, your angels or spirit guides. Most likely, you are still so unsure of your readings that you get nervous and want to read the book and that is okay for now. Once you decide to rely on the information you receive in your mind in addition to the mundane meaning of the cards, you will be amazed at how many people ask you, "How did you know that?" Just smile and say, "I'm psychic!"

Note that when you relax and take several deep breaths to clear your mind before you start a reading, you will receive intuitive information. You want to ask your guides or angels that you receive the best information for the Querent in the most positive manner that can change his or her life for the better. You can tell your Querent what information you have received, but explain that you are unsure of its accuracy because you are a beginner but that you thought you would share what you received. You can certainly question the Querent about the accuracy of your impressions or intuitive information at a later date or at the next session and then note it in your journal. Again, keeping a journal is a really good tool to help you understand where your strengths and weaknesses lie.

NOTES FROM A TAROT SAGE

READING TAROT IS a sacred experience that helps people get on their true life's path. Be sure to keep the confidentiality of your clients' readings to yourself as you may get referrals from those you have previously read including spouses, siblings, cousins or friends and co-workers. You never know. You do not want personal information getting back to a client from one of your new customers. Obviously, your ethics and morals would be in question and you would lose potential future clients because, as I am sure you know, when people have a negative experience, they share that with seventeen people. When they have a good experience, they share that with three. You can imagine how small the world is (the metaphysical world is smaller) and how many people know each other or are related to one another by blood, a common work place, organization, club, relative, neighborhood, or acquaintance. You would be surprised at how many times I have heard, "Oh, my sister Jane told me you were wonderful," or "A friend from the office said you were really accurate."

Be ethical. It is not your business to get fully invested in a reading. Yes, be interested and give the most practical and positive advice you can at the time of the reading, but be logical. If you feel the Querent is extremely negative and will take what you say too seriously, choose your words carefully and be as upbeat as possible. If you feel you cannot read for someone, suggest another Reader. If you feel they cannot take the truth, I would suggest being truthful but in the most compassionate way you can. You do not want people leaving your reading feeling more depressed and confused than when they originally came to you for guidance.

Being an astrologer, I usually ask the sun sign of the person I am reading so that I know in advance how to talk to them and how give them the information they will easily accept. It also makes me use different phrasing with positive signs than I would with negative signs. My rule of thumb is that Fire signs – Aries, Leo and Sagittarius – want to know the truth. Air signs – Gemini, Libra and Aquarius – want to know the truth, however they also want as many options as possible to be given to them so that they can choose what is right for them. Earth signs – Taurus, Virgo and Capricorn – are practical and put on a good show of being strong and detached, but underneath they are very sensitive, fearful, anxious and emotional, so tread gently with any type of challenging information. And lastly, Water signs – Cancer, Scorpio and Pisces – are the most sensitive of all the signs and really do not want to know or handle any bad news at all. If you must tell them challenging information, you must always tell them how the outcome would be much better for them and how it will push them onto a better path for a positive result or positive future. Fire and Air signs are more apt to accept change and see the big picture for a more positive future. Earth and Water signs do not like change at all, so be

HOW TO BE A TAROT DETECTIVE   ⁓47⁓

sure to use sensitivity and optimism when telling them any news that is not considered perfect. They hate change, so make change as minimal as possible.

Another way to look at it is by their positive or negative polarity. I am very direct with the positive (or masculine) signs, which are Aries, Gemini, Leo, Libra, Sagittarius and Aquarius. Out of them, the Aries wants to know the truth, but probably will not believe anything that she does not want to believe. The Gemini will go with the flow and her mind will be working overtime while you are telling her the meanings of the cards to see how she can manipulate that energy for her highest good. The Leo will just listen intently and feel that she can handle anything that comes her way. The Libra will be confused if you give them any choices at all. They will mull over in their minds over and over again to try to find a reason to select a direction. The Sagittarius will listen and do what she wants to do anyway, so you can tell them the truth as well. The Aquarius will intellectualize everything and think that no one's fate is in stone, but will listen attentively so that if a circumstance arises as you had foretold, she will be ready to deal with the situation.

Talking to the negative (or feminine) signs is another matter. The Taurus worries about everything, so even if you infer or suggest that something might happen, they will obsess over it, so be ready to smooth over your comments. The Cancerian will be all right as long as the reading does not bring about any issues concerning family, close friends or money issues. They are sensitive, but they do have inner strength. Virgos would want to know what will happen, and will rationalize and intellectualize until they figure out a way to handle the situation before it even happens. Scorpios will drink it all in, if they are getting a reading at all. Most of the mundane Scorpios do not believe in astrology or tarot. But if you get a spiritual one (the Phoenix or Eagle version), then she would think that everything happens for a reason and will try to prepare. Capricorn thinks she knows everything and that she has complete control over her life, so it would be wise not to let her know everything but make her feel as if she will still have control over the outcomes of the year ahead. Focus on the things she can do to make things run smoother in her life. And, of course, the Pisces who will listen to you, probably cry and most likely will not understand what you said or just caught a few words because she was thinking about an art or creative project or some other aspect of her life which has nothing to do with tarot and may ask you to repeat certain cards over and over again. So in my instance, I ask people's signs before I start so I know how to present the information they are seeking.

This happened to me once in the forty-two years I have been teaching and reading for clients. There was a woman from Northern New Jersey who had called for a reading. I vaguely remembered her, but being I had not met her, I thought I would give her an appointment. People who have readings by me usually stay my clients for the long haul and even if they move, they call for their yearly update so it was not unusual for someone from the past to call for another appointment. When she was in my home office, she told me she had lived in a hotel for a few years and that she was asked to leave. Then her prior readings instantly came back to me. This was a very negative person. Someone who had horrible relationships with everyone including her many siblings who would not talk to her, and after divorcing her spouse, her children did not talk to her as well. Of course she blamed everyone else. Now, she complained, that the people in her new apartment complex were giving her many problems. A pattern was quickly forming. I thought I was helping her by advising her for four long hours and explained to her that she wore very dark colors which attracted more negativity and she needed to lighten up on her wardrobe and perhaps bring in more dark greens (for money), dark blue (to help with her emotional state). She cried a lot when she was in my home for her four hour reading and I was so compassionate and understanding. The black she wore brought in more negative energy, depression and upset and the white she loved made her more like a sucker (too giving, too caring, too kind, too generous and honest, etc.). Now, I realized that the white she wore made everyone else a sucker who had to deal with her, but I was trying to be kind and hoping to get her in a more positive frame of mind since she was engulfed in negativity. Of course, she had no money so I only charged for her a one hour reading which I then came to regret.

She called me several times after her reading to check to see if she was going in the right direction and asked about the Feng Shui cures I had given her for free. I had given her a bagua mirror (an octagon mirror to dispel any negativity and to keep money in your home for free because, again, she had no money!) Finally, one day she called and I was really trying to wean her off of me as she was extremely draining and not paying me for all this added advice. She said she had put chimes on the outside of her door and her neighbors complained. I explained that she could put them on the inside of her door with the same result. Then she went ballistic and screamed at me. "You told me I was a sucker and I should stand up for myself and now you are telling me I should give in to the neighbors! Don't you know how negative you are? Why are you trying to ruin my life? You are evil and trying to put your evil on me!" Well, this went on for about five minutes and I was trying to be very compassionate because I knew she was mentally unbalanced. She also had bounced the check that she had given me for the very long session and I did want my money. But then my Leo Ascendant kicked in and I yelled back, "Who the hell do you think you are talking to. I gave you a four hour reading and charged you for one. You bounced the check, so who is evil here?" I was infuriated at her audacity of bouncing a check which included a hefty charge that the bank deducted from my account and she was yelling at me for being evil. Sometimes people see in others what is in themselves.

That was it; I was tired of being a compassionate and giving person and Reader/advisor and getting nothing in return. Although quite amazingly, her call really did not upset me because I know that I am an ethical Reader and I know I helped thousands of people throughout my career. I let it go and lost my fee, but it was worth it not to have her heavy negative energy attached to me.

I imagine she felt that I would put a curse on her, which is kind of funny since I believe there are no curses; it's your belief in the curse that makes it work. Two weeks went by and I get a letter in the mail without a return address and it is from her with a money order for half of the fee! Needless to say, she wrote me a horrible letter saying that I am a fraud and am not psychic and only read tarot cards (just like my site says) and that I live in the darkened woods of Butler, NJ because I do not want anyone to see my evilness. She said she had thrown out the bagua I had given her (for free) because it was filled with evil and that she had been to the doctor because of my trying to put evilness into her. Wow. I did not know I could do that. However, after discussing this incident with a friend of mine who is a therapist, she commented, "Do not get involved with her. She's very ill and can't be helped. Throw the letter away." I kept the letter instead to remind myself that I was used and abused and I will not allow that to happen ever again. I had a migraine for four days after she left, so if I was giving her my "evilness", I guess it backfired since I absorbed all of her negativity which made me very ill.

Why did I tell you this story? Good question. I guess it is because I want you to know you cannot help everyone. Why these crazy, wacko, troubled and poor souls are always guided to me has been a question on my mind since I started to do this work, but I asked the universe to send me emotionally stable and "able to pay" clients because at sixty-three years of age, I can no longer give too much of myself to help others. I need to keep some of my positive energy for myself and need to attract more prosperity and abundance in my life. We all need more balance in our lives and we all should help ourselves as much as we help those we counsel.

Also, remember to ask for protection of yourself while burning white sage, saying prayers or affirmations, asking for the highest good for that person and, of course, asking that you receive the information that the client needs to heal. You also want to make sure you do not keep that person's negativity attached to you, so you may clear yourself and your environment with white sage (where you did the reading) after your client has gone. I think in the situation with the unbalanced woman I had whose last name was a fruit (it figures), there was no answer. No matter what I did, she needed to blame others for her negativity, especially with relationships and ineptness. And, of course, her lack of friendships! But I moved on and never thought of her again until writing this book.

Carry black tourmaline with you because it puts a protective shield around you and repels negativity back to the person or situation that presents it to you. I had mine out in the sun regenerating that day – a mistake I will never make again! It should have been with me to protect me against Ms. Wacko's negativity and evilness.

Share business cards with other Tarot Readers so you could have a small supply of each others' cards on hand. Do not forget to share your cards with your clients as well. I always pass out two per reading so that they can give one to friends or family members. You never know from where business will originate! Many of my cards are magnetic and I have clients who told me many times that they put the card on the fridge or in the office on the metal file cabinet and always have it handy when it is time for another reading. This is a useful tool that my promotions manager gave me years ago and I have been sharing it with everyone ever since. Also, I purchased pens with my name, websites and phone number on them. Everyone loves a pen and keeps them for some time. Your goal is to expose your name out there and to have people know that you do readings so you can build up your business. Google wholesale pens and see which sites appeal to you. If you order enough, you can get pens for less than twenty cents each and people usually keep pens while they lose business cards.

Some people use tarot and astrology to replace therapy. This is regrettable and unhealthy. You are not a doctor and cannot give medical advice or medical suggestions; make this point very clear. You can always suggest to your clients that a few sessions with a counselor, therapist or social worker may benefit them in seeing another perspective of an issue or event and they will also be getting sound medical advice for their concerns. If you see something that you think requires medical attention, you can say, "When was the last time you had a check-up or annual physical?" It is a non-scare tactic and seems like a perfectly reasonable question. If it has been some time, you might suggest having her schedule a doctor's appointment. You can explain that if there were a potential problem, it would be more easily treated if caught at an early stage. You do not tell her with a voice filled with anticipation or fear; you merely state the comment in a matter-of-fact voice. I usually have business cards of my physician and a friend who is a therapist so that I can help my client further. Of course, you can say something like this doctor (or therapist) is very good. I know him/her personally, but if you would like to go to someone else, that would be good too.

Do not get caught up in having people phone you constantly to check out a particular event, circumstance or ask you more questions than your initial reading. Your time is valuable and if she needs to see (or telephone) you again, suggest she make another appointment. I have been helping people for many years and finally realized that so many people call back after one reading and get all of their advice for free over and over again by saying they thought of more questions! If you go to a doctor, the doctor does not let you call continuously throughout the next several months without having you come back for a recheck. So, neither do you.

I do not mind if there is a legitimate question, but some people take up hours of my time with a notebook of questions without ever offering additional payment. The ones who call with one or two questions and ask how much they owe me, I usually read for free. Many people understand the limitations we all have on our time, but as in all things some people do take advantage; they are the takers. Can you tell I am one of those suckers? Yes, I have always given too much; however, that has changed. I am getting better at setting boundaries and limitations in my senior years. I hope to save others who are starting out in this field a lifetime of feeling guilty that they were not giving enough of themselves or that they should read for clients or friends after a reading. I have tried it; it does not work. These people will just want more and more for free. As soon as you tell them to make an appointment, they will not bother you ever again. They realize an appointment means paying for your services – wow, what a concept! Paying someone for a service rendered . . .

(As an aside, my personal friends always pay or barter for each other's services. So if a friend pays you what you are worth, why wouldn't you expect payment from a stranger or client?).

I gave a reading to a woman who is a Libra; she was your typical air sign. She could not make a decision if her life depended on it. Again, I spent four hours with her and gave her all of my practical and metaphysical knowledge that I had for her situation. Do you know that the next morning she called and said that she still could not make up her mind. Setting boundaries, I told her that I gave her all the information I had in the four hour session the day before and had nothing more to tell her. Do you know she needed another half hour session, which I did over the phone, and when she sent me a check for the reading, she added four more questions in her note. To this day, I have not answered her. I am sure if she wants answers to these questions, she will call for another appointment. Just realize that people are always trying to get things for free. You have to set definitive boundaries. Remember that word . . . boundaries.

Giving free spiritual advice is really a wonderful thing to do if you are independently wealthy; I have learned this over the years. Those were the last four hour readings I will ever do. However, you should make it clear that you have other clients who also need your assistance. I usually book my clients back to back now so that you can spare an extra few minutes if you need to, but they are aware that your next client is waiting. If they persist, tell them what your per hour reading fee is and suggest they make another appointment to continue where you left off. As I said earlier, I used to tape my sessions and gave the tape to the clients as they left. But now, I let people bring their own tape recorders or digital ones. If they do not have one, they can always take notes the old fashioned way – pen and paper. If someone will not allow you to tape the session, then there is something wrong with the Reader. Or there is something wrong with his/her ability and does not want it on tape. Find someone who will allow this. Many Readers do allow taping of the session as it is not such a big deal if you are an ethical and conscientious Reader.

There was a time when I went through several years where clients were telling me that I said this or that and it had not come true. Knowing that I would not make such a statement, I now ask, "Really? Listen to your tape and let me know if I should listen to a particular part which states what you think I said." I have never had to listen to a tape afterwards because the outrageous claims were never made by me. As time goes on, people embellish their stories. Be careful to protect yourself and your reputation. If you are concerned because you are a beginner, remember to say that you are a beginner at the start of the tape and state that this reading is for fun and entertainment purposes only. I assure you that you will be amazed at how accurate your readings will be if you follow my clues to each card, even if you have never read for others before!

If you have clients who must cancel appointments because of financial problems, do a mini-reading for free for fifteen minutes or so. That will ensure that they will come back to you when they have the money because you were so kind. You may also ask them if they had a few questions that needed to be answered now. However, be sure these people are not users and just want another free reading. It is up to you to decide if they are really in need or if they are using their ability to take from others which they have honed since childhood.

I used to have one day a month when I did free phone readings. Even though my generosity of spirit was appreciated in many instances, many tried to take advantage of me. I recall one instance where a woman from Connecticut called to schedule an appointment for a free fifteen minute reading. I had missed her appointment, as I was helping someone else who really needed the extra time. She left me a voice mail and gave me her cell phone number and wanted me to call her back. I was outraged. I had people on welfare calling who were single parents and who truly could not afford a reading and needed guidance. This woman wanted me to call Connecticut to her cell phone (and this was when cell phones were just hitting the public, so it was not a common occurrence). When I phoned back, I told her I thought she could probably afford a reading since she had a cell phone and I did not think it was fair of her to ask for a free reading. I found out through my conversation with her that she was in her Mercedes with her rich boyfriend on the way to the airport for a European vacation. She was annoyed I would not do a reading; I was more annoyed that someone tried to take advantage of my generosity, but I stood my ground and did not give her a free reading and never heard from her again. There are always people out there who want things for free. You may give whatever you would like to whomever you would like, but value your time, your energy and your expertise and learn from my mistakes – dole out your wisdom to those who need it – and honor yourself by limiting the time you give to others vs. the money they are paying for your services.

Do not read for people who do not want a reading, who are afraid of them, or who want to prove that tarot does not work. It is not your responsibility to convince anyone of the power of the cards. They are within their own belief system as are you, so honor that in someone and just let it go. If you take away people's belief systems, what do they have left?

When I met non-believers on the web, in classes, or in other various situations, I used to argue with them continuously and try to prove that tarot was a legitimate form of divination. Now, I simply say that I have others who will pay for my knowledge so I do not have the time or patience to convince them that tarot works or to change their belief system. We all believe what we are supposed to believe. It is not worth the effort to try to convince anyone of your point of view, so avoid those situations if at all possible. My normal response now is, "That's possible." People do not know how to respond to that comment and it seems as if you are partially agreeing with them, so they will not argue with you. Besides, you know tarot works and that is all that matters.

If negative cards come out in a spread, give many options and suggestions on how to overcome those particular concerns. Each card has an answer within itself on how to overcome its negative effects. Use the cards as an aid in helping people get out of difficulties or negative situations. If the last card is, for instance, the Death Card, The Devil,

HOW TO BE A TAROT DETECTIVE

The Tower, the Ten of Swords, the Three of Swords, or any card that looks negative to the untrained eye, I believe the Querent will remember that last "negative" card, even if the rest of the reading were positive. I will usually then draw a few more cards, and draw up to twenty-one if necessary, to end on a positive note. The person is coming to you for guidance and hopefully a way out of her dilemmas. You do not want to make her feel more depressed by having negative cards remain in her mind for the next year. I call these ADDED INSIGHT CARDS which provide a better understanding on how to positively and realistically give more issue-solving clues.

You can place the added insight cards after the final twelfth card. I usually make a semi circle off to the right symbolizing the future. I briefly touch upon the cards at the end of the year-ahead reading with the variety of options and opportunities that are available to them. Sometimes you will find reconfirmation of the original twelve cards or important information to help with the current situation. One student asked if this were cheating. I definitely do not believe it is since I feel you are guided to pull these additional cards and share those particular messages shown.

When clients ask why they had only received fourteen cards while another classmate or friend received twenty-one, I tell them that they are "added insight" cards and that I was guided to pull more cards for added "insight" for the other person because their life or circumstances needed more definitive answers. That usually satisfies the person examining your abilities. This is another reason why I do personal readings without friends or family sitting in on the session. This, of course, is up to you, but I find that conversations ensue or the energies get mixed up and I am not sure if I am reading my client or the relative or friend. Besides, much of the information that comes out of a reading is so personal that no one really wants anyone else to know.

Most people need positive closure and a feeling of hope. They need to know that their negative money, career, family, or relationship concerns will end and want to know how to handle the situation, or if it is worth handling at all. As a tarot Reader, you have a responsibility to give your clients all the options, optimism and the suggestions you can possibly give and then let them decide what to do with that information.

Students and clients alike have asked if the cards are read facing the Reader or the person for whom you are doing the reading. They are always read from the READER'S POINT OF VIEW! Because of this and to avoid confusion, you may wish to have your client sit to the left of you so that you are both looking at the cards facing in the same direction. I usually ask my client to sit on my left hand side so that I will be able to absorb and understand her energy. Remember, energy comes into your body from the left side and leaves on the right side. Good tip to remember if you are ever wearing crystal bracelets. You would like the energy to help you and not a random stranger, right? So wear them on your left wrist. If you wear them on your right, you are giving that crystal's energy to everyone else.

After you shuffle the cards and give your client the cards in her left hand to shuffle until she feels comfortable, you deal them out in whichever spread you had previously chosen and place them in front of you. Therefore, the upright or reversed cards are determined by their position directly in front of you. Please be sure that the Querent shuffles the cards at least three times. Much of the energy from the last reading may still be in the cards and by shuffling only a few times, the new Querent may be getting parts of someone else's reading.

If you are doing a "Yes/No" spread, help your client focus to keep her mind on the question at hand. Sometimes, a client's mind wanders and you wonder if they are thinking of the question at all. They are in your home or office and are looking at your artwork, your certifications, your furniture, etc.; I give them a gentle reminder and say, "And remember your question is, 'Am I going to move out of state within the next six months?' Keep repeating it to yourself." Make the questions simple. If it seems too complicated, break it up into several smaller questions. For example, do not ask, "Will I marry David by the end of the year, move to another state, have a child, and live happily ever after?" You would be surprised how many clients feel this that is a single question! Those were actually four questions. Be as specific as possible with time frames, names, places, dates or anything else you might feel is relevant. It has happened many times that a client was shuffling the cards and said, "I forgot the question." In that case, let them shuffle all over again and then repeat the question with her a few times until it has been memorized. Perhaps there was too much in the question to be easily repeated or maybe it was not supposed to be asked or answered at all.

Another way of asking a question, which I use, is, "Will it be in my best interest to . . ." or "Would marrying Jeff be in both our best interests?" If you ask for both of your best interests, you will both be happy. If you are asking about your own best interest, he may leave because the relationship was not in his best interest. The best interest means that no one would be hurt by your wishes, actions, decisions or life changes. It covers everything and makes sure that the question is asked and answered for the good of all involved and for everyone's highest good.

Do not be upset if the client does not want to tell you the question. Always shuffle in the same manner and ask the Querent to also shuffle the cards. The answer to their question may come out as a "NO." Just be positive. You do not know what the question was. It could have been a question regarding Uncle Sam's or Aunt Rose's health. What if the question was pertaining to health issues getting worse in the next half year? What if they were asking if a relative or friend was going to die in the next few months? You are a tarot Reader and not a psychic (at least not at the start of learning tarot. Many times intuitive insight or psychic energy does come to you the more you use the cards!), so you do not know what people are thinking; just answer the question truthfully. If the answer comes out contrary to what they had believed, I usually read the three cards that had come out in the reading as well. I feel the actual cards in the "Yes/No" spread shed added wisdom, additional information or insight to the question so the client can understand the answer with more clarity. Sometimes the cards shown have absolutely nothing to do with the question, but still give added insight, and the Querent should be told what the cards have revealed. You will have to see which way works best for you.

On a last note for this chapter, I would recommend that you not use a deck of cards longer than five years. Put the date on the outside of the box so it will be easy to determine when to change them. I use eight decks at the same time with a few decks being in a sunny window with their crystals being re-energized for full strength at the same time. They sit in their wooden box to remove more negativity. If cards are used for many readings over many years, the negative energy from the readings drains them and it will be hard to perform a positive and accurate reading. Of course, during the five-year period when the cards seem to be inaccurate or just not giving you good vibes, it may be that they just need to be re-energized. How do you do this? You do this "very simply."

Put them in a wooden box on top of their plain colored silk; place the crystals on top of the cards and put them outside in the sun for the weekend or in the window where the sun could shine on them. Cards need the positive or masculine energy from the sun and the negative or feminine energy of the moon. The deck will then have balanced energies and you will then have accurate readings. But like batteries, this can only be done a certain number of times before they cannot hold the charge any longer. If you feel that they are no longer "recharging" from the sun and moon, then it is time to invest in another deck. A way to test this is if you do Yes/No questions and all the answers come out NO, then you know that the cards are no longer holding a positive energy charge.

One added insight: you should have one deck to read for others and another deck to use for personal readings. You may get a smaller or mini deck that you may be able to slip in to your purse or briefcase. I carry a pocket deck with me at all times in my purse and have a few decks in my car ready to go if I need to do an emergency reading. Yes, you never know when an emergency tarot reading will be needed as was often said to me while I worked in corporate for over thirty years. There are tarot emergencies, so be ready for them.

CRYSTALS

I T IS BEST if you go to the store and hold your own crystals in your left hand before buying them. The left side of your body receives energy in while the right pushes energy out! So, if you hold crystals in your left hand, you will generally feel if this crystal feels right to you.

The first group of crystals you should get as a beginner would be an amethyst, clear quartz, rose quartz, black tourmaline, citrine, hematite, carnelian and agate. This is a nice mixture of various energies which could help you to deal with any issue.

Next put them in a sunny window for the next three full days (meaning the sun's "masculine" energy in the day and the moon's "feminine" energy through the night). After the UV's clear your crystals, you can put them in your pocket, purse, drawer, up on a window sill, in a room on a table, etc. You can place them anywhere you need that crystal's energetic presence. Crystals radiate energy six feet in all directions. If you buy a round crystal, the energy will be evenly distributed; however, all crystals have a powerful and good effect on humans and animals.

You may also hold your crystals near white sage if it is being burned to get rid of negativity or any entity that may be residing inside of your crystal; however, the sun/moon combination is the only cleansing that energizes your crystals as well.

Remember, crystals are like batteries. They require re-charging from time to time if you feel they are lacking energy. Just place the crystals back in the window for a full day and night and they will be recharged and raring to go.

Just as an aside, crystals can help everyone who displays them. If you keep them in your purse, pocket, drawer or hutch, they will certainly give your energy to those areas and not for you. Take them out some of the time. Use them, hold them and feel the power they can give you.

Crystal therapy is a great modality to help bring in the energies you need and balance the energies that are not favorable. They broaden the positive energy and minimize the negative.

HEALING CRYSTAL MEANINGS

T HERE ARE MANY more crystals to choose from; however, these are the ones that I normally use and are familiar with.

AGATE

This crystal is a very grounding and balancing stone which helps with protection, abundance, hope, harmony, fertility, artistic and creative energy, acceptance, and centering. Lace agate helps to strengthen and tone the body and mind.

AMAZONITE

Amazonite helps build confidence in one's self; this is a soothing stone to calm anxieties and instill trust. This stone also represents intuition and warm, gentle, unconditional love. Amazonite is known as the stone of hope as it inspires both faith and hope to the individual carrying it. Amazonite can balance the emotions, perfect personal expression as well as verbalization. It may also align the heart and solar plexus chakras.

AMBER

Amber is a very cleansing stone with good energizing properties. It helps one focus and deflects radiation from computer monitors and any high tech equipment that may give off EMF's (electromagnetic frequencies). This stone is useful, as it contains information from Atlantis, cleanses the Thymus Gland, heals, and balances. This is an essential New Age stone.

AMETHYST

Amplifying contact with Spirit guides and the higher self, amethyst energies include wisdom, guidance, and direction in personal affairs. This stone helps with indecisiveness and brings love, peace, and harmony. It also helps strengthen the endocrine and immune systems. Amethyst is an excellent stone for healing on all levels: mind, body and spirit. This stone helps to raise vibrational frequency and protects against negative energies.

ANGELITE

Angelite is an excellent stone for communicating with spirits and angels. It can promote compassion and understanding. Angelite can increase telepathy and also can enhance astrological understanding. This stone can alleviate psychological pain and help you speak when the truth is difficult.

AQUAMARINE

This is a lovely stone for creativity that also amplifies personal strength, confidence and cleansing the soul. Aquamarine is associated with joy, happiness, humor, and removing guilt, judgment, and denial from your being. Aquamarine can aid in compassion as well as tolerance in a situation or with others. This stone can also facilitate communication with others and with the deeper self. It favors creativity, confidence, serenity and attunement to the spiritual realm. This stone is said to help safe and prosperous sea voyages.

ARAGONITE

Aragonite is a stabilizing stone that centers and grounds one's physical energies. This stone has been said to ease adaptation to different situations as well as people. It provides insight into the causes of problems and can also bring tolerance and patience without losing a sense of self-worth.

AVENTURINE

This stone is used for luck, money, gambling, growth, change, flexibility, connections with intergalactic energies, travel, telepathy, enhancing mental powers, stimulating muscle tissue, and helping ease anxieties. Aventurine is associated with improving eyesight, diseases of the eyes and the Thymus gland. This stone is also known as the heaven stone and is considered a healer of everything (emotional, mental and physical). Can help to balance, soothe and heal a wounded heart. Aventurine has been said to increase opportunities, motivation and intelligence. Aventurine can bring luck and prosperity to those who carry this ancient stone.

AXINITE

Axinite can amplify the ability to focus and find creative solutions to issues. This stone can develop courage as well as independence. It is best used for fearless thoughts and clarity of mind. Beneficial to carry as one goes through changes and transformation.

AZURITE

This is a good communication stone, also used for endurance and helping relieve severe illnesses, such as Parkinson's disease, epilepsy, and bone marrow problems. Azurite is also connected to the planets, and space travel.

BLACK ONYX

Black Onyx is an excellent grounding, strengthening and centering stone. It can be used to balance a person's mental and emotional aspects. It can assist you with specific tasks in which strength is required, and can also help to calm fears. Are you on a diet? Onyx is believed to increase a person's self control, guide them in making decisions as well as help to increase self confidence.

BLOODSTONE

Bloodstone purifies the body and aids organizational abilities. It helps with prosperity and ridding yourself of sadness, disappointment, judgment, arthritis, menopause, and radiation. It also cleanses the heart Chakra. Bloodstone is known as a balancing stone which creates harmony between conflicting personal emotions. It calms fear and anxiety and can help to deflect arguments. Bloodstone can be used for blood problems including circulation and diseases, ease menstrual pain and prevent miscarriage. Bloodstone can be used in channeling energy to others.

BLUE CHALCEDONY

Blue Chalcedony banishes fear, hysteria, depression, sadness and also mental illness. It can also promote calm and peaceful feelings. This stone drives away nightmares, fear of the dark when placed beneath the pillow and night visions. Blue Chalcedony can also be used for beauty, success, strength, and energy. It will protect its bearer during times of travel, from physical attack, and negative magick. Also has been said to prevent accidents.

BLUE LACE AGATE

Blue lace agate is an excellent healing stone. This crystal can be used for overcoming obstacles and is a potent wish stone.

BLUE ONYX

Blue Onyx corresponds to the throat chakra and is used for higher inspiration.

BLUE TIGER'S EYE

Blue Tigers Eye is also known as Hawk's Eye or Falcon's Eye. This stone can enhance integrity of communication as well as practical communication. This crystal can help to gain perspective to see and face situations fully, seeing the overview clearly and then helps with difficulties in decision making. Blue Tiger's Eye deepens meditation. It can help a carrier to speak more and gain more confidence. Blue Tiger's Eye has also been said to relieve pain, helps with shivering, and hormonal hyperactivity.

BOTSWANA AGATE

Botswana Agate has been said to provide protection for super sensitive individuals. (Specifically in crowds) The agate has been said to strengthen the immune system. It can strengthen sexual energy, ease the pain of loneliness, liberate mental feelings and provide emotional understanding.

CALCITE

Calcite enhances psychic abilities, trust, perception, spirituality and intuition. This stone is said to also be a deep intellectual cleanser, getting rid of despair and promoting clarity and intuitive abilities.

CARNELIAN

Carnelian is used for prosperity, individuality, and is a great stone to take worries away. *(This stone loves to be rubbed.)* It is also used for grounding, staying in physical reality, creative visions, and deal with nervousness. It helps one appreciate the earth and all of its beauty. Carnelian is useful to counteract doubt as well as negative thoughts and can be used in spells which relate to either of these problems. Carnelian has been said to help the timid and shy overcome their issues and boost one's self courage. It can help with public speaking to ease the anxiety as it strengthens the voice and provides confidence and eloquence. Carnelian can help to prevent nose bleeds, insanity and to boost general health.

CHRYSOCOLLA

This stone relieves nervous tension, allowing peaceful compassion and emotional balance to fill your being. It helps with chronic depression, bringing about forgiveness and lessening feelings of guilt. Chrysocolla can ease blockages of the heart energy such as loss, anger, fear and sorrow. This stone can increase inner strength, and also may bring about acceptance and tolerance. It may help with acknowledgment of inner sensitivity and alleviates feminine problems.

CITRINE

Creativity, communication, action, and the Arts are citrine's specialties. It also sharpens and directs the mind. This stone is helpful in getting rid of nightmares, especially for children. It is also used for protection and pulling in prosperity from unlikely sources. It aids the colon, liver, heart, kidneys and gallbladder in assuring good health. This crystal rules the solar plexus and a center of your intelligence. It should bring light and joy into your life. Citrine sharpens your wit and also helps you assimilate change. This is an extremely creative stone and helps those stuck in indecision. Business decisions are this stone's specialty. Citrine is good for issues involving kidneys, colon, gallbladder, liver, heart and digestive organs. It is said to help to open the conscious mind to intuition and aids with psychic and physical digestion and assimilation. It diminishes self-destructive tendencies as well as raises one's self esteem. It helps one adjust and adapt to processes and changes. Citrine helps one feel confident and secure. Good for use to obtain cheerfulness, hope and lightheartedness. It also strengthens the will, stimulates communication and promotes mental clarity.

DIAMOND

This symbol of duration in our society relates to the seventh chakra, the crown chakra. This is a purifier and amplifier of good thoughts. It is the most durable of all gems and the most sought after stone for jewelry.

EMERALD

This is a heart stone which has healing properties. It can act as a purifier stone like the diamond and helps balance issues and concerns. It is the stone of abundance and prosperity in all things. Emerald is a good stone when dealing with bringing love into your life. This stone is also used for advantages in money and/or business ventures. Emerald has been said to aid perception as well as inner clarity, healing, and problems with the eyes.

FLUORITE

This freeing stone rids one of limitations and fears with cleansing energy while drawing out denial and brings about clarification of the soul. Fluorite is called the "stone of discernment" as it discourages chaotic growth. This particular crystal balances the positive and negative aspects of the mind. It can also help to produce order in the mental, physical, emotional, and spiritual systems. Fluorite is useful in the treatment of flu, colds, staph, and strep infections as well as canker sores, ulcers,

Herpes and similar infections. This remarkable stone can also be used in the early stages of tumors.

GARNET

Garnet is used for energy, vitality, and productivity. It enhances unconditional love and calms angry feelings. Garnet is a stone of love and passion. This stone gives courage and confidence, boosts energy, and guards against depression and melancholy. It brings constancy to friendships and success in business.

- **Green Garnet** dissolves bitterness, regret, helps all forms of Cancer. It also helps with eye problems and dissolves any visual problems or irritations.
- **Red Garnet** aids circulatory system, Leukemia, blood tissue, stroke, low vitality, and heart conditions. It is a balancer and purifier to the second chakra. It will harmonize any imbalance with emotions. This crystal will inspire deep devotion and love.

HEMATITE

This wonderfully grounding stone balances mental, physical, and spiritual energies. Keep it in the car or carry with you when you are on an airplane; in this way, you will always be connected with Mother Earth. Hematite helps relieve lower back pain, activates the spleen, and has a positive effect on the bloodstream. It is used for grounding and protection as well as it strengthens the connection with the earth. This stone can be used for courage, strength, endurance and vitality. This crystal is a "stone for the mind". Hematite stimulates concentration and focus, enhancing memory and original thought.

HERKIMER DIAMOND

This is used for dream work, memory, and telepathy, developing psychic power, aiding astral travel, and amplifying the powers of other crystals.

HOWLITE

The energy of this stone primarily aids in creativity and artistic endeavors.

JADE

Jade is used for strength, protection, luck, wisdom, money, contentment, bliss, health, and material well being.

JASPER

This is a healing and balancing stone. Red Jasper is a root Chakra cleanser; this is a powerful healer, helping the liver, gallbladder, and bladder.

KUNZITE

Kunzite unites compassion and acceptance with strength and determination. It opens the heart Chakra, grounds Star Seeds, and purifies the blood.

KYANITE

Kyanite is a balancing stone which is known to be a natural pain reliever. Its high vibration can help raise the consciousness level of those who carry it. It can enhance creativity and broaden the wearer's perspective. This is one of the few stones that never will require cleansing. This crystal is used for past life recall; Kyanite is also connective and useful for learning.

LABRADORITE

This stone is used for potency and fertility, getting rid of childhood blocks or trauma, and freeing oneself of judgment.

LAPIS LAZULI

Lapis amplifies psychic abilities, and is great for promoting objectivity in emotional matters. It is a true healing stone, and aligns Spirit and will. It also aids in integration and clairvoyance and is used with third eye energies. Lapis Lazuli can be used in rituals to attract spiritual love. This stone is used in the Brow Chakra for healing. It can also be used for eye strain, difficult pregnancies, and trouble in expressing yourself and for tension.

LEPIDOLITE

Lepidolite promotes harmony, peace, and spiritual awareness. It is useful for working in silence, helping ulcer problems, and for those who need an acid and/or alkaline balancer.

MALACHITE

This stone is for shy or reserved individuals. The dominant and aggressive energies of malachite recall past issues and yet help with flexibility. Do not use this stone if you are a dominant, aggressive individual, as the energies will amplify those characteristics. This stone promotes health, endurance, action, purpose, masculinity, energy, and strength, power, and warrior qualities. Malachite will always reflect how you feel. If you feel happy, carry malachite with you to increase this feeling. This crystal can aid in the success of business deals and projects. Malachite is good for balancing relationships. This stone has been said to protect travelers.

MOONKAITE

Moonkaite is an ideal for settling animals and children into a new home. This is an excellent crystal for inducing self-healing, especially for strengthening the immune system and detoxifying the blood. This stone is a protective shield against negativity as well as against others who play head games. Need to concentrate? This stone will help reduce distractions and allow you to see opportunities as they present themselves.

MOONSTONE

Moonstone is very empowering to women, promoting psychic awareness, balancing, and helping with inner growth, strength, and psychic potential. This crystal also helps you to forget and forgive past wounds from family, significant others and friends and lets you reconcile your feelings about the negative situation. Moonstone is a used to represent the God and Goddess. This stone is good for traveling, calming energies, cramps, balance and harmony. It can also help with insomnia, dreaming, feelings and emotional tension.

NEPHRITE

Nephrite can stimulate all the senses while increasing the life force energy to one who carries it. This stone can also bring abundance and prosperity. Ancients often wore this stone to remedy diseases of the kidneys.

OBSIDIAN

This is an excellent grounding stone, helping one focus on inner vision and self-awareness. It dissipates negativity in particular situations or the current environment.

OBSIDIAN (Snowflake)

This crystal is very calming for anxious, hyper people. This stone dissolves old belief systems, expels and releases darkness through acceptance, and helps release burdens that others put on you. It also reduces stress and benefits the stomach and intestines. Snowflake Obsidian is an excellent aid for anxiety and stress as well as for purity, divination, grounding and balancing.

ONYX

Onyx helps with security issues, while it stabilizes and calms feminine energy. It is also used for protection and keeping negativity at bay.

OPAL

This stone helps attract good energy and people, aids in visualization, and is used for power, receptiveness, and sexuality-related issues. Opal focuses energy, atmosphere, and light.

ORANGE SELENITE

Orange Selenite can help one to connect with Angels and Spirit Guides. It has the ability to clear negative energies and can be used to reprogram other crystals.

PEARLS

Pearls bring wisdom and are good for dream work. They have to do with getting to the root of your feelings and emotions and it also purifies the Spirit. Pearls also help remove blockages in the emotional body through the heart Chakra.

PERIODOT

This renewing stone reduces stress and nervousness. It also purifies the colon and intestines.

PINK MANGANO CALCITE

Pink Mangano Calcite is a stone of empathy. It allows one to attune to the energy fields of others. It offers a soft feminine comfort that helps in releasing fears and grief. It is beneficial to anyone who has suffered trauma or an assault.

PRASIOLITE

Prasiolite has been said to release blockages on the emotional level by clearing the heart chakra and promoting self-love. This stone has been said to alleviate anger and fear. It can also help in the expression of one's originality. Prasiolite promotes higher states of consciousness.

PREHNITE

Prehnite can help to dissolve avoidance and substitution mechanisms. This stone can also help us face avoided images and memories as well as dissolve unpleasant feelings connected with these feelings. This stone is also known to stimulate the metabolism of fat and accelerates the removal of toxins stored in it.

PYRITE

Pyrite shields from negative energies and assist in seeing behind facades. This stone can help to overcome fatigue and also increase stamina. It is a grounding stone that acts to put concepts into action. This mineral is used to ease anxieties and attract money.

QUARTZ

This is a very basic crystal you should have in your house or with you at all times, especially if you have just started collecting and studying crystals. All quartz transmits energy in thought forms and helps one focus.

- **Clear Quartz** activates the pineal and pituitary glands and helps stimulate the brain. Clear Quartz is known as the stone of power. This is one of the most widely used crystals because it can enhance inspiration and creativity, increase confidence, clarify thoughts as well as repair auras. This stone has been said to balance emotions as well as dispel negativity. It can be used for guidance if searching for purpose and meaning in your life.
- **Rose quartz** helps kidneys and circulatory systems and aids fertility. Rose Quartz eases stress, grief, anger and fear. It can be used to soothe a restless child or animal. Rose Quartz has been said to ease pain and tension. It is helpful when detoxing or aiding in complexion issues. Rose Quartz has long been said to protect against intrusion and other spirits. When placed under the pillow, it will protect one from nightmares. This is a very useful stone for children's nightmares. Can be used in magick for peace where there is war.
- **Snow quartz** helps aid in the healing of the stomach, spleen, and pancreas disorders.

RAINBOW MOONSTONE

With qualities known for exploring balance, harmony, and intuition, let the rainbow moonstone aid your divination. Pendulums are frequently made of this type of moonstone for harmonious readings and answers.

RED JASPER

Red Jasper has been said to be helpful with menstrual and menopausal issues. It helps detoxify the blood and liver. Red Jasper aids in circulation as well as warms the body and joints. It increases one's energy and aids in keeping up stamina. Good for promoting cheerfulness and assists in making an individual more outgoing. Red Jasper protects against psychic attacks, bullying and physical threats. This crystal is used to help remember dreams.

RHODONITE

This stone's energy projects elegance and a high standard of living. Rhodonite can help us to forgive and brings about reconciliation. This stone can liberate those carrying it from deep mental pain, shock, confusion, panic and fear. This stone can also help heal wounds and reduce scarring as well as relieve arthritis.

RUBY ZOISITE

Ruby Zoisite is a powerful stone that changes negative energy into positive. This stone can relieve lethargy and boosts physical energy. It offers stamina to the mental processes, facilitating advancements of the wearer's goals.

SAPPHIRE

Sapphire's energies are inspirational, purifying, and enlightening. This stone is also used for all faith work.

SERPENTINE

Serpentine is a very strong source for energy. This stone can bring a sense of protection and increase psychic abilities. Serpentine is also known to bring balance to one's emotional state and can help to resolve conflicts peacefully. Serpentine can also aid in detoxifying the blood and body.

SODALITE

This stone is used for deep thinking, and it detoxifies the body of harmful substances and aids in general good health. Sodalite is excellent to increase confidence, and enhance creativity. This stone can be used to assist in medical treatments, help prevent diabetes and assist with digestive system issues. Sodalite is used by those who wish to enhance self expression and communication.

STROMATOLITE

Stromatolite can bring heavy persistence, stability, connection to the essence of life, resilience and versatility. This stone is also known as the stone of longevity and perseverance. It can help relate to universal principles and developmental stamina.

SUGILITE

Sugilite aids in spiritual endeavors and allows the bearer to be more receptive.

TIGER'S EYE

This is a protection stone whose energy is filled with practicality, and helping to soften stubbornness. It also aids to strengthen the pancreas, colon, and spleen, and grounds and centers your emotions. Tiger's Eye has been said to balance energy levels as well as the metabolism. It detoxifies the body and also aids in energy flow throughout the body. Tiger's Eye can reduce cravings or addictive behavior. It has been said that Tiger's Eye can be used to protect one from psychic attacks as well as psychic vampirism. It can help to bring prosperity and also aids in grounding.

TOPAZ

Topaz is used for learning and positive thinking.

Dark blue: helps with the expression of creative energies.

Light blue:	brings about spiritual growth and psychic ability.
Clear:	manifests desires on earth plane.
Golden:	aids you in the generosity of spirit and good humor.

TOURMALINE

Use tourmaline's energies for good health, balance, and relieving feelings of fear and negativity.

- **Black** protects against negative energy. Black tourmaline is a favored stone for crystal healing practices as well as similar New Age and magical endeavors, where it is helpful in protecting individuals from negative influences and offering balance. This stone has the ability to attract spiritual energies and to calm restless thoughts. As it provides peace of mind, it is a good stone for meditation and to promote serene dreams.
- **Blue** aids with communication.
- **Blue Green** allows tolerance and open mindedness.
- **Dark Green** attracts prosperity and balance.
- **Watermelon** enhances balance and stability.
- **Yellow/Brown** assists in intellectual processing.

TURQUOISE

This stone is used for strength, wisdom, positive thinking, protection, humor, wisdom, and dreams.

ULEXITE

Ulexite gives a philosophical outlook to its owner and helps with handling challenges in a positive manner.

UNAKITE

This stone is used for power, assertion, and the ability to stay in control in a given situation. Unakite promotes healing, balances breathing, and benefits the heart. Unakite is used to bring consciousness to the present. This stone helps to go beneath the physical symptoms of disease to find the root cause. It also balances the emotional body and helps one deal with their past. It can help with weight gain and is also used in the treatment of fertility issues.

Remember that crystals are like batteries. The more you use them, the more their energy is drained. If you feel your crystals are not giving you all the energy or help you need, just put them in a sunny window for a few days and nights. They need to be re-energized and then you will have all the power and crystal strength you need. Crystals work best when they are balanced with masculine (sun) energy and feminine (moon) energy.

As an aside, I have been known to put a small dish of crystals in the rear window of my car when I knew the car would be out all night. You can bring them with you and have the crystals recharged as you go. Also, if it is raining, you will still get the energy of the UVs (ultraviolet rays from the sun) to charge your stones. The sun is always shining and its energy is always available to us here on Earth.

Which stones are you attracted to? It is believed that crystals pick their owners, so whichever ones you are attracted to put into your left hand and see how it feels. If it feels right, then all you have to do is purchase and energize it, and use it to help give your deck the proper vibrations for accurate and spiritually guided readings.

COLOR INTERPRETATIONS

THE FOLLOWING ARE the colors I recommend for silk handkerchiefs which should be wrapped around your tarot deck (in and out of the box) to influence your deck in the most positive way. There are many colors available, but I have chosen to talk about some of the more basic colors which I frequently suggest and use. You want to be sure to obtain a plain colored silk handkerchief since wrapping the cards in a print or crazy design would make the vibrations, energy or chi given to the cards erratic and bizarre. Your readings would reflect that crazy energy. Readings would also be more difficult to interpret and you would probably start to wonder why things were not making sense with that variegated silk handkerchief. You can get a silk handkerchief in a men's department in your favorite clothing store, or if you are lucky, you can find bulk silk at a local fabric store. I have found many pieces of silk for sale on eBay throughout the years. You may wish to look into that. Your pieces only need to be large enough to wrap around the tarot deck, so it should be easy to find.

I have found that if you purchase the bold or vibrant shades of all of the colors listed below, you will be able to control the traits of that color easily. You will also resolve all the issues of that color. However, if you buy a tint or pastel of the color, you will have all of the problems associated with that color.

If a color touches your skin in "real life", then you are absorbing that energy. I always recommend beige under garments if you wish to be more grounded, secure, stable and focused. Most women wear white, the sucker color (see below). You may also use under garments that are made out of many colors for a balanced energy field which will support your life and goals.

BEIGE/BROWN/TAN/MAUVE

These earth tone colors are the best colors for positive foundations. Earth tones are something you can rely on because it makes you feel as if your foundation is grounded and centered, secure and stable, organized, focused and well thought out. It represents sturdiness, balance, durability, calming energies, reality, practicality, efficiency, and order; dark earth tones can seem almost business-like and non-emotional. This is a great help to balance people who are flighty, too scattered or who cannot make a decision.

- Burning brown candles invoke the Earth, grounding energy and animals. It would also neutralize negativity and bring around the status quo in situations which are in flux.

BLACK

Black usually denotes secrets, hidden agendas, and things going on behind the scenes or behind your back, lies, negativity, mourning energy, sorrow, guilt, hidden meanings, insecurity, and darkness, lack of confidence, instability, and hesitation. This color also represents depression, sadness, feelings of being overwhelmed and stressed, confused and indecisive. It feels as if the responsibilities and weight of the world are on your shoulders. If you wear black long enough, you will believe that you are living under a black cloud and you would be right. Many teenagers wear black and do they seem like happy campers? You absorb and take on the vibrations of the colors that are around you, so when choosing the color of your clothing, pick the colors that will directly benefit you such as bold and bright colors.

- Burning black candles will get rid of negativity and worry in your life. Be sure to take the residue and throw it into a stream or river which runs away from you and your home so that the negativity will not stay attached to you. It also absorbs negativity and is correlated to the 1st Chakra.

BLUE

Blue is usually connected with empathy, sympathy, compassion, serenity, calmness, and depth of emotions, sensitivity, happiness, positive outcomes, wisdom, clear sailing, harmony, peace and going in the right direction. It is also the most emotional and sensitive color in the deck. If there are many blue cards in a spread, then it reflects an emotional future by being *too* empathetic, *too* sensitive and *too* emotional. Also, if blue cards (emotions) in a year-ahead spread are not balanced with yellow cards (intellect) to offset them, life may be emotionally unbalanced, scattered and confusing. You will be too sensitive and take everything much too seriously. Even though you may feel like it, not everyone is out to get you or hurt your feelings. Be more logical and less sensitive, so that you can make good choices and decisions for the good of all involved.

- Burning blue candles attracts tranquility, peace and a meditative state. It invokes the 5th Chakra.

GOLD

Gold has always represented beauty, God and Goddess's love, serenity, calmness, brilliance, and the highest earthbound vibration relating to Heaven. Gold relates to healing, the realm of creation, and channeling energy from the Pleiades. This color has always been associated with a Supreme Being, Angels, and a Higher Power (no matter whom you believe in) and Heaven. It also connotes riches and financial security, abundance, protection and beauty.

GRAY

Gray has been linked with a faulty foundation, confusion, uncertainty, indistinguishable issues, vagueness, ambiguous concerns, doubtful energy, blurred or cloudy vision, or as if you are driving on a foggy road. A common thought on this color is that: *You know you are on a road, but cannot see far enough ahead through the fog to see the exit signs to get off to your destination.* Gray also represents not knowing how you will achieve your objective, aspiration, dream or goal within your present situation. Hopelessness and concerns, worries and negative thoughts surround you. You may be in the middle of a situation and cannot decide which course of action to take because you cannot make a final decision. It promotes anxieties, fears, and doubts, worries, being overwhelmed, confused, indecisive, procrastination energy, mild negativity and/or depression through procrastination or being afraid of the ramifications connected with a decision. Deal with procrastination issues since unfinished or negative projects and/or relationships that go on for too long without any love or hope for a positive future will only attract more negative energy.

GREEN

Green depicts harmony, a bright future, new growth, money, prosperity, wealth, financial security and compensation for a job well done. It also represents money won in a lawsuit, inheritance or lottery as well as happiness, success, and new ventures which will bring in more money. This color almost always relates to harmony, peace, abundance, and joy as well as fertility and growth for those looking to become pregnant or who wish to do well in a career.

- Burning green candles brings in prosperity and financial security. You should light the candle and then write a list of things you want the universe to bring you and place the list under the candle as it burns. You should ask the universe to at least provide you with enough money to pay your bills and live comfortably. This color brings in healing, growth, fertility and correlates to the 4th Chakra.

INDIGO

Indigo brings with it soothing surroundings, relaxation and healing attributes. It cleanses and calms the person who wears it. This color usually denotes a calming environment, as if you were on holiday or a vacation, and the handling of situations in a more sensitive, and quiet yet determined manner.

MAGENTA

Magenta connotes vision, empathy, compassion, love, and opening up to forgiveness and higher spirituality. Being in the pink/red family, it also stands for passion, love, harmony, and asserting your life energy to get whatever it is you feel is important to you. It can make you adamant, stronger, more persistent and forceful so you are equivalent to your partner's strength.

- Burning pink/red candles also brings in love energy and romance, so purchase four inch candles quickly if this is what you feel you need to make your life complete. Burn them (and use a candle snuffer to stop them from burning if you need to leave the candle unattended for any length of time) and just relight the candle and let it burn all the way to the end. You can write your wish for love, happiness, and joy, etc., and put it under the candle or you can put all of your energy into the wish after the candle burns. See which way works best for you.

ORANGE

Orange is a color which represents change, success, energy and vibrancy. It correlates to mental activity and occasional tactlessness. It also stands for those who feel as if they are always right and do not often listen to others' opinions or advice; someone who feels as if she is self-sufficient and often seems too stubborn and obstinate for her own good. It brings challenges as well as a new beginning and new energy into your life so that you can move forward towards your goals, aspirations, objectives and dreams.

- If you burn orange candles, you are asking the universe to make you successful in your personal and business life. It could be great success in any area of life as well. You are also welcoming change. Bury the residue on your property to keep that wonderful successful energy around you at all times.

PINK

Pink is a romantic color; it is a color of idealism and dreams about love and romantic partnerships. It represents the idealist who uses fantasy as a life boat and believes in love and happiness ever after no matter what they have endured. This is someone who is waiting for Prince Charming or Princess Charming, whichever the case may be. This color is healthy, happy, romantic and very fanciful. It tends to relate to seeing what you want to see and hearing what you want to hear in a love relationship, but it is rarely the whole truth. However, you are still living in a lovely world where nothing can harm you or go wrong in any way. If it does, it is ignored and you go on to the next step in your life. Pink is the innocence of love, the forging of a new relationship with many hopeful dreams and aspirations in the most romantic way possible.

- If burning pink candles, you are invoking love (romantic love) and asking for love to be brought to you, into your home and into your life. It also brings in happiness, self-love and self-esteem and correlates to the 4th Chakra.

PURPLE

Purple has the highest vibrational rate of all the colors. It represents dignity, unity with God and Goddess, the higher good, the proper path, higher aspirations, service to humanity, and a humanitarian and selfless nature. It represents Heaven. This color is usually interpreted as having to do with guidance, counseling, and advising, or being guided by Spirit to help those on this third dimensional plane of existence. It is a color most metaphysicians or spiritual people seem to be drawn to at a very young age and then find themselves in the spiritual world helping, healing or counseling others later in life. The counseling and help can be from medical professionals to metaphysical and holistic practitioners.

- Burning purple candles represents the highest vibrational rate which correlates to the astral plane, Heaven and the galaxies. It brings in connection with the universe or a connection with the Deity of your choice. It also is connected to intuition, wisdom and knowledge, and spirituality. It correlates to the 6th Chakra.

RED

Red always means desire, ambition, aggression, assertiveness, conflict, motion, action, reaction, making things happen quickly, authority, quick wit, bad temperament, temper, anger, impatience, lust, and someone who "wants what they want when they want it – which is always yesterday!" It can be too bold, tactless, violent, invasive, offensive, antagonistic and hostile. A very dominant and assertive person should limit themselves by wearing this color sparingly as it will amplify these traits and characteristics which would probably be too harsh for others to handle.

- Burning red candles indicate the physical world and your community, but most importantly it also represents passionate love and lust. If you wish to add some spice to your relationship, then red is the candle for you.

SILVER

Silver is used primarily for artwork, creative endeavors, and channeling. It is sometimes attributed to Mercury (quicksilver), representing speech, a quick mind, intelligence, and communication. Reports have come out that said that Americans favorite color for cars, according to the car industry, is silver so perhaps we are evolving in the right direction.

VIOLET/LAVENDER

Violet denotes unification with God and Goddess, royalty and regality, the higher self, spirituality, confidence, control, wisdom, integrity, and honor.

WHITE

On clothing, white always means that the person wearing this color is a sucker. By saying that, I do mean that the person is too good, too giving, too loving, too caring, too kind, too generous, too honest, and does way too much for others and gets little in return. This person has to learn how to say no, set boundaries and not allow others to drain her energy. These types eventually will become a doormat if this pattern is not broken or changed. They have learned the lesson of giving and must now learn the lesson of receiving. Accept all gifts given to you, especially if you want to gain back some of your power, heal your weakened auric field and move on.

- Burning white candles would invoke protection and clarity and spiritual guidance. It represents the 7th Chakra.

YELLOW

Yellow represents the intellect, logic, analytical and methodical abilities. It also represents your reasoning ability by the number of yellow cards that are chosen in a spread. It depicts thoughts and actions, mental activity, thinking, decisions and weighing the pros and cons of a situation without emotion. There may be a possible need for balance between the intellectual and emotional decisions that need to be made. It represents being systematic, critical, and rational, an investigative type of person and using your common sense and reasoning abilities to get to your conclusions.

- Burning yellow candles invoke communication and clairvoyance. It also makes one more logical, intellectual and allows that person to use her reasoning ability and common sense more now than in the past. It is connected to the 3rd Chakra.

PREPARING THE CARDS

PREPARING THE CARDS is very important. It means that you will be making these cards yours alone. You will need to get a small wooden box. This box can be an unfinished box from a craft store or it can be a family heirloom. The only prerequisite is that it has to be one hundred percent wood. Then you need to get a silk handkerchief to wrap your deck in and the crystals which were previously explained; however, I usually recommend a beginner's grouping of crystals for the deck and eventually you may add whichever other crystals resonate or call to you. The beginner crystal cluster is clear quartz, rose quartz, carnelian, hematite, Sodalite, citrine, and the most important one, black tourmaline. If you can only afford to get one crystal at this time, get the black tourmaline. It will protect you from negativity and place a boundary around you so nothing can harm you in any way. The crystals may be polished stones or rough cut. It is up to you. What do you like?

Once you get the box, you will put your deck into the box and on top of the silk (some people believe that 100% cotton will work as well, but I prefer a plain colored silk) and put them in a sunny window for three full days and nights. Your deck will get the positive energy from the sun (masculine energy) and the negative energy from the moon (feminine energy). In that way, your deck will be perfectly balanced and will be ready to become yours and will give amazing readings.

Burning white sage over them cannot hurt. It helps eliminate any negativity that may have been associated with your deck and makes it more positive and undoubtedly yours.

(Just know that you should have one deck to read for others and one deck should be used by you alone, so in essence you need two boxes and two decks. There are all sizes of decks, so just pick a pocket one for you so you can take it with you and a regular size one for your clients and guests. Two decks should not be in the same wooden box at the same time. The energies will get mixed up and it may impede your readings.)

INTERPRETING THE CARDS

ONE IMPORTANT BIT of information for the long-time tarot student is that with the dawning of the new age right around the sixties and seventies, many Readers decided not to read reversed cards as negative. I am one of them. Upright cards were read in the most positive way and reversed cards were frequently read as a totally opposite negative meaning for that card. I go a step further and use them for the second part of the time frame in which you are working. For instance, if the Two of Pentacles was upright, it might mean that the client would have to balance his money and budget more in the upcoming months or year-ahead. If it were reversed, it used to suggest that the client would not be able to balance his money and would get into further financial debt, perhaps using credit cards to pay other credit cards and eventually losing his good credit rating, or possibly claiming bankruptcy, etc. So reversed cards present the second part of the time frame. In this instance, the balancing of finances would be more probable in the next seven to twelve month period. With this knowledge, the Querent can then budget his money until such time as he could pay off his debts.

THE FOUR OVERVIEWS

ONE OF MY students, Annie Hall, came up with a great way to remember the four overviews. CRUMS which stand for Color, Reversed/Upright cards, Major Arcana and Suits! This is a brilliant and easy way to remember them. My students are always teaching me something new with each class. Thank you, Annie. It's a great acronym.

- The Major Color of the Sky

Decide which color is the predominant color of the skies of all the cards in your reading. If you have too many blue cards, the Querent will be too empathetic, sympathetic, emotional, super sensitive and compassionate. If the major color for the skies is yellow, then the Querent will be more intelligent, logical, analytical, methodical and able to use her reasoning abilities and common sense. If there are too many gray skies, then the Querent is stuck with fears, doubts, worries, anxieties, being overwhelmed, stressed, confused, indecisive, procrastination energy, and feeling as if she is going on a long desolate road in a fog. She cannot see what is ahead of her and cannot make out the signs to get to her destination. If there are too many cards with black skies, the Querent will go through rough times including feeling like the weight of the world is on her shoulders; she must handle many responsibilities and obligations and will experience arguing with family, friends and co-workers as well as sadness or depression. If the skies are balanced in number, then the colors will most likely balance themselves. It is especially important that if there are too many blue cards balanced by a few yellow cards that no matter what that person does for the next year, her decisions must be logical to balance the blue energy. If there are too many yellow cards, then the Querent must balance the energy with more compassion, sympathy and empathy. In other words, she must make a decision from the heart. If the client does not follow this suggestion, many of the decisions she makes will be totally wrong.

- Reversed and Upright Cards

How many cards are upright? How many are reversed? Even though I do not use reversed cards as negative in the twenty-first century, I still make note of them because they may still be areas of potential challenges that the Querent may or may not be aware of. The more upright cards, the easier the next year will be. The more reversed cards there are means the more challenging the year will be. Word your statements carefully. (For instance, if you have eight reversed cards and four upright, you can always say, "I see you have had many challenges this past year. It does not look as if they are all going to be resolved immediately, but it seems that you will be working on handling them a little at a time and will have a much more positive year-ahead." I also like to say, "If you are more proactive about your choices, you will minimize the time frame in which your issues will be resolved."

So, we now use upright cards as having an additional meaning for a time frame which is the current date of the reading through the next six months ahead. The reversed cards means that the actual energy associated with the card will not happen until seven to twelve months from the date of the reading. Or you can imagine that it is used as half of the time frame. For example, if I were doing a reading for a month and I observed reversed cards, they would mean that those particular energies would manifest in the second half of the time period, in this case, the second half of the month or week three and four. If it were a day, upright would be from midnight until noon and reversed would be noon until midnight. Get the picture?

For every positive action you take to complete, handle, or finish anything, the Querent will be taking one month off the amount of time she has to get rid of any of the negativity around her. If she has eight reversed cards that means it will take at least eight months to get into a more positive energy field. With every pro-active move she makes, she gets rid of one month of worries. In essence, she has to take eight steps forward to get rid of all the negativity in her life. If the Querent would like to change the things around her in a very positive way, she can get into that positive energy field much quicker than the eight months depicted by the original reading.

It is much better than saying, "This year looks worse than last year." Be selective in which words you use and give as much hope as possible to your client, friend or family member. With hope, anyone can change their future in a very positive light and that should be the goal.

- Major Arcana Cards

Notice how many Major Arcana cards are in the spread. Prayers will always be heard and many times answered, even if there are one or two Major Arcana cards in a spread.

- No Major Arcana Cards

No Major Arcana cards mean that God and Goddess have decided to let you handle your own responsibilities and issues within the next year. This is the time for you to take charge of your own obligations and concerns and take control of your life.

- One or Two Major Arcana Cards

Only one or two Major Arcana cards usually signify that God and Goddess, Angels, Spirit, The One, The Source, The All, The Universe, or whomever your client believes in, will be there if she needs guidance, but she must ask for that help or pray for assistance. The client may also need to reconnect to their place of worship or meditate. Be sure to find out if your client believes in God and Goddess, Angels, Spirit, etc., since there is no faster way of losing a client's attention and interest than when you start referring to something in which they do not believe. If you are reading for an atheist or a Pagan, try using God and Goddess or Universal Energies as their spiritual force.

- Three Major Arcana Cards

Three Major Arcana cards mean that God and Goddess has decided to guide you in the upcoming year since you may have already gone through too many challenges and decisions during the past year and have still not made a positive decision about your future. You will be guided on the right path (or given a cosmic kick in the pants) and given the information or intuitive insight needed to succeed and get on with your life in a positive manner. It is your job to let the Querent know what is going on in her life and what help, if any, will be forthcoming in the way of guidance from God and Goddess.

Another easy way to make decisions now is to accept the fact that the first thought that comes into your mind about a particular decision or choice is from God and Goddess and take the advice as gospel. If you can remember what the first thought was about a choice you had to make, just go with that thought. It is when you go back and forth and keep changing your mind about a decision is when things will fall apart and there is more room for error. If you "what if" yourself to death, that is the wrong decision. If you vacillate and keep changing your mind out of confusion or indecision, that too is the wrong answer. Remember your gut feeling or your first impression of the thought is the right thing to do.

- Four or More Major Arcana Cards

If you have four or more Major Arcana cards, you are truly blessed. It explains two very important pieces of information for the Reader. One is that you have had a very difficult year (starting yesterday and going back at least a year). However, this year is going to be so much better because God and Goddess are pushing you on the right road. God and Goddess are tired of you being on this particular path and may make some drastic changes in your life or give you very important choices. In this way, you will have to take risks and move forward. If you do not take risks, the good opportunities will pass you by and never return again.

The more Major Arcana cards you have in a year-ahead spread, the easier your year will be. Give positive insight and information to your client whenever you can. Your clients need to know that their hardships are nearly at an end and that they have the ability to change their life in any way they wish. Emphasize free will.

- Major Suits

A major suit is the number of wands, pentacles, swords and cups you have dealt in the spread. If you have more wands, the issues will be about your career, health and education; if you have more pentacles, your issues will be about money, related issues, security, stability and problems with finances; if you pull more swords, it relates to having too many things to do at once and you will be arguing and fighting with family and friends; however, if most of the swords are up, you will win most of these arguments. If you have more cups in a spread, then it relates to love, happiness, prosperity and joy, inner peace, guidance, strength, wisdom and knowledge and everything you need to be happy. As you can guess, I consider cups the luckiest of all the suits; however, no matter which one(s) you have, there is a message for you on how to solve these issues in a positive way.

Then to continue with your interpretation, look at the card. Is it a happy or sad card? Blue and yellow backgrounds (skies) are usually considered the happier cards, while the gray and black cards are more often considered the more fearful, anxious, and obligation cards.

What emotions or feelings do you intuitively get from the card in front of you? Is there a focus on a particular part of the card? How would you feel if you pulled this card out of a deck for yourself? What would you tell someone you were reading for when they got this card? There are no wrong answers, only varied and individualized interpretations depending upon the Reader's point of view and education in the field. Go with your intuitive nature and have fun. Spirit will guide you.

QUESTIONS TO ASK

YOU SHOULD ASK these questions as you are reading the year ahead spread (or whichever spread you are using).

What is the predominant color of the card? We judge this by looking at the color of the sky.

Blue, Yellow, Green, White, Orange, or Black

Look up the meanings of the colors that are dominant in your spread to get the flavor of the year ahead. Too many cards of one color background (within the sky) indicate an imbalance in whatever the color represents. Not enough of a particular color suggests that there is not enough of the lacking color's quality or energy to balance the situation or event.

- What are the people doing in the card?
- Are the people in the cards sad, depressed, or fearful? Are they happy?
- Are the expressions of surprise or contentment?
- Do the figures look as if they are celebrating?
- Do the figures look obstinate or disinterested?
- Is (s)he sitting on a cement throne or standing at the edge of a cliff?
- Is (s)he facing the past (left), present (center) or future (right)?
- Not looking at a house, castle, tower, or city indicates that the Querent will not get the love, happiness, prosperity, and

joy, inner peace, guidance, strength, wisdom, knowledge, self-confidence, self-esteem and everything else needed to be happy.

- So what are they looking at, if anything?
- Are they looking straight ahead to the Reader? Then, this information is happening right now.
- Are they looking to the right or the future?
- Are they looking in the wrong direction to the left or the past?
- Is the figure holding onto a wand in the past (left hand side) for security, a paycheck or benefits or are they seriously looking to improve themselves by finding another rewarding position?
- How many Minor Arcana cards?

These cards indicate mundane concerns and issues, not those of a spiritual or esoteric nature like the Major Arcana. The more Minor Arcana cards, the more practical advice the Querent is seeking. These cards usually indicate that the Querent or Significator should take control of her own life rather than look elsewhere for help. It is time to learn the lessons that must be handled and deal with responsibilities. By doing this, you can get on with your life handling tiny speed bumps along the way instead of road blocks. Mundane issues can be a job, health, relationship, projects, chores, money, etc.

- Are there any Major Arcana cards?

If there are three or more Major Arcana cards in the spread, spiritual matters are indicated for the year ahead or whichever time frame you have chosen. This is a time of divine intervention when the God and Goddess, Source, The One, All, Guardian Angels, Universal Energies, or your Spirit Guide (whomever they believe in) will guide them onto the proper path without hesitation. The Querent's job is to accept the guidance. As I have already shared, I believe that when faced with a decision, the first thought that comes into your mind will be God and Goddess properly guiding you. It is when you start doubting the received or perceived information that you become unsure of your next step. Then negative forces keep trying to push you into the wrong decision by making you question your choice. Being indecisive will let you realize that you are on the wrong path. When you start weighing pros and cons over a circumstance or issue, be assured, you are being lead astray. Once indecision is apparent, procrastination follows. Always try going back to your first thoughts on the situation because those are correct answers which will be for your best interest. Nothing else matters.

- What are the predominant suits?

How many wands, pentacles, swords, or cups do you have in the reading? What are the two predominant suits in the spread? Cups and pentacles are usually fortunate cards, while swords and wands signify challenges.

- What must the Querent, Significator, Sitter or Client do to counteract this particular card's energy?

The issue and concern is apparent in every tarot card, but so is the solution. Look at the card. If it has too much blue, it means that emotions may be your downfall and you need more logic or analytical thought to help with this instance. If it is too black or gray, denoting sadness, anxieties, fears, limitations, responsibilities, etc., then what you obviously need is more yellow, to handle things in a more methodical, rational, logical and analytical manner. You may also add more blue, to add a bit of emotion, compassion, sentimentality, empathy and sympathy to the situation or circumstance.

Remember that it does not matter whether the figure in the cards is a man or a woman. Whomever you are reading for is represented by the figure's energy in that particular card with only a few exceptions. By working with the cards, your intuitive insight will help determine which individuals the cards are representing, your client or someone else in her life (perhaps a spouse, partner, sibling, family member or even a boss, colleague or co-worker).

Below are some of the basic questions I ask my students to consider to get the general flavor of the reading. If I am doing a reading, I keep these questions in my mind as I explain the implications to the Querent.

- What is the main figure doing in each card?
- Is (s)he holding onto one or more of the suit?
- Are figures holding onto each other?

- Are they chained or linked to each other in a negative fashion?
- Is the main figure in between columns, trees, people, houses, castles, or money? This means that something needs to be balanced.
- What is the balance issue? Figure out what it is by the color of the objects.
- What color is the sky?
- Is the sky clear?
- Does it have clouds?
- How much of the card is taken up by the sky?
- Are clouds brewing behind the figure in the card?
- Are they puffy or streaking clouds?
- Are there mountains in the card? What color are they? Are they to the left, right or across the whole background of the card?
- Memorize the meanings of the colors so you can quickly interpret each and every card you choose in a reading.
- What colors are the figures wearing? What is the first color covering the skin? (White, yellow, blue, etc.) This is important as the person reflects these energies whether positive or negative.
- Are other pieces of clothing covering up the color closest to the skin?
- Are the figures creating their own problems? (Body parts in water?)
- Is there a sun/moon combination in the card so that the Significator does not see things clearly or is being deceived in some way?
- Is he living in illusion and delusion?
- Is there a great deal of water expressing an individual being overly emotional and sensitive? The more waves or ripples the water body has, the more emotional and sensitive the person is over the issue. What effect onto the client does the water have in this card?
- Are animals, birds, trees, ships, or anything else BEHIND the individual? This means that there is something hidden from the person or that secrets are going on behind their backs. How large or small these animals are determines how big or small the secrets will be.

- Is there an animal in front of the figure(s) in the card that they are not paying close attention to? This could mean there is something going on in plain view, but they choose not to deal with it at this time. They may also know of the situation but do not think that this situation warrants any attention; it may just go away on its own.
- How many figures are in the card?
- Who are they? What is their relationship to one another?
- What are they doing?
- Are the figures celebrating or do they look depressed and sad?
- Is there a path leading to new adventures and surprises?
- What color is the path? Is it straight, winding, or does it just disappear into the past, future, or center (meaning the future is not written yet) of the card?
- Where does the path go and who or what does it pass along the way?
- Are there obstacles that must be faced to get to the goal?
- Is the ground rocky or is it smooth, like the cement ground? This is the most secure, balanced, sensible, well-adjusted, centered and stable ground to stand on.
- Is there a combination of many colors throughout the cards?
- Is the figure in between the suits? When a figure is standing in between wands, pentacles, swords and cups, they are actually putting themselves in the middle of that particular situation which is represented by the suit in the card. Sometimes, she is the one causing the problem.
- Is there a house, castle, tower, tent or town anywhere in the card? Is it in the background or foreground? Is it in the past, present or future? Is the figure looking at it or concentrating on something else wondering why her home life is not happy?
- What other personal questions would you like to ask the cards?

After reading the above information, you will have a good deal to consider and interpret. Take a few moments to look at your spread and compare the notes above with your cards. Are you seeing a theme or pattern in the spread?

As you practice reading the cards, you may come up with specific questions of your own. Remember, we all get information differently and this was just the information that I get while reading for family, friends and clients. You may get totally different meanings for the symbolism in the cards, which is okay for you. Everyone connects on a different level and Readers get diverse interpretations or impressions from God and Goddess. Whatever you get is the information you are supposed to receive, so share it with your client and make sense of the whole spread in front of you. You do this by reading the cards in order and explaining everything you can about each card as you interpret them one by one from left to right in the Beginner's Year Ahead Spread or by following the numbered diagrams later in this book.

For instance, one student told me that every time she did a reading and pulled the Temperance card in a spread, she knew her client needed to go to the dentist. Wow, that was a new one on me, so I tried it several times. It never worked for me, but apparently she was very adamant that the person always needed to visit the dentist and it always worked out that her clients did need to go to the dentist. I did not get that reference for the card at all and each time I tried expressing that concern, I was wrong. I always say that if we all read alike, there would be no reason to have so many Readers or so many tarot decks to choose from! Currently, there are over one thousand tarot decks that you can choose from and more are being invented each and every day. Find the one that works for you and experiment with them; however, if you are looking to begin your journey through the tarot, I would definitely choose the Rider-Waite deck which is the most spiritual deck and the one with the most symbolism as well as the easiest to learn.

SYMBOLOGY

IT IS VERY important to look over the list of symbology below so that you will become familiar with many of the symbols within the cards; in this way, you will be able to do accurate readings. You are taking the symbols or clues in each card to come up with a unique interpretation. In this way, you are like a tarot detective.

Some of the most common ones that are found in the cards are included in this list with my interpretations. If you find something within a card that is not in this list, you can either ignore it or decide what it means to you.

ARMOR

Any figure wearing armor is simply protecting himself from hurt or pain in some way. He was hurt in the past and is taking precautions so he will never be hurt again. He can be protecting himself against any number of things but inadvertently, he wants to feel secure and stable and not at all vulnerable during this time. I use "he" since the Knights (which display the armor) are male.

BEARD

A man with a beard is enlightened, wise, and honorable, has much integrity, spirituality and knowledge from Above.

BIRDS

The Querent must take a necessary risk to achieve his or her goal. If (s)he does not take the risk, then the opportunity will pass by and will never be repeated again. Bring this bird to the Querent's attention since (s)he may need a push in the right direction to feel comfortable about taking that risk. Once an appropriate risk is taken, everything falls into place and is in the Querent's best interest. These are not the black birds that are in the court cards which are noted in black animals below.

BLACK ANIMALS

Animals denote hidden meanings, secrets, lies, issues, problems and concerns. Where the animal is located in the card can help one understand if the Querent's issues are in the past, present or future. Is (s)he noticing the issue, avoiding it, or not seeing it? Also, how small or large the animal is indicates how big the problem will be. Most of the black animals within the cards are the black birds in the court cards, but there are several other black animals throughout the cards. See below.

BLACK BIRDS

These tiny black birds indicate hidden secrets or negativity that is yet unseen. (Notice which part of the card they occupy -- past: left; present: center; or future: right). If they are in the past, then their ability to cause problems has a slim chance of affecting the present or the future. If it is in the center of the card, then the issues of the birds are happening now. If the birds are in the future, then you should warn the Querent that destructive issues are bound to happen if steps are not taken to counteract this negativity. Always remind clients, friends and family that we all have free will and we can change anything that we do not like in our lives. We are in total control of our own lives.

CASTLES

The castles indicate love, happiness, prosperity, and joy, inner peace, guidance, strength, wisdom, knowledge, self-confidence, self-esteem and everything else you need to be happy. (This also applies to towers, houses, tents, cities or any place in which one can live). If the castle is behind the figure in the card, one must pay closer attention to his home life to reap the wonderful benefits of having a castle in the card at all. Is the castle in the past, present, or future? Facing or getting to the castle, home, tower, or tent is the goal of the Querent. If one is not looking at the castle, none of the benefits are received. It does not matter where the castle is in the card; the Querent must find her way there or will never reap any of the benefits and rewards. (Does this meaning sound familiar? It's exactly the same meaning of the Cups suit.)

CEMENT

This is the best foundation on which to sit or stand. It indicates determination, security, stability, focus, organization, endurance and being totally grounded.

CHAINS

Chains signify feeling imprisoned, helpless, restricted, or limited in some way. These are self-imposed chains or feelings, not reality. The chains may be removed at any time by the Querent so that they can move forward towards the future without feeling the guilt, restrictions or problems that (s)he have felt with the chains around them. (S)he must remove the self-imposed chains, open the door under the Devil and completely get out of the situation. Let the person (s)he is trying to help figure out his/her own issues and leave the negative situation. The one trying hard to fix the situation is actually enabling the person they are trying to help. Once the person hits rock bottom, they will be able to start again and do well on their own. This man or woman has to want the drastic change or it will never happen no matter how much assistance and help they receive from others.

CIRCLES

Circles stand for completion, eternity, oneness, wholeness, following a total cycle from the beginning to the end of a situation, the one, the all, and totality. For instance, the journey from the Page, Knight, Queen and King finish a complete circle which is a cycle of life from beginning to end. The Page begins a situation; the Knight continues to learn about the situation; the Queen has a good grasp of what is going on and is in control and the King is handling anything that comes his way. He is in charge and knows what to do next in the best interest of everyone.

CLIFFS

Cliffs are self-explanatory. If you do not look where you are going, you are bound to fall off of the cliff and find it very hard to recover. However, if you are trying to balance, you know of the dangers that lie ahead of you. You tend to be cautious and are preparing for the upcoming adventures or opportunities. If a cliff is ahead of you, it may be a bit difficult to climb up to the top, so plan on moving one step at a time in a cautious manner. There is also the possibility of a "Leap of Faith" off of the cliff as in The Fool card. If you believe that whatever you have to do is a necessity, even though you know there may be other options, you are willing to take that leap of faith. If you do, you will be guided in the right direction – just believe and it will be given unto you.

CLOTHES

Clothes are delineated in layers. The clothing closest to the body or touching the skin is how the person truly is and anything on top of that clothing, such as a tunic, cloak, cape or coat is explains what the Querent has to do to overcome the negative energy of the first colored piece of clothing. A possibility is that the Querent knows that in the past he was too caring, giving, loving, kind and compassionate and now is wearing a robe of red, as in the Magician card, covering his first white garment. Two things are going on here. One, the generous and selfless person knows now that he has been going in the wrong direction in the past and is trying to become more courageous, ambitious, passionate and adventurous. He is also craving more attention, may anger easily, and has a dramatic flair for the future. If you look at the distribution of colors, it looks as if the Magician is wearing a bit more red than white. The red color is more dominant in the present and is overpowering the old attitudes of being overly helpful, gullible and innocent. In this case, is the red helping the Querent or hindering him? It will help him since the reason he has not obtained all that he wants (what lies before him on the wooden table) is that he had been taken advantage of time and time again and did not have the insight or stamina to focus on his desires and goals. He needs to stand up for himself and his beliefs to get everything that he deserves. Red is an issue about "me". What do I need to do to help myself? Once the white sucker color and red aggressive color is balanced, he will have good health and a wonderful job (wands), all the money he needs to live comfortably and pay his bills (pentacles), resolve his conflicts (swords) and the perfect love will come into his life (cups).

- Here is an interesting note on people and their clothing: when the figure in a card is wearing a particular color, it makes that color very important as it is the way they behave. Even in real life, the color of the outfit you wear every day has an unbelievable effect on your behavior and choices. As long as the color is touching your skin, the vibration of that color is being absorbed into your aura, your energy system and your soul. I warn students and clients alike that underclothes are usually the first thing to touch your skins. If you wear white, you will be a sucker for the whole day. Do not forget that white socks also mean you have a sucker foundation to your whole day as well!

As you weed through your under garments, try to buy a little more beige or multi-color items. If you need to be assertive, wear red. Do you need to be more intelligent or logical, wear yellow, etc. If you want to attract more prosperity, wear green. If you want to be more spiritual and intuitive, wear purple.

- The pastels cause the problems of what the color represents. The bold, deep dark colors bring all the positive energy, opportunities and choices from the quality it represents.

CLOUDS

Are there clouds in the sky? The higher a cloud is in the card means that the problems and concerns are at their peak, but when they start moving downward, situations and conflicts get resolved. Are there more clouds in the past, present, or future area of the card?

CLOUDS–FLUFFY

Fluffy clouds mean that secrets are brewing behind you. Be prepared for life to get a little more complicated in the near future. The lower the clouds are in the card, the closer you are to having those issues resolved.

CLOUDS–STREAKING

Streaking clouds mean that you are in the middle of arguing and disagreeing with someone as the cards are being read; (in rare instances, it can be within a week or two from the reading). Circumstances have escalated beyond your control. You must quickly take hold of the situation or it will spiral into countless issues and problems that will be difficult to stop or change.

CROWN

A crown symbolizes royalty, regality, knowledge, and high status in life. What color is the crown? If it is yellow, it denotes the person is very intelligent and logical and needs to use those qualities to find a solution to the issue at hand. If the crown is white, then there will be a good deal of spirituality and enlightenment given to that person from Above so that he can share it with mankind.

CUPS

Cups represent the water signs of the zodiac: Cancer, Scorpio, and Pisces. They signify nurturing love and a desire to be thoughtful, kind, compassionate, and sensitive. They also represent love relationships with partners, family and close friends. It brings in good health, prosperity, affection, attention, good luck and positive opportunities which encompass love. This can be a love of a partner, child, friend, neighbor or someone who is special in your life.

DOG(S)

The beloved house pet symbolizes fidelity, loyalty and trust of family and friends around you. It always suggests secure and faithful people will always be ready to help you in any circumstances.

FEET/SHOES/SOCKS

The color on the figure's feet is their grounding energy or foundation.

- Blue would indicate that the Querent is compassionate by nature and can be easily swayed by emotion, empathy, sympathy and sensitivity.
- Black would indicate that the figure has a great deal of responsibilities and obligations; she would need to be very determined in moving past the heavy energy she has attracted and would want to bring in more light and resolutions to problems and issues. Being pro-active is the key.
- Brown would indicate stability and grounded energy.
- Red would indicate a fiery temper and an extremely vocal, arrogant and passionate individual.
- White stands for naiveté, goodness, purity, gullibility and ignorance. It is also the sucker color, as we know, which means the person is too giving, caring, loving, kind, generous, honest, too trusting and does too much for others and not get anything in return.
- Yellow means a very intellectual foundation with logical, common sense and practical choices. No emotions are used to make decisions.

FLAMES

Fire represents Spirit, passion, a burning desire, and a consuming energy. Fires can erupt and be put out. Fires may also burn out of control or start more problems than was originally anticipated. Flames can be hurtful, cause pain and are always feared. It also indicates that people or things come into your life quickly and leave just as quickly. It makes an impact on you in some way.

FOUNDATION

The foundation is what the figure in the card is standing or sitting on and it can also be the color of the shoes the figure is wearing. Foundations are very important. They indicate what is really holding or not holding the person to a particular situation or outcome. Interestingly enough, your feet are the foundation of your body so what color shoes or socks do you wear each day? Maybe knowing what energies you need to bring into your life will help you decide which foundation color would be right for you at any given time.

FRUIT

Fruit indicates fruitfulness, prosperity, abundance, fertility, growth, ideas, and being productive. If you are wearing fruit, you will be fruitful in the respect of being able to have healthy children. If you are starting a business, your business (which would be like your baby) will also be healthy, abundant, stable and secure. No matter where fruit is in the card does bring in fruitfulness and abundance. Wear fruit designs in clothing in real life to add some prosperity and abundance as well as deep green colors.

FUTURE

Anything on the right side of the card is in the future. This represents everything that is possible if you take a step in the right direction. The right direction is always the future. Remember, we all have free will so any step you want to take will change the outcome of your future. Be bold. Try something new and move to a new tomorrow with confidence and pride.

GECKO(S)

This small creature which is usually black in these cards represents challenges or obstacles that must be overcome. If they complete a full circle by biting their tales, the concerns and issues are at an end. In addition, when a gecko has hold of his tail in his mouth thus forming a circle, the obstacles and problems are either self-contained or being properly handled. If there is a space between the tail and mouth, then the issues have not totally been resolved and will continue. If there is a break from the mouth to the tail, additional problems may come into your situation unless they are promptly or properly handled.

GLOVES

Gloves covering the hands indicate hiding the truth from those around you. It also states that the one wearing gloves is not being honest, not telling the whole story, and keeping secrets.

GROUND

The ground is very important in tarot. Is the ground level? Is it rocky? Is it filled with water? Is the figure in the card standing on firm cement? Are cliffs or mountains in the card? Where are they located? Rocky ground indicates that your life is on "rocky ground" or that it is uneven, unsteady or not centered at the present time. You are afraid to move ahead since you are petrified to stumble or at the very least fall into the water and become your own worst enemy. Cement is the most firm and stable foundation or ground in which one could be standing. You tend to be obstinate, certain that you have made the right decision, persistent, unyielding, and feel extremely safe and secure in the knowledge that you cannot be persuaded against your will. You know you have made the best decision or have taken the most favorable action given the facts of a particular situation. Your foundation is sturdy and secure, grounded and focused on which to build your life and dreams.

HEAD

Anything on the head of a figure in the cards such as a crown or head covering has added significance. The hair color is an indication of the figure's motives or temperament. For example, a white crown on the head indicates spirituality and goodness, a sharing and caring nature while red may indicate someone with a fiery nature who is passionate, aggressive and controlling in the way they handle circumstances. However, white hair indicates that the Significator is too giving, caring, loving, generous and honest and lets everyone take advantage of her. This person needs some boundaries and limitations. Yellow hair always indicates intelligence, logic, analytical and methodical thought. It is good to be in tune with the color of the hair in the card so you know how this person really thinks and reacts at all times. In this way, you will never be surprised.

HORSES

A horse is often seen carrying the present figure back to the past or ahead to face the future. The horse's color is also important for a proper interpretation. Horses help carry the person to the next level of their journey throughout the cards. Horses attain success in the area that the color influences.

- For example, beige or brown would be a grounded, centered, focused and stable influence.
- White would be someone who is now in control of her spirituality or has taken a step towards not being taken advantage of any longer.
- Black means that the person has now taken control over the problems, negativity and depression in her life while gray means the Querent will easily handle all the fear, doubt, worries, and anxieties as well as being overwhelmed, stressed and exhausted.

FIGURES

It is very easy to tell whether or not something has happened or is about to happen by the position of the central figure in a card.

- If the figure is facing left in the card (going in the wrong direction), then she is looking in the past or is focusing too much on past events and needs to look ahead into the future to accomplish anything.

- If the figure is looking towards the right side of the card (going in the right direction) or the future, then she is on the proper path, proceeding in the right direction.
- If the figure is looking directly at you as the Reader, then the Querent needs to make a decision about which path he will take.
- You will notice that several cards have the main figure going in both directions at the same time. One part of the body is looking in the past and the other towards the future as in the Seven of Swords. This usually indicates that things are confused and does not know if she is coming or going. Maybe she is trying to continue to serve the past while thinking of grasping the future.

It suggests that this person is trying to handle too many things for others and has less and less time for herself. She may look towards the future and see everything that she needs to do for herself, but it seems that those issues will have to wait because she is over-burdened with all of the obligations and responsibilities from the promises she had made to others. Look at how she is handling the swords – from the wrong end which indicates that she will get hurt by her decisions to help others. She definitely is uncertain about which direction she is going or needs to go. It would be in the person's best interest to let go of the past and turn around to fully face the future and accomplish what needs to be done. The only proper direction is to the right of the card or the future.

FIGURES "IN BETWEEN" ANYTHING

If a figure is "in between" anything, whether it is a tower, trees, columns, etc., something in the Querent's life is out of balance. However, sometimes getting in between two towers also showers luck on the Querent by the very nature of the meaning of towers, castles, homes and cities. Pay attention to the objects the figure is standing in between. If you have to reach the two castles, then you would be doubly blessed with all the good tidings of the castles once you reach them. If you are standing in between things already in place, then that could be a double trouble issue.

HOW TO BE A TAROT DETECTIVE   105

LEAVES

Depending upon the color of the leaves, they usually represent fertility, growth, prosperity, and new beginnings. Add the color of the leaves to the position in the card for a more precise meaning.

MOON

The moon stands for illusion/delusion, not seeing the truth, seeing what you want to see, or hearing what you want to hear because it is easier than facing the truth. Just imagine how different a road may seem if you were driving down it at midnight as opposed to 3 PM. Life takes on a different meaning with the moon and being your subconscious is ruled by the moon, you may be in for a wild ride. Ask a trusted family member or friend if the situation you are in sounds odd or ask for an opinion from someone you trust.

MOUNTAINS

Mountains across the whole card usually mean that there are so many amazing opportunities to choose from, and that you have to choose one. Sometimes too many choices are confusing, but if you think of what your most important issue is and deal with that first, your other circumstances will start to change as well. No matter which choice you make, it will be the proper one. Notice the color of the mountains, as they give clues on how to handle a particular issue.

- For example, if the mountains on the left side of the card were blue, it would indicate that the issues are emotional ones and should be handled with logic and common sense. (Again, this position is from the Reader's point of view and who is the Reader? You!) Mountains on the left are definitely going in the wrong direction and mean that there are procrastination issues at hand. If the Querent procrastinates, then there will be more negativity and he will not attract positive energy until action is taken. Generally, I have found that if mountains are to the left, then the objectives or goals have either just started or have not come to fruition. The more mountains that are represented in the card, the more procrastination issues that have to be resolved. Procrastination breeds negativity because the energy is stagnant and lifeless. One must take a step in the right direction and then they will be pushed into a positive energy field filled with wonderful opportunities and options in the future.

- If mountains appear across the whole card, it means that there will be wonderful opportunities and choices just waiting for you. If you do not take the opportunity or gift, it will disappear forever (and never be given to you again!).
- If the mountains are to the right of the card, then your goals, aspirations, ambitions and dreams will be easily met.

PAST

Anything on the left side of the card indicates the past. If the figure in the card is looking to the left side, then you are going in the wrong direction. You must handle the issues of the past, turn around and get on with your life by taking steps into the future.

PATH

Be sure to note if a path is straight, crooked, or going off into the sunset or mountains. Usually paths are put into a card to show the Reader (if you are doing a reading for yourself) or Querent where she has come from or where she should go. Also, take note of the color of the path. For example, if the path were yellow, you would follow the path of intellectual and logical thought rather than emotional thought, etc. If it were beige or brown, then you would need to be extremely grounded and focused to get to your goal at the end of the path.

PENTACLES

Pentacles correspond to the earth signs of the zodiac: Taurus, Virgo, and Capricorn. They represent prosperity, abundance, inheritance, possessions, and money. It indicates how you take care of your finances; if you are stingy or generous and how much money means to you in the scheme of things within your life.

PRESENT

If the figure is looking directly at the Reader, then it is in the present so whatever is going on is happening at this particular time. This indicates the way things are now, whether good or bad, and possibly a current situation you may need to handle to change the energy if you feel it is not appropriate.

RABBIT

A rabbit connotes someone in a hurry to conclude a situation or to get on with a particular concern or issue. It represents not looking before you leap. However, if the rabbit is running towards the left of the card or the past, then it is someone who may be going in the wrong direction. It could be someone who is confused and starting to go in one direction but then follows through in another. All this leads to procrastination and confusion.

ROADS/PATHS

Where does the road lead? What color is it? Is it a rocky or smooth path? Are there any obstacles in the road? Does it run in between castles or orchards or lead into the unknown? A straight path means an easier road to follow; conversely, a crooked or winding path may lead to a few surprises along the way or delays in reaching goals.

SERPENTS

Having a serpent in a card means trouble, secrets, hidden problems or concerns, mistrust and negativity. Make people prove themselves to you before you totally trust them.

SHOES

The shoes are the foundation of the wearer. Notice if the shoes are the same color, or the same kind, and all of the other possible combinations including the color of the socks. If there are two different shoes or two different colored shoes, then there is an imbalance of some sort and confusion. Look to the suits and the background for more insight. Notice what color shoes the figure is wearing in a card. The color can be very insightful into that person's true feelings or motivations. Are the shoes beige/brown, letting you know that this person is a very grounded and focused individual who is dependable in any circumstance? Are the main figure's feet firmly planted on the ground? Is the figure walking? Is the figure in the card standing with his or her feet in a stable and secure position or not? Are his feet under a garment so that the Reader does not know what is going on with the shoes? Are there different shoes on each foot?

SKIES

Clear skies indicate clear sailing, happiness, harmony and peace. What color is the sky in a particular card? This indicates in which area your good fortune will come to you. Is it a happy blue or intelligent yellow or perhaps a negative or depressed black or a foggy gray? Yellow skies always mean that it would be in your best interest to deal with the matter at hand in a very logical or analytical manner as opposed to the blue of sensitivity and making decisions based on emotion alone. Is the sky muddy or murky indicating that focus is needed to help balance a situation or make the situation clearer? Is it orange indicating a lot of grounding energy around the Querent which should be used to make decisions? Is it mauve indicating a spiritual energy? A clear blue sky is a happy and fortunate background for a card, especially if the figure in the card is looking at it. There is no hint of deceit, treachery, or negativity. It is an optimistic, happy, and stable card. A sky with clouds is another matter. See note on clouds above.

SNAIL

A snail connotes that you will proceed with extreme caution or will not move fast enough for others. You feel as if "slow and steady" wins the race. It depends on many other things, but sometimes this is true.

SNAKES

Those afraid of snakes will be afraid of learning new knowledge. Snakes always represent wisdom and knowledge, so being afraid of snakes means you will miss the opportunity to learn something from the experience.

SOCKS

Is the figure wearing yellow socks indicating that he is intelligent, yet hiding his knowledge? Are they red, indicating that this person will only be pushed so far before breaking into a violent outburst? The color of the socks shades the personality of the figure after the foundation in a very subtle way.

STARS

Stars represent choices or decisions. Take note of the color and number of stars. White stars indicate spiritual guidance; while yellow mean that the Querent must remain logical and rational while making this big decision. The bigger the star is, the more important the issue will be. Prioritize your decisions and make the most important one first and all the others will fall easily into place.

SUN

The sun stands for vitality, goodness, optimism, illumination, focused energy, new beginnings, an optimistic attitude and clearly seeing reality. It also helps one from procrastinating.

SUNFLOWERS

Like the sun, these flowers represent new beginnings, fertility of ideas or creative energy, new ventures, new journeys, new career and new growth.

SWORDS

Swords correspond to the air signs in the zodiac: Gemini, Libra, and Aquarius. Swords represent arguments, fighting, responsibilities, obligations, conflicts, concerns, limitations, creative thinking, ideas, action, and energy. The color is even more important if it is on the head of a figure, as said before. White usually indicates being (a sucker) too giving, caring, loving, honest, generous, etc., but when on the head, it represents spirituality and enlightenment (as it is with white suns, moons, stars, and snow).

TOWERS

Towers in general mean love, happiness, prosperity and joy, etc. It is where your partner and family live and where you feel nurtured and loved. If anything is in between two towers, columns or people, something is out of balance or needs to be balanced. Notice the colors of the towers or columns. Who are the people you are in between. For instance, if you are in between two Towers, then you need to balance your home life which consists of love, happiness, prosperity and joy, inner peace, guidance, strength, wisdom, knowledge and everything to make you happy. If life is unbalanced at home, you may be headed for a divorce or your spouse may try to find comfort elsewhere. So what can the problem be? Are you at work too much? Do you work from home and never leave? Do you regularly compliment your partner? If you are in between two gray columns, it might mean that you have to balance all the negativity in your life including fears, doubts, worries, anxieties, being overwhelmed, stressed, confused and living on a foggy road not being able to read the signs to get off to your destination.

TREES

The green leaves on trees indicate prosperity, abundance, good health, possessions, and things concerning finances. The brown trunk of the tree stands for grounding and clarity of purpose in regard to finances. If, however, the tree is black, it represents negativity, issues, concerns or depression. Is the tree in the past or the future? Wherever it is will tell you whether it is over (from the past) or still coming to you (in the future).

WANDS

The suit of Wands represents the fire signs of the zodiac: Aries, Leo, and Sagittarius. This suit represents career, jobs, education, training and health. If you are a stay at home mom, that is your job. Retired, that is your job. If you are a volunteer in your community, that is your job.

Whatever you do for the better part of the day is considered your job or vocation, even if it does not bring in a wage.

WATER

Having water on the ground usually indicates emotional issues, especially if the figure in the card is placing a body part into the pond, stream, ocean, or any type of water. It is more profound if the figure is in between bodies of water or if she were pouring water out of a vessel which would indicate that it would be best to deal with the situation in a logical and intelligent manner now before things get much too emotional. Also by pouring or touching water, it seems to indicate that she should try to be in more control of her emotional side.

Situations around water always tend to be too emotional and sensitive at this time. Calm water usually means that emotional issues are calmer or nearing an end; however, do not be fooled by the serenity of the water. Still waters run deep. There may still be issues, secrets, things hidden beneath the surface, and pain that is buried very deep inside the individual's soul. It may show hidden emotion and immeasurable sensitivity. Water that is still also indicates being too compassionate or sympathetic towards others and not taking care of oneself. It is a giving element and is filled with never ending selflessness. Be aware that you can be drained easily, so start setting limits for everyone in your life.

Rain usually indicates crying or tears. Ripples and waves indicate that problems are brewing. The larger the ripples or waves in the water are, the bigger the upcoming emotional obstacle or challenge. Is one side of the water rough and the other calm? Is the figure in the cards moving towards the rough water or away from it? Is any body part of the main figure shown in the water indicating someone is creating his own problems?

There are so many depictions of water throughout the Rider-Waite deck, but in particular, it stands for emotions. Calm water indicates secrets and emotions below the surface. There could also be hidden agendas. Ripples in a body of water mean that troubles or negativity will be coming into your life. If a body part is causing the ripples, the Querent is causing his own emotional problems. If the water is very wavy, there are rather serious and upsetting issues to handle. Turbulent water means that your emotional life is out of control.

WHEAT

Wheat symbolizes fertility, growth, abundance, fruitfulness, bounty, and plenty.

WHITE LILIES

These flowers are indicative of purity, naiveté, kindness, and being overly giving, and trusting. If there are too many lilies in a card, it may indicate that the Querent is always being taken advantage of and tends to be gullible and innocent. One must stand up for themselves and try to say "NO" more often. Strong boundaries and limitations need to be put into place.

WHITE SNOW, SUN, MOON AND STARS

Other than on clothing and white flowers, white represents new beginnings, hope, trust, loyalty, enlightenment, honesty, good-heartedness, great opportunities, and openness to new ideas. To those who still believe that white is a spiritual color, it can be viewed as such. I do not use it very often unless it is represented as a white sun, stars, or snow. I envision this as spirituality or enlightenment, and wisdom and knowledge from Above through the person to help others on this earthly plane.

WOOD

Wood is the second most grounding substance to stand, lean, or sit on. This brown color also brings one in connection to the earth or Mother Nature indicating being centered, grounded, stable, organized, secure and focused.

YODS

These are the small flames that appear on some of the cards (for instance, The Tower card). They are considered blessings from God and Goddess, Spirit guides, Guardian Angels, The Source, The One, The All, The Alpha and Omega, etc. I believe in God and Goddess and refer to the Aces and Yods as having God and Goddess's blessings.

I do not wish to offend anyone. It is a personal belief system; however, you can substitute your own belief system into this part of the cards' divination. These small, usually yellow flecks of light are blessings in the suit that has been pulled. If Yods are present in a card that looks negative, this always indicates that God and Goddess is blessing that person and pushing them into a necessary change. There is usually a gray sky connected with the Aces, the gifts from God and Goddess are evident, but the Querent is still stuck in fear and doubt that she does cannot understand how this blessing can come to pass. God and Goddess will handle it for you, so stop thinking in a negative fashion or you will limit the help offered to you. So when you think this is the worst day in your life, it will actually become a pivotal part of life which will be remembered for making you proceed in a much more positive direction even though you are unsure of why you were heading that way. You will succeed as long as you try.

Add this extra little knowledge of the symbology of the cards into the puzzle of the reading. As one of my good friends and colleagues, Trish Woods, always says, "Tarot is like a giant jigsaw puzzle. Each card represents only a little piece of the puzzle and it takes a qualified Reader to put it all together to make sense of it."

TIMING OF EVENTS

THERE ARE MANY different ways to time events. Play with the few methods below and see which one works accurately for you. Many people get different information and there is usually a pull towards one spread over another or one method over another. Keep a journal to see how accurate you are while practicing to learn which methods work best with your energy.

Major Arcana cards usually indicate that the circumstance or event will <u>happen soon</u>.

Aces signify in which season the situation will happen.

We use the proper order of the suits to calculate the seasons: fire, earth, air and water. There are two methods listed: my method and the traditional method. A fair test would be to see which method works for you.

TOTALLY TAROT TIMING METHOD

Astrological Order: Fire, Earth, Air Water

Wands present SPRING

Pentacles represent SUMMER

Swords represent AUTUMN

Cups represent WINTER

I HAVE DEVISED MY interpretations using astrology as a blueprint of the elements' order. You may try whichever method you prefer, but I would encourage you to try the Totally Tarot Method first. If you feel it does not work for you, you can always try the traditional method. However, the traditional method has no rhyme nor reason as to why it is supposed to work and in my experience has always been wrong.

TRADITIONAL TIMING METHODS

Pentacles represent SPRING

Cups represent SUMMER

Wands represent AUTUMN

Swords represent WINTER

YOU MAY SHUFFLE the cards as usual. Then make two piles. Pick the top card of either pile of the cards. Notice the suit and number of the card you have chosen.

Wands represent days.

Pentacles represent weeks.

Swords represent months.

Cups represent years.

So if you choose the Two of Wands, it will take two days. If you choose the ten of Swords, it will take ten months for that event to happen. Even though this method may sound a bit vague, I have learned quite a bit about when things were supposed to happen. Remember, we all have free will and if you put positive energy into any of the projects, issues or decisions that need to be made with good intentions, you can handle anything that comes your way especially in the time frame that is represented above. Of course, with determination and persistence, you can actually change the timing of events to a shorter period of time.

- The easiest way to find out a time frame, in my opinion, is to ask the cards: "Will I marry Michael by the end of this year 2015?" You should be able to get an answer you will understand. Again, see which method works better for you and try to remember to write the results in a journal so you will know which method has been more accurate. In the future, you would know which method is most accurate and only use that particular one.

Minor Arcana – Court Cards

This is another traditional method which never made any sense to me. How can you get an answer of days, weeks or months? This method is not very precise, so I never use it. I tried this method when I first started out in tarot over four decades ago and they just did not work for me, but you can try them and see if the universe works with you in this method.

Pages

When you pull the Page, it indicates that the event, project or decision will happen in 11 days, weeks, or months.

Knights

When you pull the Knight, it indicates that the event, project or decision will happen in 12 days, weeks, or months.

Queens

When you pull the Queen, it indicates that the event, project or decision will not happen unless you take an active role in moving the issue forward.

Kings

When you pull the King, it indicates that the event, project or decision will not happen and the universe cannot give you a specific answer because the energies have not connected. You have to push this energy forward to get to your conclusion.

Aces

When you pull the Ace, it indicates that the event, project or decision will happen almost immediately. Remember, Aces are blessings from God and Goddess.

MAJOR ARCANA INTERPRETATIONS

THE MAJOR ARCANA refers to "large hidden secrets" and your spiritual quest or soul's purpose on this karmic journey here on the third dimensional plane. It also represents your secrets, feelings and how you see things from your own perspective. Others may not know how you really feel about certain things because you keep this side of yourself hidden from others.

When I talk about he or she in the cards, I am referring to the figure in the cards. If the card is drawn for you, then it is describing what is going on in your life! If you draw it for the Querent, most of the time that energy of the card refers to him or her. Occasionally, it will refer to another, such as a husband, brother, boss, sister, Mother, etc., but not very often. So for now, use it for the person for whom you are doing the reading.

In the way I read cards, white is the "sucker" color. Most people do not like this description, but it is easier to say than the person is too giving, too caring, too loving, too kind, too generous, and too honest and does everything for everyone else. You eventually become a doormat and never get your goals accomplished. So please do not be offended when I use the word "sucker." Just know that I think all spiritual people are suckers in this lifetime. It takes many years and a get deal of maturity to realize that "we" are just as important as everyone else and should be receiving reciprocal energy for our services. We do have to take care of ourselves and our energy field. Boundaries and limitations need to be set.

(These are the cards guided by God and Goddess, Spirit Guides, Guardian Angels, the Source, the One, the All or whomever you believe in).

The Traditional Meanings are taken from the actual Rider-Waite deck.

Major Arcana Scans - 1

Major Arcana Scans - 2

0/XXII
The Fool
(Major Arcana – 22/13/4)
(Exception Card)

Zero is not a number, so we use The Fool as the last card in the series of Major Arcana cards as number 22 for numerology purposes. In the Rider-Waite deck, The Fool comes before the Magician.

There are many interpretations for this card. You should have an open mind, lots of dreams are within reach, and endless possibilities are available to you for your life. You must take a leap of faith to get onto a new path that has been your goal for some time. If you do not take that leap, then you will fall off the mountain and find it very hard to recover.

THE LEAP OF FAITH CARD

Notice all of the yellow in this card indicating intellectual thought, not only in the background, but also on the man. The sun is white showing that spirituality is shining on his life. He may be on a crossroads at this time and looking for a spiritual path. This is a very important time of life because he has to make a choice of either taking a leap of faith or taking foolish risks. If he continues to live with his head in the clouds, he may eventually fall off the cliff and find it hard to recover. It is time for a major decision; occasionally, it could also be a time of running away from problems or upsetting situations and looking for a better life or path. The spiritual white snow on the mountains in the background indicates the desire and aspirations to get on with life in a positive fashion and using his faith or spirituality to achieve those goals.

It also represents that he is being guided by Spirit with enlightenment and universal knowledge. He must think logically and methodically about all of the future consequences relating to these changes. Friends and family will be supportive as is represented by Fido, the dog, a loyal and faithful companion. Although the ground is very stable and secure, there is a cliff that he can fall off of at any moment if he does not look where he is going. The pole carrying all his necessities of life shows he is willing to make changes and leave most of his material possessions behind or that he is taking everything he needs with him and leaving the rest behind. This is not a card of abundance or seeking to gain more in the material world. He is seeking a spiritual direction, although up until now he may have been going in the wrong direction (to the left of the card). The Fool must go in the opposite direction, decide on a course of action, take that leap of faith, and get on with his life in the most spiritual and positive manner possible. New beginnings will come to him and open many new doors for a bright and interesting future. He needs to make a decision quickly before falling off of the cliff and finding it hard to recover. Making the proper decision in a timely manner will save him from issues and concerns in the future.

THE MESSAGE OF THIS CARD is that you must take a leap of faith and go after your dreams. Do not have your heads up in the clouds because you may not see the road ahead of you. Plan and then decide on a future and go towards it with confidence and resolve.

TEENAGER MEANING: If you feel you should go in a different direction than everyone else has planned for you, you need to check out your options and once you have done all the background work, decide with confidence what your next steps will be. Do them with determination and assurance, and you will be successful in your dream or goal.

KARMIC LESSON: The Karmic Lesson of The Fool is one of constant new beginnings and learning how to go with the flow when life gives you lemons. It is about not getting too attached to people and things that show up in your life. This card is about seeking the challenges your challenges directly and knowing that nothing is forever or permanent and that change is usually for the best. This card is all about taking a leap of faith and going in a new direction. It suggests that we must trust Spirit to guide you while you find your new path. Loyalty of family and friends is with you as you venture on this new path. You may hesitate or find it hard to change, but you feel in your heart that you must make a drastic change to move forward. Procrastination is a big issue which must be resolved. If you do procrastinate, you may fall off of the cliff and find it very hard to recover. Do not be the giving person you have always been and start dealing with your own life and its future. Set more boundaries, try to say "no" a lot more than usual and make sure your life is just the way you want it and not the way others want it for you.

ASTROLOGICAL CONNECTION: Uranus

MEDITATION/AFFIRMATION: Change is inevitable and I am at the stage in my life when positive change will be in my best interest. I will take a leap of faith and move forward to my new ventures and new beginnings that will be in my best interest. I know my loved ones will always support and love me, but now I will think of my destiny and move forward to my goals with the best of my ability.

TRADITIONAL MEANING: This card means that you are unpredictable, open, spontaneous, adventurous, a free spirit, and a dreamer. You are free of responsibility by choice and do not like restrictions. You have the soul of an entrepreneur. This signifies the start of a new phase of life. Trust in your own ideas and plans no matter what others may say.

I
The Magician
(Major Arcana - 1)

Logic should be used when deciding your future. Exercise wisdom, confidence, assertiveness and will power to get what you truly need.

EMPOWERING YOURSELF CARD

You are the master of your fate! You must take control of your life so that your career, job or position prospers. You must balance everything on the table before you. The background has a predominantly yellow sky that suggests intelligence, logic, analytical and methodical skills, reasoning ability and common sense must be used to accomplish goals, dreams, wishes and desires. The Magician is wearing both red and white, indicating the desire to get what he wants, but he is going about it in a very roundabout way hoping not to step on anyone's toes. In reality, the white (sucker color) is against his body, which means that this is how he is and is slowly, replacing that benign attitude with a more assertive, aggressive, passionate and adamant nature (red). Everything he desires is on the table before him. The wooden table is the second best foundation or grounding element in the cards. The tan color is very grounded and focused indicating that if he uses more passion or assertiveness towards his goals, he will have adequate money (pentacles), his conflicts will be resolved (swords), have the perfect job, education and health (wands) and love (cups), and happiness, inner peace, wisdom, strength and joy will be his. The scepter in his right hand is bringing the knowledge, intuition, and enlightenment from the Universe or Akashic Records down through him and into the earth (or his daily life). He is spreading knowledge to those in need as well as to the situations or areas of his life that require major decisions or changes. The eternity or infinity sign over his head indicates his spiritual nature, but it can also be a lifelong concern or responsibility to handle; he will ultimately succeed. The foliage bordering the card indicates abundance and prosperity if he follows his dreams and stops being too giving, caring, loving, kind, generous, and honest and letting others take advantage of him. As long as he uses his mental abilities to attain these goals, everything he ever wished and worked so hard for will become a reality.

THE MESSAGE OF THIS CARD is that you have resolution to all of life's issues before you if you can be more grounded, centered, focused and assertive. You need to handle one area of life at a time. Start saying no to unreasonable demands of your time and energy, so that you may concentrate on getting everything you need for your future. For those who cannot say no to a request from a taker, you may say, "I would love to help you, but . . . And then finish with, "I will get back to you when I have time." Unfortunately, you will never have the time and believe it or not, after bothering you a few more times, (and keep to your guns), these people will find someone else to burden. You are receiving enlightenment from Above, so balance your energy, set boundaries and limitations. Do what needs to be done in order to have a happy and rewarding life. You deserve it!

KARMIC LESSON: The Karmic Lesson of The Magician is to balance your life and stop being a sucker. In my opinion, a sucker is someone who is too giving, too caring, too loving, too generous, too kind and honest and is usually taken advantage of by others. A sucker can never say no and is always doing for others and rarely has anyone helping them in return. These people usually say that they do not need help or never accept gifts or anything in return that are offered. In this way, they are telling the universe that they do not need its help. Accept any help that anyone wants to give you in any way. If someone wants to buy you lunch, a cup of coffee, pick up something at the grocery store or whatever it is, you can now just say, "Thank you." You will be getting reciprocal energy for all of the favors you have done for them. Just accept their gift of time or in doing an errand as a thank you for all of the past good deeds you have done for them. You should take the spiritual or religious path as you are being directed by Spirit (or whomever you believe in) to help humanity and the world. Try not to be so naïve, vulnerable, innocent and gullible and be sure to use your intelligence, logic and common sense in life to make the proper decisions and you will succeed in many areas of life.

TEENAGER MEANING: This is truly a battle between you always giving in to make everyone happy and trying to be assertive enough to let your feelings and thoughts known. You are going on a spiritual path in this lifetime; however, being we live in a third dimensional world, you should take care of your school (and health), learn how to save more for the future, handle your issues and conflicts in a positive manner and then you will be guided to more love, happiness, prosperity and joy. Abundance is all around you. If you are within a working age, it also denotes that a part time/full time job will be very beneficial to you if you apply yourself. It could help your career move forward or you will get more money in order to save for a car, college or anything else that is important to you.

ASTROLOGICAL CONNECTION: Mercury

This planet deals with communication whether it is in writing, artistic pursuits, acting, singing or public speaking. It is an extremely intelligent, creative and imaginative planet.

MEDITATION/AFFIRMATION: I need to act on my beliefs and inspirations. I am resourceful and flexible in all things. I work with my body, mind and spirit to gain knowledge, perceptions and feelings to help me achieve everything that I need to be successful and happy.

TRADITIONAL MEANING: You are well-suited to business, science and high-tech fields. You are a risk-taker and an overachiever, highly organized with tremendous powers of concentration. You are flexible and creative. Determination and the strength of your personality will overcome problems. Take charge and take action. This is the card of personal power.

II
The High Priestess
(Major Arcana - 2)

The card indicates a female reaction or inspiration, feminine energy, protection, and emotional issues that she has stored from others. This card also stands for secrets and silence in protecting those secrets.

THE THERAPIST CARD

I call this "The Therapist Card," as everyone talks to and confides in The High Priestess. This person needs balance in her life. The gray pillars indicate that you need to balance the fears, doubts, worries, anxieties, being overwhelmed, stressed, indecisive and procrastinating energy around you. You must try to find a way to get off of the foggy road of all of your clients, family, friends and colleagues, etc., and move in a direction that you are comfortable with. You are not letting go of everyone's negative energy so you are overwhelmed and a bit disheartened. She must bring balance into her life to attract a peaceful and harmonious state of mind. You worry too much about the welfare of others. The pillars represent black and white, severe and mild, day and night, right and wrong, femininity and masculinity, deceit and honesty, each an opposite. This woman is draped in blue and white, indicating a great deal of sensitivity, emotion, compassion and empathy; she is too giving, caring, loving, and kind, generous, honest and does everything for others and no one does anything for her. Being too emotional, compassionate, and overly sensitive may cause additional issues. The High Priestess is the person everyone comes to for guidance and advice, but she does not listen to her own good counsel; in fact, she has no one to share her burdens with. The High Priestess is protecting all the secrets that her friends, family, partner and acquaintances have shared with her; all seek her advice and know it is safe to tell her anything as she will die with the information they have entrusted to her. One helpful hint would be to limit the advice she gives to others, and to be more cognizant of her own health. She needs rest.

The High Priestess has all the compassion and goodness associated with the moon; she is the Nurturing Mother. Any time you have a crescent moon facing towards the sky, it indicates that the woman would help everyone just as a mother would and this nurturing energy is above and beyond the norm. Her robe is draped like a waterfall over her knees, indicating the emotional turmoil of others, and being able to keep secrets below the surface of the water. There may be some concerns surrounding her, but she will hold her ground in protecting the secrets that were entrusted to her. The sky behind the "fruitful" drapery is clear blue, meaning that there is clear sailing, harmony, and peace and going in the right direction. Pomegranates on the drapery behind her reflect good luck; however, the luck is given to the people who see them in front of them, not to the one whose back is towards them. (Remember, if you do not see it, you do not get it – no matter whatever it is.) The river behind her indicates that there is a great deal of the compassion, empathy and sympathy for others and their secrets. Emotions are flowing and never ending. Water always forces things below the surface. Perhaps there could also be some of the tears and concerns she keeps "below the surface" of her emotions when she is totally drained and burdened with others' problems.

I have found too often that this card represents a doctor, nurse, or therapist. It is a "to be of service" type of a card and many times it represents the person for whom you are doing the reading who is in the healthcare field in some way. The message should be that it is wonderful to help others and be so compassionate regarding their issues, but all that concern should be turned around and used to guide her in her own life. With the water behind the curtain and all around her, in addition to the wearing of her blue outfit, it would be a helpful suggestion to say that she needs to be a bit more logical, intelligent and use common sense and her reasoning ability rather than making emotional decisions alone. In fact, if she makes any more emotional decisions, they will all be wrong!

Notice the elaborate white Triple Goddess crown. Yes, she is a spiritual person who guides and helps others. Perhaps if this person helped only those who truly needed the help and had some time to deal with her own issues, she would be much better off. She retains the negativity of those who share their problems with her and does not know how to balance or disperse them. The High Priestess needs someone to listen to her for a change. She needs rest and relaxation as well as some alone time.

THE MESSAGE OF THIS CARD is to start taking some of the advice you give to others. You need some time to unwind, relax and prioritize your future. Do not let others take up all of your free time. You need to reenergize and become physically, mentally and spiritually strong once again. Be aware of those you are helping. Are they continually coming back to you with the same issues that you had already given advice on? If so, it is your cue to let them go. Tell them that you have told them everything you could possibly tell them on that issue and there just is not any more advice you have to give them. They will go find someone else to bother. Empower them to take care of themselves. You have already done too much to help them.

TEENAGER MEANING: It is fine to help those you like and love, but school, after school sports, your part time job, health and family obligations should come first. It is very important not to continually help others and leave yourself drained of energy which could lead to health issues. If you get exhausted, it is time to take a break and relax. You can chill with your friends, go to the movies or go out to eat as long as it does not include giving more advice to others. Stop agreeing to do things for others. You are the most important person in your life and you should treat yourself with more respect.

KARMIC LESSON: The Karmic Lesson of The High Priestess is for you to be the spiritual being you were meant to be and continue on the road to enlightenment; however, to do this, you must think of yourself now and let others help themselves. You are stuck in the third dimensional world in a role of a therapist to all of your family, friends, colleagues and acquaintances. Your understanding of life is so great that everyone thinks that your role in life is to help them with their worries and concerns. Balance is the best karmic lesson you can learn. You have to stop being everyone's Mother. Stop giving your advice so freely without any concern for your own well being. You can keep secrets well, but this is at a cost. You may become depressed and overwhelmed easily because you hold too much deep inside your soul. Meditate or pray the negativity away from you. Everyone trusts and confides in you. The problem here is that no one comes to you when there is happy news, so you are continually bombarded with negativity. Balance your spiritual, mental and physical bodies so that you may continue to evolve into the enlightened being you were meant to be.

ASTROLOGICAL CONNECTION: Moon

The feminine power of the moon represents emotions, thoughts, illusion, delusion and mother energy. It is a creative energy force which also controls your subconscious mind. The moon is sensitive, very compassionate, empathetic and sympathetic. It represents the God and Goddess energy, nurturing, caring, love and intuitive insight.

MEDITATION/AFFIRMATION: I trust in my feminine intuition and inner wisdom. I have learned to balance my life in all things and with everyone. I now know how to differentiate between illusion and reality. My strong sense of acceptance and serenity brings me total peace of mind in all things.

TRADITIONAL MEANING: You have strength and inner peace. Your way is a passive path which seems to be best for you. If you remain calm while others overreact, the outcome will be in your favor. Rely on your gut feelings and you will always be right. A mysterious and/or attractive woman may enter your life.

III
The Empress
(Major Arcana - 3)

This card represents a need for stability, motherhood, family values, and love. This card also means fruitfulness, the unknown, and occasionally doubt or ignorance. All in all, a very nurturing person who wants to help everyone and not only her family and children. She may become others' representation of the Mother because she tends to take care of everyone and handles problems, responsibilities and obligations without complaint.

THE PREGNANCY, FERTILITY AND CREATIVITY CARD

This card usually is considered to be the pregnancy card; however, the Empress could be pregnant with ideas involving creativity or dreams about the future. It represents fruitfulness. The sign Venus in a heart at her side indicates femininity and Venus-like characteristics (love, support, relationships, helpfulness, and harmonious conditions and beautiful surroundings). The yellow sky and grass below her indicate that she does not think by emotion alone. She is intelligent, quick-witted, and can see through most deceptions. Being seated on an orange cushion and a red pillow indicates her stability, security, focus, prioritization, comfort, organization and assertiveness. The red pillow is her desire for a fruitful existence whether it is in having children with the right person or making a project come to fruition. Her white and red garment indicates the desire and wish to accomplish this. It also shows that she is a "sucker" to her children to a degree, but does have some boundaries (with the red on her dress). The white still indicates a "too giving" existence by helping everyone and never getting anything in return. With more fire, assertion, aggression, passion, and maybe some anger at how she has been treated in the past, she may get past this doormat mentality. The black trees in the background reveal secrets or circumstances that is unknown to her at this time, (because she does not see them or is not facing them), but they will eventually surface and impede her plans. Many times it can indicate an unwanted pregnancy with negative repercussions, as perhaps with a teenage pregnancy and the teen's mother has to take on all of the responsibilities with this issue.

The waterfall in the future background would then certainly indicate the emotional upsets of the unwed couple, their parents, and all involved with the teens' circumstances. Decisions may have to be made regarding abortion, adoption, marriage of the young couple, or being a single parent that would certainly be an extremely emotional situation for anyone. Of course, this could mean a pregnancy that was not wanted by an older couple as well. If you do not want children, do not take any unnecessary risks. Protection is required at all times. This card may also represent someone that you know who may get pregnant like an older child, neighbor, family member or friend. The crystal wand is indicative of her calling on higher powers, wisdom and knowledge from Above; the stars on her crown represent the ever-present hopes, dreams, and wishes she would like to attain as well as all the knowledge of the twelve constellations in astrology.

THE MESSAGE OF THIS CARD is that you should be trying to balance your Mothering instincts. You need to be more grounded; handle whichever situations come your way in a very logical fashion and listen to your inner voice which is guiding you from Above. Creativity is a wonderful outlet for forgetting concerns.

If you are trying to get pregnant, this is a very positive card and within a year's time, you will most likely become pregnant. If you are not trying to get pregnant, be very careful. One slip and you will have a baby on your hands. Be responsible.

TEENAGER MEANING: This card literally means that if a couple chooses not to use protection, that they will conceive a baby. This card never fails, so be extremely careful. If protection is used, then it refers to the creativity and artistic ability which will be available for either or both parties to help them in school or in a career.

KARMIC LESSON: The Karmic Lesson of The Empress is to stop being everyone's protector in the guise of The Mother and try to limit the amount of responsibility you handle for others. You need to balance your overly compassionate nature within yourself with assertiveness so that no one can ever take advantage of you ever again. You hold the secrets of everyone and it brings negative energy into your life. Let them go and live your life. Deal with your plans for your future. Let others take care of themselves. You do not have to be everyone's mother.

ASTROLOGICAL CONNECTION: Venus

Venus is the planet of love, happiness, harmony, joy, partnerships, relationships and positive emotions.

MEDITATION/AFFIRMATION: I nurture all who need my help and provide a basic foundation for their growth and well being. I know the pleasure of giving and receiving and will balance this energy daily. I love unconditionally and with wisdom. Those who need my guidance will always be in my care and protection within the boundaries and limitations that are good for my own well being.

TRADITIONAL MEANING: The Empress represents self development, creativity and personal growth. Success brings freedom, security, material comfort and protection. Wealth may separate you from your roots and sense of self. You spend too much time indoors and should get outside more. You are interested in sexual pleasure. Fertility. This is the pregnancy card. You will have excellent physical condition and health. Loving relationship between mother and child.

IV
The Emperor
(Major Arcana - 4)

Maturity is a dominant characteristic of this card, as well as a sense of justice and male values. Do not give up. Things will work out for the best if you take charge of the situation and stay adamant. Here there is a very stable figure representing logical reasoning and conviction with a flair for a controlling and critical attitude. Even though he does not give compliments easily, he is really trying to protect and guide you on the right path. He does not want you to make the same mistakes he has made throughout his life. The Emperor cares deeply for you, but just does not know how to express his love.

RESTRICTED EMOTIONS
CONTROLLING ENERGY CARD

This Emperor is seated on a throne of cement. I always give cement a very concrete aspect, no pun intended. It can be stubborn, unforgiving, unmoving, stable, secure, fixed, unyielding, and unstoppable once a decision has been made. Notice the red garb. This man is a very dominant and aggressive person who usually gets his way. The garment is covering a suit of armor that indicates that he is willing to fight for his beliefs, but it is also showing that he has been hurt in the past and will protect himself from hurt again at all costs. The four rams' heads indicate many Aries tendencies: persistence and dominance, always needing to be right, taking risks, trying new things, needing everything done now, being the center of attention, losing patience easily and demanding control. Also, this person needs to be the most important or most valuable piece to the puzzle in any situation. The scepter in his right hand indicates he feels that he has the right to be the leader because he has Divine intervention. In reality, he is getting wisdom and knowledge from Above and enlightenment as well but may not know what to do with this knowledge. The orange background indicates being grounded, but also indicates his fixed ideas and unyielding, stubborn nature. His white beard denotes the wisdom and intelligence guided by Spirit that he has in his possession to share with the world if he can get past some of his control issues. He is seated between two mountains. As always, when the figure in the card is in between two objects, there is a balance issue at hand. The Procrastination Mountains are yellow indicating that he must deal with his issues on a mental plane, but perhaps only things of scenarios for resolution instead of doing anything about them. The orange mountains in the future suggest that with more grounding and a sense of stability, he could reach any of the goals he has set for himself in a very positive and decisive manner. Maybe he is just happy about where he currently is in life. However, for now he is rigid and inflexible, so one must proceed with caution when asking for assistance. Ask for help from this type of person; never demand anything or you will be on the losing side. Carefully choose your words.

As an aside, this person usually has all of these controlling issues and may be overly critical; however, this person really cares for you on some level and is telling you what you are doing wrong because he does not want you to make mistakes. The way he does it is not to your liking, but nonetheless, he wants the best for you.

THE MESSAGE OF THIS CARD is to listen to another's point of view because you cannot always be right. Balance in your approach to relationships and daily life will help tone down your assertive nature. This façade may be keeping important people at a distance since they are not quite sure how you will react to a particular issue or news. You are too volatile and unpredictable. Be more open and listen to others before responding with your own brand of words of wisdom.

TEENAGER MEANING: An older person with more wisdom and knowledge is very judgmental of you and is very unforgiving. You are seeking guidance or approval from this person, but may be too sensitive to digest the information that was given to you from this very assertive, no nonsense person. It could be a parent, older relative or just someone who is older but it is someone that asked for advice. This person your best interest at heart (depending upon who it is); however, his communication skills lack in compassion and sometimes they can be considered demeaning.

KARMIC LESSON: The Karmic Lesson of The Emperor is to be objective and know that he cannot always be right. Others have opinions and want their points of view heard as well. Be more expressive in love and stop hiding emotions from the ones you love. Those around you need your love, affection and attention, so this would be a good time to show how you really feel about them. Do not worry about which words you use to get your emotions across; they will come once you start trusting in yourself that you only have that person's best interest in mind.

ASTROLOGICAL CONNECTION: Aries

This is a very forceful, energetic, dominant and arrogant sign. They usually get what they want and stand up for themselves with no problem at all. Arians are the natural leaders of the zodiac and want what they want when they want it! Preferably yesterday.

MEDITATION/AFFIRMATION: I am strong and can make all of my dreams come true. I hold onto order and structure and create stability and security for my family and friends. I can reason and plan my future and succeed in all of my ambitions and dreams. I contribute too many accomplishments in life and in being a teacher and mentor; I help many others achieve their goals and dreams. I will try to be more compassionate and empathetic to those I help without criticism or disapproval.

TRADITIONAL MEANING: There is a loving relationship between father and child. You are the master of your own emotions. You have leadership ability as well as authority, willpower and self control. Projects or ideas will fall into place. You are in control of all situations. Dreams will finally be realized. You will be in a position of responsibility. You will defend and protect those in a weaker position.

V
The Hierophant
(Major Arcana - 5)

This is a practical card and can represent magic applied for practical purposes. It stands for tradition, power of the mind, and ritual. It can also stand for a marriage alliance (not particularly for love) and mercy or goodness coming from an unexpected source. It is a higher spiritual path which pushes you to help those in need or to give guidance when appropriate.

BALANCING LIFE ENERGY CARD

The Hierophant is seated high on a throne and wearing the wisest of all the headgear in the cards. This truly is an intelligent and spiritual card. Look at the two people in front of him. They could be monks, or represent anyone who is seeking guidance, help, advice, opinions or want to learn from his overflowing fountain of knowledge. The white underneath his robe indicates that he is too giving, caring, loving, kind, generous, and honest and does too much for others and yet, the red robe is indicative of his trying to balance the energy and become more assertive, passionate about his own life and what he wants. He demands time for himself despite others' trials and tribulations. Red and white seem to be very common in the Major Arcana cards indicating dominance, desire, control, aggression, and passion combined with purity, goodness and hope. Being in between the two gray pillars indicates that no matter what is going on, the people who come to him for advice, etc., are filled with fear, doubts, worries, anxieties, being overwhelmed, unsure of their future and need someone to guide them. Guess what? The Hierophant has been elected to the job without running for office. If you notice the exaggerated cross in his right hand, you can see that he has been spiritual or religious for most of his life with a few stops on the way to balance his mundane existence. The vertical part of the cross means spirituality and enlightenment; the horizontal part of the cross means handling mundane and everyday tasks and chores. So if you look at the cross, one sees that The Hierophant has stopped at least three times in his life to deal with mundane issues such as personal or family concerns. Now the vertical part of the cross is continuing upwards again, so he is back on his spiritual quest.

(This is a powerful blessing card giving the Querent all the grace needed to get on with life. Notice the keys beneath the Hierophant. Could they be the keys to your happiness if you let the Universe provide the answers? This may also be an issue with close relationships in your life since you are between the two priests. Could it be a religious struggle or issue? Are you looking for more direction, enlightenment, or spirituality, but just do not know how it all fits into your life at this time? In all, The Hierophant is bestowing a blessing upon you, so gracefully accept the situation or circumstance and continue with your positive plans).

THE MESSAGE OF THIS CARD is that you should strive for balance within your spiritual and mundane lives. There are many people who need your time and attention. Others look up to you. You are in the middle of so many issues and concerns; however, you just need to relax and help those you can. You also need more rest and entertainment in your life. The more energy expended on others means the less for you. Set clear boundaries.

TEENAGER MEANING: You are seeking answers in so many areas of life. What is life all about? What is your part in it? And yet, you are very much the role model for many, so show yourself in the best light so that others may follow your good example. Help your friends or people who need assistance.

KARMIC LESSON: The Karmic Lesson of The Hierophant is to balance your life and the amount of time that others seek your wisdom and advice. You are a very intelligent person, but still have so much to learn. You are on a spiritual journey, but it seems as if your challenges continue. People look up to you because you are a strong symbol of courage, strength and compassion not only to gain the wisdom and answers that you seek, but to help those who also need closure or insight into their lives.

ASTROLOGICAL CONNECTION: Taurus

A feminine/negative polarity fixed sign. This means that Taureans rarely change their minds unless it makes complete sense to them to do so. Taureans can be stubborn, persistent and adamant about their dreams and goals. They are also one of the best nurturing parents as well as being very family oriented and creative. Taurus rules the throat and many famous singers are born under this sign.

MEDITATION/AFFIRMATION: I keep cultural traditions alive within my family and generation. I can form a bridge between this human experience and Heaven, a connection between right and wrong, black and white and the positive and negative. I offer each generation a chance to decide what they will preserve for future generations.

TRADITIONAL MEANING: You are well suited for a career in education, religion or medicine. Increased knowledge, education and skills will be forthcoming. There is much spiritual growth. Teamwork is necessary for job contentment. Bend to authority and do what is expected of you. Watch out for ethical conflicts. Be sure to choose the moral path. Your need for social approval affects your decisions.

VI
The Lovers
(Major Arcana - 6)

You could be on a crossroads in a relationship, although this card usually represents agreement after tremendous sacrifice and compromise. You will, however, need to compromise on this issue for the rest of your life. It is not easy, but it is possible. The emotional and logical sides of the brain need to be balanced. It also implies that a decision has to be made between the couple which does not necessarily mean it is a romantic couple. It could be siblings, family members, a best friend, etc., that you are having the concerns with, so the faster you fix the issues, the quicker a resolution will be found between the two of you.

COMPROMISE CARD

I do not use this card to represent The Lovers as it does in the traditional meaning. Actually, I use it quite the opposite. Taking up a good third of the card, the sun represents mental properties, power, reason, logic, new beginnings, optimism, vitality and growth. However, it is also giving life to the situation and is helping it flourish, as well as spreading all of this vibrant energy. Raphael the Archangel is blessing this relationship and wants it to lovingly grow. Sometimes, depending on the circumstance, I have found this card to mean that the people involved are very honest with each and break down the other's defenses. Naked people in the cards are extremely vulnerable, innocent, naïve, gullible and easily hurt. They should try to set better limits and boundaries so that others will not have the ability to take advantage of them as a couple and as individuals.

The woman is facing the right (the future) while the man is facing the left (the past or wrong direction). The ground is green, full of fertility, abundance, and good health. If you look at the man, he is almost questioning the woman as to what is going on. He is clueless of the issue. He does not understand what is going wrong in the relationship, while she, on the other hand, is looking upward towards Heaven praying for guidance and asking why he does not understand what is going wrong.

He is full of ambition, life, and energy, indicated by the flames behind him. She possesses much insight and a calm way of handling matters, indicated by the snake (wisdom and knowledge) on the tree behind her. Also, the fruit indicates her resourcefulness and fertility in allowing the relationship to grow and the handling of all matters that need her special touch – nurturing people and life. The largest mountain in all of the cards stands between them. This indicates that there is a large issue which will always be between them; it must be actively dealt with. Only compromise will help this situation. An example might be if a married couple's in-laws did not like the partner their son or daughter may have chosen. The problem will always be evident, but the couple would have to deal with it. Does the wife/husband call the in-laws on holidays, invite them over, send birthday cards and just chat on the phone or do they do nothing? Should they deal with this awkward situation for as long as they are married? Let us look at it from the wife's side. She would have to make up her mind about how to act around the relatives, but in order to keep the marriage healthy, she may have to compromise and go to family gatherings or invite in-laws to her home. Perhaps the other half of the time, the partner could go to family functions on his own or not at all. This would have to be worked out in the compromise. The clear blue sky indicates clear sailing, harmony and peace and going in the right direction even though the mountain is between them. So if either party makes the effort, it will be a very positive step in keeping the relationship intact. Can this work? Yes, but as I previously said, there will be a tremendous amount of compromise on both parties.

The brown mountain indicates stability and security, so therefore with some work, compromise, and maturity, their aspirations and dreams can come to fruition. Their problems may be solved with hard work, perseverance and determination. It is not an easy task, but this can work.

THE MESSAGE OF THIS CARD is that a couple seems very vulnerable. The man seems clueless as to why things are not working out while the woman is seeking spiritual guidance from Above. The huge mountain in between them indicates that there is a major issue or concern that will always be a bone of contention. Someone will always have to compromise in this relationship until the issue is dealt with more openly. This compromise may be for the rest of your life. Sometimes both parties have to compromise or come to some sort of a truce on a particular matter. If they do, then things will work out for the couple's best interest.

TEENAGER MEANING: Both parties see life, situations, circumstances and reality differently. It will be very hard to compromise, but it can be done if you feel it is worth the challenge. This could be a partner, sibling, parent, teacher or friend. If you do not agree with what is being said or done, open your mouth and let others know how you truly feel about the situation. Then and only then can compromise help both of you feel as if you have gained some ground.

KARMIC LESSON: The Karmic Lesson of The Lovers is that you must always see situations and life from another's perspective. Know that you are being blessed from Above. With compromise, anything is possible. Even though there are large issues to overcome, you can make things work. Know that you are too vulnerable, innocent, naïve and gullible, stand up for yourself and when you feel you have compromised as much as you can, you need to stop being taken advantage of and hold your ground. If compromises cannot be attained, maybe it is time to let the situation or person go.

ASTROLOGICAL CONNECTION: Gemini

MEDITATION/AFFIRMATION: I am attempting to make this relationship work by compromise, positive commitments and forgiveness. There are difficult choices ahead, but once I learn to accept life's limitations, I will be ready for the opportunities that are destined for me.

TRADITIONAL MEANING: This is the card of physical beauty. Beginning of a romance. You have a beautiful soul. Temptation, sexuality, attraction, lust and love. In order for a relationship to work, you must leave your parents. Represents a period of good times and adventures. An important decision must be made.

VII
The Chariot
(Major Arcana - 7)

The Chariot represents the worst procrastination energy in the deck. It also represents control, self-control, inaction, and lack of movement. It denotes that emotions are the driving force behind your inaction. You also continue to waiver about making decisions and taking care of responsibilities. Then you wind up doing nothing. This card should give you a cosmic kick in the pants to take decisive action so that your life can move in a positive direction.

PROCRASTINATION CARD

Yellow is the predominant color in this card which indicates that there is always intellect, logic, analytical and methodical thought, common sense and reasoning abilities that you can rely on to make decisions if you stop procrastinating. There are two castles in the background. Whenever there are houses or castles in a card, they represent love, happiness, prosperity, and joy, inner peace, guidance, strength, wisdom, knowledge and everything you need to make you happy. However, the figure is not looking at the castles; when you do not look at a castle (or anything in these cards), the person does not get that gift or energy. In fact, he is looking away from them indicating that the things he seeks are not within his grasp. They are back in the home. The castles on either side of him would seem to conclude that home life is a balance issue. Should he be at home more? Should he make home life a priority? Does he work from home and therefore should he be there less? He should concentrate on what is behind him to make him happy and not seeking pleasure, romance, and excitement away from his home base. He may wish to travel, but will be going nowhere fast in a cement chariot. The black and white sphinxes lying down in front of the chariot certainly indicate the yin/yang philosophy of balance by showing a little light in darkness (negativity and problems) and a little darkness in light (purity and goodness). They are twiddling their thumbs waiting for the chariot driver to make some sort of decision so they can take him to his destination; however, his decision never comes. The rippled water in the background represents that several emotional concerns or challenges lie behind him. Perhaps he is unable or unwilling to face them at this time. He would like to get on with his life, but has to make a major decision or choose a direction. His chariot is on top of the green, abundant and healthy grasses and he is wearing clothing of blue, yellow, black, and white representing all his sensitivity, honesty, integrity, devotion, mental acuity, and his strong, dark side if needed. He will accomplish what he must to fulfill his plans, but he must first make a commitment to take that first step forward and handle the issues that may be hard for him to face, particularly surrounding his family and home life.

THE MESSAGE OF THIS CARD is that you are going nowhere fast. You are in a cement chariot because you want to explore or travel the world, but have many responsibilities and obligations at home that you must handle and you feel stuck. This becomes a conundrum. This is also a card of indecision, so planning goals and objectives for the immediate future would benefit the Querent and his family who reside in the two castles behind him. Could it be there are two families that he must deal with? Maybe there are extended family issues? This decision is very puzzling to him; however, if he makes one major decision, the universe will push him forward in a definite positive manner.

TEENAGER MEANING: This is a terrible procrastination card which means that you will never move in the right direction if you do not make important decisions. You need to move forward by taking a risk, following a dream or discussing your goals with others until you understand what you have to do. In the end, you are the only one who can have the perfect future after making good choices, and following through with your plans. If not, you will stay in the original circumstances that you started in.

KARMIC LESSON: The Karmic Lesson of The Chariot is that you must choose and make a decision. Then you must take a stand on whichever position you feel is right. Your procrastination will keep you from accepting good energy and positive opportunities because you are confused, remorseful or guilty about something that you have to do, but because of obligations or responsibilities, you find it very difficult to move forward. Be the change. Live the change. Move forward and try to resolve issues which can only be dealt with on an intellectual level. You have the resources to do it so just know that you are right by moving forward and leaving indecision behind you.

ASTROLOGICAL CONNECTION: Cancer

MEDITATION/AFFIRMATION: I will overcome any obstacles or confusion that keeps me from attaining my goal. I am in charge of my life and how it proceeds and I wish my life to move forward in a very positive way.

TRADITIONAL MEANING: This is a card of success, confidence and determination. Victory over illness, financial problems and enemies. Goals achieved through self-control, willpower and discipline. Focus on the battle at hand. Take satisfaction in your accomplishments, but guard against arrogance. Your reputation will be established. Respect is earned.

VIII
Strength
(Major Arcana - 8)

This card illustrates a trusting soul that is not aware of all the perils around her. She tries to be a friend to everyone and by never questioning anyone's motives; she usually is the one who gets hurt in the end. Jealousy and envy is all around her and yet she does not see it. Wild animals always turn so she needs to be very careful that she does not trust people too easily.

THE TRUST CARD

Notice the yellow sky, which takes up more than two-thirds of the card. Mental activity, intelligence, cunning, ability to be versatile in all situations and logic are found throughout this card. The woman is playing with the lion, not struggling with it. She is learning how to tame "the beast" and have control over a situation or person at the same time. The woman is dressed in white that stands for her being too giving, caring, loving, kind, generous, and honest and doing too much for others and nothing for herself. She is a good person trying to take command of a situation through teamwork or cooperation. The green grass she is standing on has some bumps in it, so she has to be careful not to falter. However, if prosperity and abundance issues arise, she knows she will be fine since the prosperous and abundant foliage is around her waist giving her a good foundation for plentiful financial security opportunities. She is facing the lion (situation, circumstance, obstacle, or challenge) in a different fashion than usual. However, she is facing the past or the wrong direction. She is trying to see all sides of the situation and is making an attempt to handle it with the least opposition. The blue mountain in the left background indicates that she has procrastination issues relating to emotional matters. Is she facing the issues at this time? The eternity or infinity sign above her head indicates that the knowledge and wisdom of the universe is hers if she wishes to use it. This shows what a spiritual soul she really is; yet, it makes one wonder if someone wearing all white (the color of being taken advantage of over and over again) is using her intellect in playing with this lion. After all, it is still a wild animal and may turn on her at any time. So be cautious, and she must not believe everything that is being told to her. She should also be prepared for the unexpected. Do not trust people with sensitive information unless you trust them one hundred percent!

THE MESSAGE OF THIS CARD is that the person is too giving, caring, loving, generous, honest and kind. She needs to face the future, not live in the past, and realizes that everything is not as lighthearted and fun as she may believe. The lion is still a wild animal, even if she seems to be playing with it. At some point, the lion may turn on her. Handle all procrastination issues to get onto the proper path. Be cautious in exposing your personal life with new people. If gifts or actions from others seem too good to be true, they probably are.

TEENAGER MEANING: You must be very careful about making new friends who want to know all of your business. Even if it is the most popular kid in school, you must set boundaries and not talk about anything personal until you are one hundred percent sure that you can trust that person. If someone else finds out about your secrets or personal information before you know them, it will be spread throughout the school so fast and you will be hurt or embarrassed in some way.

KARMIC LESSON: The Karmic Lesson of the Strength card is that you should really consider putting up sufficient boundaries around you since you are not very good at protecting yourself. You do too much for others and not enough for yourself. You are too trusting and will always find yourself getting hurt and never understanding why. Take control of your life and what you want in it and start attracting those energies. Procrastination only keeps your life on hold, so consider dealing with the issues you keep pushing into the background. Not making a decision is not a decision. If you do not make decisions, then the universe will push you into a direction it thinks you should go instead of the one you think you should be on. Try harder to be in control of your own destiny.

ASTROLOGICAL CONNECTION: Leo

MEDITATION/AFFIRMATION: Even though I trust everyone immediately, I will be more aware of others and their motives. I cannot let other people manipulate me or make me do things that I know are not in my best interest. I will be strong and confident and in control of my life at all times.

TRADITIONAL MEANING: This is the card of tolerance, character and compassion. The ability to endure adversity. You can face any problem with inner strength. When challenged, maintain control of the situation by reacting calmly. Do not get angry. Have patience with others' weaknesses and do not allow them to become your problem. Look for support from a strong woman.

IX
The Hermit
(Major Arcana - 9)

This card represents a very spiritual life and the spiritual teacher. It sometimes represents a deeper wisdom and understanding from a deeply spiritual point of view. You must keep a clear mind to deal with upcoming situations. These are not your situations or concerns, but those of everyone else whom you are helping by lighting the way for them to come up the *mountain of enlightenment and wisdom while you stay in the past helping others and not furthering your own objectives and dreams.*

THE SPIRITUAL TEACHER CARD

The Hermit is someone who has taken one step at a time through his life to get to where he feels comfortable or has reached the spiritual enlightenment he desired. He is at the top of the world. He can stay all alone enjoying solitude, while leaving his former life or challenges behind him. Or he can help guide others to a life much like his own, where they would be happy, content, and able to share wisdom with others seeking the true path. Holding the lantern high for all to see, he is shining the light of knowledge downward towards humanity. Friends, family, and strangers will come forth seeking his wisdom, knowledge, and advice. He is ready and willing to help. In this regard, he may be selfless. The sky is a dusty shade of blue (blue and black mixed together) without clouds, so his life is proceeding on track even though there seem to be a few mysteries incorporated into the color of blue and black combined. The snowy mountaintops represent his spirituality and enlightenment and how hard he has worked to reach it. The yellow wand is bringing mental activity or reason to the advice he is giving others. Notice he is facing in the wrong direction. Facing the past may indicate that he is so busy helping others that he has neglected his own emotional and spiritual well-being. He needs time to disseminate his wisdom and knowledge. Cloaked in a gray robe, he is trying to protect himself from harm, negativity, and from those who drain his positive energy so he can continue guiding others to the best of his ability; however, everyone else's negativity, fears and doubts are still stuck to him. He needs to release all the negativity gained from others and truly lead a more solitary life. He may need only one close family member or friend to help him stay grounded and focused. He may be able to use the wisdom and enlightenment he has gained throughout the years to help himself as well as others. He needs time to re-energize and concentrate on his goals in life.

THE MESSAGE OF THIS CARD is to balance your life by not only guiding others, but by helping yourself as well. You have much wisdom to share, but need to keep some of the universal energies for yourself.

You are trying to protect yourself by covering yourself in the robe; however, others' negativity is still stuck to you – that's why your robe is gray. You must release it quickly by prayer or meditation. Making yourself more of a priority without forgetting others is your task. You must release the negative and embrace the positive. Your future is one of your top priorities.

TEENAGER MEANING: Most of your friends find you very helpful, insightful and always to be counted on to give a kind word or advice for their bizarre and negative circumstances. It would be wonderful if you could help those who truly need the help and let others help themselves. You should also take your own good advice and do what makes you happy for a change. Setting boundaries is very important.

KARMIC LESSON: The Karmic Lesson of The Hermit is to stop helping others all of the time and spend some of your time getting to your goals, dreams, desires and aspirations. You have taken care of others and helped them reach their goals for far too long. You attract their negativity and failures and have a hard time letting go of their "stuff." Look to the future and know that you are as important, if not more, than the people you help. When is it your turn to shine?

ASTROLOGICAL CONNECTION: Virgo

MEDITATION/AFFIRMATION: Even though I know it is my mission in life to guide others to the top of the mountain and get them on the correct path, I also know that it is important for me to help those who cannot help themselves but let them find their own way. I know it is best for me to look towards my future goals and dreams and start going after them because I am just as important as those that I help.

TRADITIONAL MEANING: This card represents the search for answers to life's problems. Withdraw in order to find the answers to your questions. Peace and quiet is needed. Make decisions cautiously. Take advice from others. Predicts a meeting with someone who will defend, inspire, or protect you. Possible vacation or sabbatical. Follow your heart, not the crowd.

X
Wheel of Fortune
(Major Arcana – 10/1)

This card presents many things that you must do and a few risks you should take to make your life better, happier, bring in more opportunities and positive energy. If you do them, you will be going onto a more positive path where most of your dreams will come true.

TAKE A RISK, CHANGE YOUR LIFE

This interesting card has so much symbolism in it that I recommend you study it and see which images stand out in your mind. It involves knowledge, strength, wisdom, independence, and stubbornness. The four fixed astrological signs are Aquarius, Taurus, Leo and Scorpio as are shown in this card one in each corner. The figures in the card are resting on clouds. The top left corner, Aquarius is represented. It means that the Querent must gain more wisdom and knowledge, such as in attending classes in formal education, lectures, seminars, workshops or training in some way possibly for a new profession or interest. In the lower left corner, we have Taurus the Bull indicating that the Querent is stubborn, but needs to be more persistent and tolerant in dealings with others in order to attain future goals. The lower right corner holds Leo the Lion which suggests that if you are more confident and call upon your inner strength and courage, you are on your way to the successful outcome of this card. Finally, the top right of the card is Scorpio and although it does not look like a Scorpion, it is one of the three phases of Scorpio, the Phoenix. Any time there is a bird in this particular deck other than the black birds, it means that a risk needs to be taken in order to achieve goals, objectives, dreams and aspirations. An Egyptian with a sword is protecting the TORA and you. Here we see him protecting integrity, honor, pride, and understanding. Notice that the word on the Wheel which can be seen as other aspects, such as TORA, ROTA, meaning wheel, and TAROT. It suggests much knowledge and an ever-changing meaning depending on your belief systems. The billowing clouds can represent some negativity or disbelief on the Querent's part as to the nature of his good fortune. The blue sky is evidence that there will be happier times and enjoyment once the person for whom the reading is being done can accept that good things do happen to nice people. Stop waiting for the other shoe to drop. Take positive action to receive positive results. All the good fortune will be yours if you gain more knowledge, as indicated by the angel or the sun sign Aquarius; if you are more persistent and tolerant, as indicated by the Taurus bull; if you call upon your inner courage and strength, as seen by Leo the lion; and if you take a risk, as indicated in the top part of the card in the future position. These fixed signs of the zodiac are stable, centered, grounded and focused when it suits their needs; however, they also represent stubbornness. Perhaps this is a chance to change your mind and look at other perspectives and alternatives to the same choices you continually make. Many people ask what the risk is in this card. The Reader may never know, but when faced with a situation or circumstance, the Querent will.

THE MESSAGE OF THIS CARD is that anything you want will come to you IF you gain more wisdom (by reading, TV, audio tapes, formal education, seminars, lectures or training); be more persistent and tolerant; call upon your inner strength and courage and lastly, take a risk that is appropriate to the situation. Only then will you be able to change your course and move forward in a very positive way.

TEENAGER MEANING: Whatever you think the happiest thing in your life could be at this time is what you will get and achieve. If it's passing a grade, getting a part time job, a part in the school play, on the sports team you wanted or attracting the partner of your dreams . . . whatever is your happiness ever after is at hand. Go after it and put your attention and energy into obtaining it.

KARMIC LESSON: The Karmic Lesson of The Wheel of Fortune is to take that risk, get new information or education and take chances. You should be determined and persistent, confident and have courage to take all the risks you need to get what you feel is important to you in this lifetime. Otherwise, your life will continue down the same path with little or no change making you feel as if you live on a perpetual treadmill.

ASTROLOGICAL CONNECTION: Jupiter

MEDITATION/AFFIRMATION: There are so many choices in life and once I focus on my vision and dreams, I will get further education or training, be persistent and tolerant of others and use my confidence and strength to take the risks that I need to get for the outcomes I desire.

TRADITIONAL MEANING: This card represents the ever-changing cycles of life, both good and bad. Your luck is turning and a new phase of life is beginning. Period of personal growth and extreme change. Success after failure. Destiny and fate will allow you very little control over coming events. All you can do is go with the flow. Promise of a better future.

XI
Justice
(Major Arcana – 11/2)

Justice, balance, and equality are denoted in this card. Are your dealings with others considered to be too fair and compromising -- not just by you, but by others as well? This card suggests the possibility of going to court, dealing with lawyers or important legal papers, such as some kind of contract or lease. At the very least, this warns of speeding tickets, so slow down. The other aspect of this card is for you to finally stand up for yourself and stop giving away too much. You are just as important as others. Anything that comes your way will be handled easily now, so enjoy your new found independence and strength.

FAIRNESS CARD

This card represents a person who is very fair and just. He is holding a scale of justice (as the symbol that represents Libra, the Scales) in one hand representing fairness, openness, goodness, and equality; however, in the other hand he is defending himself with a Sword. This King knows that occasionally one must fight for what he believes in. This is another balance card (notice the two columns). Also notice the drapery behind him. Justice is protecting something or perhaps someone. This represents situations that are unknown to the general public or persons involved with that situation. In other words, there can be secrets and lies behind the drapery. The King is using his intelligence and logic to handle the matter (yellow crown and scales); his red robe is indicative of his passion, love, strength, assertiveness, power, and desire to handle all in a fair and honorable manner. The yellow background indicates that all will be handled intelligently and logically with little conflict. It will also be resolved because he is sitting on a cement throne between columns and his feet are grounded on a cement floor. He is a very stubborn and persistent man, but that white shoe comes peeking through showing the giving, kind, loving, and caring nature in these important circumstances which may get him into trouble. Holding the sword up in the air indicates that he can handle anything that comes his way.

This is also the only law-related card. It could represent seeing a lawyer, being involved in a court case, or getting a parking or speeding ticket. This would also indicate signing contracts, leases, or prenuptial agreements. I would suggest careful scrutiny over any contract given to you for signature, just to be on the safe side. Remember, there are things you are unaware of behind the drapery. This card would reveal any aspect of life pertaining to law.

THE MESSAGE OF THIS CARD is that you would like to conclude circumstances in a friendly and honest manner; however, you will use whatever force necessary to make sure you are being treated fairly. This is the only card that pertains to the law, lawsuits, court cases and court appearances, getting tickets and lawyers in general including signing important documents or going to see one for a general consultation.

TEENAGER MEANING: This is a card that attracts speeding tickets. For those who speed, watch out! If not, this is a great time to set boundaries and only do whatever feels right for you. Be careful not to be so giving, caring, loving, and kind, etc., that you are always doing for others and no one is helping you in return. You need balanced energy as well as defined limits and boundaries for yourself. Be very selective about the people you help and the secrets you hold for others.

HOW TO BE A TAROT DETECTIVE
151

KARMIC LESSON: The Karmic Lesson of Justice is that you have always been so fair and compromising and to what end? You have a good heart, but others may see this as a weakness and want to take advantage of you whenever possible. It is time to stick up for yourself, and do whatever you must to set boundaries and limitations which are in your best interest. It is time that you reap the rewards of what you have sewn into the fields of life. This is not a time to keep giving, but a time to start receiving and restoring your energy.

ASTROLOGICAL CONNECTION: Libra

MEDITATION/AFFIRMATION: Balance and boundaries are the keys to making good choices. I will only compromise when absolutely necessary, but will take control of my life so that I will attract the things that are important to me and not worry so much about everyone or anything else.

TRADITIONAL MEANING: This is the card of personal integrity and fairness. Take responsibility for your own actions. Every action you take will have an effect. Be decisive. Move forward. Contracts, agreements and legal disputes are resolved in your favor. If you have been wronged, Justice is assured.

XII
The Hanged Man
(Major Arcana – 12/3)

This card represents positive change after deep contemplation. A new, more spiritual outlook is needed. You might want to look at your concerns from another point of view. You may be on the right track, but you need to think about your life from another perspective. Take your time in making important decisions. (Most people who are not familiar with this card automatically assume he is upside down. Make sure you know if the card is upright or reversed before reading it so that the timing is right for your predictions).

DIFFERENT PERSPECTIVE CARD

The Hanged Man is not in pain, nor is he being punished. This is easily noticed by studying his face. His face is peaceful and tranquil. He is on the road to enlightenment, but perhaps needs time to think about his future plans or objectives. His head and shoes are yellow which means that intellectual insight guides him through thought and logic is in his very solid foundation. He has a relaxed appearance and although the sky is gray (which could be filled with some negativity, fears, anxieties, and doubt), his red tights indicate that he is strong enough to make the necessary changes. A calmness or serenity will come over him (denoted by his blue shirt) when he finally decides what course of action should be followed. It also indicates that there is an imbalance between the assertive side and his compassionate side. It seems like the compassion, empathy, sympathy, sensitivity and emotion are overpowering the red of passion, assertiveness, and being more adamant and strong. The tree is brown which grounds and centers him and the green leaves are prosperous and abundant. He is in between the green leaves which mean his money situation or health (or both) may be an issue and something may need to be resolved in those areas.

The "T" on the top of the tree indicates his materialistic tendencies or reality as opposed to the vertical tree trunk indicating spirituality, enlightenment and wisdom from Above. He needs to look at circumstances from a different point of view, perhaps one that does not make sense to him at the present time. He needs to explore various options, as the old ways of thinking are not working any longer. He needs to grow, pursue a dream, or cling onto a different philosophy or belief in life. The Hanged Man is ready for his spiritual awakening and anxious to begin his journey. His legs resemble an upside down "4" or the glyph for Jupiter, the best luck planet. So even though the sky is gray, and he is in the middle of a financial or health issue, he will be very lucky in pursuing the future on his own terms and resolve any concerns that may hamper his future goals and dreams.

THE MESSAGE OF THIS CARD is to look at all things from a different perspective. It does not matter how things were or how they used to be done, you have the ability to think "outside of the box" and should use your intelligence to see beyond what others do. This is also a very spiritual card, which may push you into a new philosophy of life.

TEENAGER MEANING: You may not always be right about everything, so this card is asking you to see another side or another perspective to the present situation. You need balance between your logic and emotions so you can try to find out what the right thing is for you to do at this time. You need more money, perhaps for a car or college, and it is possible that you are doing too much without rest which may compromise your health with possibly getting a cold, flu, bronchitis, pneumonia or allergies, etc., until the universe has you resting in bed to make sure you get well.

KARMIC LESSON: The Karmic Lesson of The Hanged Man is that it is time for you to start looking at different points of view and other perspectives. Believe it or not, you are not always right. You need to deal with your mundane (or everyday) issues and may have to leave spirituality aside for now, but it will always be there when you are ready for it again. Balancing your finances and/or health would be also a good start towards seeing things from another perspective. Try to budget and pay for purchased items with cash so you do not get caught in the old credit card money pit. If it is a health issue that you are concerned about, be sure to see a physician or you will be run down and exhausted and the universe may make you stay in bed until you are better.

ASTROLOGICAL CONNECTION: Neptune

MEDITATION/AFFIRMATION: I am flexible enough to look at other points of view and to see other perspectives. I do not need to be stuck with the same old ideas and thought patterns that have not helped me go forward. I will move forward by seeing all sides of every situation and only then will I make great progress in reaching my goals.

TRADITIONAL MEANING: This is the card of contradictions. Confusing time ahead. Do the opposite of what you're doing. Peace of mind comes from making the decision. Put aside any selfish interests. It may be necessary to sacrifice in order to achieve success. Instead of trying to control situations and people, leave them alone.

XIII
Death
(Major Arcana – 13/4)

This card stands for transformation, renewal, and change. The old dies and makes way for the new and better and rises again like the Phoenix. Old habits die hard, so you should undertake or expect a complete turnaround. It could stand for the end of a particular road in life and moving forward on a new path. It also stands for acting as if people are dead in your life so you can move on to a better future without them. This is a card which suggests that you de-clutter your life of the people and things that are no longer useful to you in any way. It is a shedding of anything negative and you are being blessed as you move to your new beginning.

THE TRANSITION CARD

This card usually causes fear and worry because of the word "Death" at the bottom of it, so if this comes out in a reading, assure the Querent that it does not necessarily mean a physical death, but it could be the death of an old way of life. The skeleton in black armor needs to let clingy people go in his life as if they were dead. He needs to leave the past behind so he can find a brighter, new future. If one looks closely at the card, he will notice that there is a religious figure (or some prefer universal energy) in yellow (mental activity, intelligence, and analytical and logical thought, common sense and reasoning ability) blessing him on his positive journey to the future.

The sun is peeking through two castles in the background inviting the Querent to pay close attention to the meaning of the castles. Because there are two castles with the sun emphasizing them, it means that there will be double the meaning of the castles. (Castles always mean love, happiness, prosperity and joy, inner peace, guidance, strength, wisdom and knowledge and everything to make you happy). These are the same castles that are seen in The Moon card. Once the skeleton gets beyond fears, worries, illusions, delusions, and takes the road of logic, then he will wind up here in the new beginnings. The rising sun focuses on his new life, and even though the gray sky foretells of negativity and a fear-based situation, he may not be able to see the future clearly. The blue water indicates that emotions are involved and sensitivity, sympathy, empathy, and compassion are heightened to the matter at hand. The water has small ripples, which denotes further complications and obstacles if not properly handled. Although the skeleton is wearing black armor and carrying a predominately black flag with a huge white flower on it (another balance issue), the white spiritual horse on which he rides represents purity, goodness, enlightenment, wisdom and knowledge from Above as well as rebirth. The image presents a mixed blessing and a balance of opponents, mental activity, goals, and objectives. Success is assured if he tries to accomplish his goals and handle the negativity (black) which is being driven out by the religious figure (or the universe). While the rider is surveying his options and moving very cautiously to the future, he is going in the right direction. The Querent should go forth in confidence since there are many new adventures on the horizon.

(Combined with the Devil card, The Tower, the Three of Swords or any of the health issues cards, this card may possibly mean a physical death, but I rarely use it for this purpose. As a beginner, you should <u>never</u> use it to represent the death.)

THE MESSAGE OF THIS CARD is to let go of the past for now; it is behind you. Move towards your new beginnings where love, happiness, prosperity, and joy, inner peace, guidance, strength, wisdom, self-confidence and everything else you need to make you happy await you. Everything that has been negative in your life is now just a memory, so continue cautiously on the right path to make your life happy and successful.

TEENAGER MEANING: You must leave friends behind as if they are dead to you. If people continuously use you and take advantage of you without giving you anything in return, it is time to let them go. It would be best to move on to new beginnings with friends who will be available to help you in any situation. Go towards the future with great hope since your life will be very positive and upbeat from now on.

KARMIC LESSON: The Karmic Lesson of the Death card is that you really have to let some people go in your life as "if" they were dead. They no longer serve you in a positive way and their energy is such that it is overwhelming and heavy for you to deal with. Shed all encumbrances and be ready to attract new opportunities and surprises. It would be wise to only help close family members and friends. Then set strict boundaries for others so that no one can use up your time, energy or good heart ever again. Allow others take care of their own life so you can take care of yours.

ASTROLOGICAL CONNECTION: Scorpio

MEDITATION/AFFIRMATION: Even though I am moving forward, I wish to prioritize my goals and dreams. There are many people who rely on me, but who give me nothing in return. As I move forward, I will shed the psychic vampires in my life so that they can handle their own lives and I can move forward in a much more positive way. I can then reap the benefits of all the good deeds that I have accomplished.

TRADITIONAL MEANING: This card signifies either the metaphorical personal rebirth followed by great change in your life or the literal death of someone you know. Renewal. Personal growth through honest self-examination. And of an era - put the past behind you. Fear of the unknown, of change, and of being out-of-control. Focus on the essentials of life. Simplify.

XIV
Temperance
(Major Arcana – 14/5)

This card represents making all of your decisions from your heart. You constantly go back and forth until you are so confused that you cannot even make a proper decision. You procrastinate too much and the universe would like you to finish whatever you have started so that you can attract more positive energy for into your future.

YOU ARE YOUR OWN WORST ENEMY CARD

The woman has her foot in the water, causing ripples and thereby, her own emotional problems. The figure is in between the two cups, trying to balance her emotional state of mind or circumstances; however, in reality, she is churning the water between the cups and causing more problems rather than correcting them. One foot is on the earth trying to be grounded, centered and focused, the other is in the emotional waters. She is confused and desperately trying to handle all of her challenges in an intellectual manner. The white robe indicates the goodness and honesty of the person trying to make a fair decision and take control of the situation. As in all figures wearing white, it is a color meaning the person is too giving, caring, loving, kind, generous, honest, helpful, and doing too much for others while no one reciprocates the energy in any way. Limits must be set or the person will continually be drained of energy and eventually get physically ill or mentally depressed. Angels are guiding the woman at this time, but the black in the wings show that their protection is waning. Temperance needs to ask for exactly what she needs and must use wisdom to help make this decision. A new beginning will come soon, shown by the sun peeking in between the twin blue procrastination mountains in the background. Are they emotional procrastination issues? Of course there are and we can tell that because the mountains are blue. The sun is also showing that these procrastination issues must be dealt with quickly if she is to straighten out her life. The gray sky is confusing matters, not allowing her to clearly see the road ahead of her. The green vegetation with yellow flowers shows abundance in the future, as well as the intellect needed to obtain that goal. There is a road leading to a new beginning, a new path in life, and the unknown. Miss Temperance has come from a much grounded path from the past to the present. She must make her emotional decisions quickly, not let others control her, and get on with her life. Telling this type of person to be a little more assertive and strong would be good advice.

THE MESSAGE OF THIS CARD is to try to be more logical in your approach to life's situations. Handle your procrastination issues and try to make your most important decision quickly, so the rest of them will fall into place. Do not let others take advantage of you as you are still perceived as being too gullible, innocent and trusting. Indecision is unacceptable. Take control of your life and move forward with it now!

TEENAGER MEANING: Make a logical decision and keep your emotions on hold. You seem to be your own worst enemy, so take a moment to figure out what you have to do to resolve the situation around you and keep your emotions under wraps. Try very hard to make boundaries that you will follow and know things are headed in a much more positive direction.

KARMIC LESSON: The Karmic Lesson of Temperance is that you are your own worst enemy and need to start thinking in a more rational, logical and intellectual way with reason and forethought. You should limit your emotional responses and choices because many of them will be wrong at this time. Logic, analytical and methodical thought, common sense and your reasoning ability will aid you in making proper decisions for any of the choices you need to make. It is more of a yes/no, right/wrong, or I'm doing it/I'm not doing it, kind of time. It is a more black and white time which should get you on the right track.

ASTROLOGICAL CONNECTION: Sagittarius

MEDITATION/AFFIRMATION: I try very hard to handle everything and I now know that everything is about balance in my life. I cannot control the world. I can only control myself. If things bother me, I will deal with them with a positive attitude and a compassionate heart. I will try not to make more problems for myself, but will become stronger and more dedicated to being a strong link in the chain of life to help those who need it and to allow those to help me when they offer.

TRADITIONAL MEANING: This is the card of flexibility, change and adaptation. One who works well with others and has good management skills. Achieving balance and control over your own life. Many ideas and experience synthesize to form new ideas. Compromise to secure cooperation. Possible reconciliation.

XV
The Devil
(Major Arcana – 15/6)

This card indicates materialism or the choice of money or material possessions over spirituality. It could possibly indicate an obsession. It is a battered wife or husband card which also stands for repeated addictions to sex, drugs and alcohol. This is a card where the people under the Devil are wearing self-imposed chains meaning that one or both of them are chained to a negative person or situation. The most helpful one who is always there for the addict must let take off the chains and escape through the door below. Only then will the person hit rock bottom and then will succeed in rebuilding his life.

CHAINED TO A NEGATIVE PERSON OR SITUATION CARD

This is another one of the cards that gets people anxious. If this card should appear in the spread, just assure the person it is not as bad as it seems. Yes, negativity is in the card, represented by the Devil and all the black in the background, but the people attached to the Devil have voluntarily chained themselves to him. In other words, they wear self-imposed chains. They are afraid to change or let go of material possessions, a negative situation, or an abusive (physically or emotionally) person or situation. If you look closely, you will notice that the chains around the couple's necks are very loose - so loose, in fact, that they could easily lift them over their heads and escape through the door underneath the Devil. This card usually represents one partner having to deal with another's addictions (alcohol, drugs, or sex), abusive behavior, or at the very worst, it can indicate a violent rape or incest. All seems desperate around you, indicated by the totally black background. It can be a frightening experience with seemingly no resolution in sight. Either the man or the woman will have to decide what or who is the negativity in their lives. If they check closely, they will note the block or stand on which the Devil is seated. In reality, it is an unlocked door leading to a more positive life on the other side. Either party has to be brave enough to open the door to see what is on the other side. Seize the opportunity to start a new life or new positive adventures and do not look behind you! Unfortunately, the only way to deal with this card is to put this negative circumstance or situation behind you as it will not get better. (Notice the woman is looking to the future with the fruit or abundance behind her and the man looking in the past with the flame consuming him. In this instance, we can gather that the woman in the card is going in the proper direction and the man is not.) If you feel "chained" to a particular circumstance or person, perhaps it is time to decide which changes would be in your best interest.

(As an aside, many times as an addiction card, I have had mothers or family members and yes, even some friends, trying to help a person by putting them into rehab or staging an intervention. When the person comes out of rehab, it is only a few weeks before he is addicted again. At that point, the mother, friend, etc., has to let the child or person hit rock bottom and they have to completely leave the situation by not taking responsibility for it and escaping through the door under the Devil. Once this is done, the person usually bounces back because (s)he realizes that no one is left to help. Tough love is indicated with this card.)

THE MESSAGE OF THIS CARD is to get out of whatever situation or relationship that you are bound to. You have self-imposed chains around your neck. Take them off and escape through the door underneath the Devil. This situation rarely gets better, so the only way to protect yourself is to get out of it as quickly as possible and stop empowering others to make you into a person who feels as if they are obligated to them through guilt or worry.

TEENAGER MEANING: You are hanging around negative people who will bring you down if you let them. You continue to try to help depressed people who bring much more negativity and problems into your life. Let go of this person and the all encompassing situation and only then will you be on the right track. This is also an addiction card such as being addicted to sex, drugs and alcohol, etc., so be careful not to get caught up in this harmful and deadly game.

KARMIC LESSON: The Karmic Lesson of The Devil is that you can help as long as you feel you need to, but at some point, you have to get out of the situation. It will not get better and your help is either not wanted or needed. It is a card which puts more strain, pressure, obstacles and negativity around all parties involved with that person or situation. You must be strong enough to let go and let the other person (who has the problems) deal with his or her issues on her own. You have done your best and now it is time for you to live your own life.

ASTROLOGICAL CONNECTION: Capricorn

MEDITATION/AFFIRMATION: I must learn that everything is not under my control. I cannot continue to help others when there are no positive results in sight. I will free myself from the bonds that keep me attached to this negative person or situation and know that it is okay to move on with my life and let others take care of their own issues, fears, doubts and demons.

TRADITIONAL MEANING: This card denotes a greedy, materialistic, selfish person. Disregard for others. Beware of someone who tries to control you. You're caught in an unhealthy situation. The card of sexual perversity and dark secrets. Sexual addiction. Overspending. Substance abuse. Compulsions. Judge people by their values, not their outside appearance.

XVI
The Tower
(Major Arcana – 16/7)

Your plans are about to be altered. There is a sudden change, shift, and some sort of struggle that you must overcome in your life. There is opposition to your plans and bumps in the road that you have not foreseen. If you feel it is the worst day of your life because of this change, think again as it will wind up being the best day of your life by the time the situation is resolved. Just go with the flow and everything will work out for the best. Do not fight the change. God and Goddess have plans which are much better than yours, so keep the faith that everything will be all right.

GO WITH THE FLOW CARD

This is certainly not one of the more peaceful looking cards; however, it is a very important card for people who find it difficult to make change. It is similar to a "square" in astrology. It pushes you into a change that you would have never made on your own and is long overdue. It gets you out of a rut. The black background shows negativity, despair, and hopelessness while the gray clouds add worries, fears, doubts, anxieties and concerns. The castle or tower is gray indicating that your circumstances seem dismal at best and you cannot handle them in an appropriate manner. There may even be confusion surrounding your circumstances. Everything you know is being challenged, changed, pushed, ended, or forced to be different in some way. The yellow lightening (showing mental activity) is causing this unexpected change. It forces the figures to leave (fall out of) the tower, which indicates the foundation of your life, business, or money, seems to be knocked out from under you. It is pushing everything into the unknown and into something new. The small yellow Yods floating down around the figures in the card are blessings from God and Goddess. So we know that the changes, although uncertain at the present time, will be for the benefit of all involved. The blue dress of the woman shows that things will be calmer and more serene as she gets closer to her goal (the ground!). The man is also wearing blue, but has a red garment over it. This indicates his desire for change, but perhaps not knowing how to accomplish it. He may make rash or impulsive decisions. For instance, this card may come up when you are unhappy at a job, but you will not leave because of the security of a weekly paycheck or benefits. Then all at once, there is a big layoff or cutback and you find yourself without of a job. You are forced to look for another position and in doing so, find one that pays more money, has better opportunities, and many more benefits than the position or situation you recently left. Do not be afraid to face the unknown because in the long run, it will bring you the happiness and security you need.

THE MESSAGE OF THIS CARD is that sudden, unexpected change pushes you into new situations because you are in a rut and would not make the change on your own. Welcome the change as it will push you to make important decisions which in turn will bring good opportunities and positive energy into your life.

TEENAGER MEANING: Even though it seems as if everything is not going your way, just kind of go with the flow. Whatever you thought was in your best interest may not be. God and Goddess have bigger and better plans waiting for you. You will wind up in a much better and happier place once you see where the universe has taken you.

KARMIC LESSON: The Karmic Lesson of The Tower is that sometimes, you just have to go with the flow and allow the universe to move you onto a path where you will flourish, even if you are unsure of the outcome at the time. You have been afraid to make the change for so long, so let the universe push you into the direction it feels you need to go to make your future positive and happy.

ASTROLOGICAL CONNECTION: Mars

MEDITATION/AFFIRMATION: Even when my life gets confusing, upsetting or feels out of control, I trust in God and Goddess (or whomever you believe in) and know that there is a plan for me. I will go with the flow to find the new path that I am now supposed to follow.

TRADITIONAL MEANING: This card has long-held beliefs and ideas are challenged. Overall chaos, sudden crisis and misery. Natural disasters. Grief over a broken relationship. All aspects of your life are open to disaster. Take action. Trouble ends only after you get rid of something or someone. Later you will realize that these changes are for the best.

XVII
The Star
(Major Arcana – 17/8)

This card indicates that you are your own worst enemy. Decisions need to be prioritized and quickly made. Procrastination needs to be dealt with and risks need to be taken in order to move forward in a positive way. If you do not deal with your emotional issues now, notice the five extra ponds you will be making in the future. Things will be much more chaotic in the future if you do not straighten out your emotions and sensitivity now.

PRIORITIZE YOUR LIFE CARD

This is a lovely card filled with blues, greens, and yellows. It is a card that gives you the opportunity to make choices to change whatever needs to be changed. It involves balance and trying to decide whether or not to live on the land or in the water. Land represents the grounded and centered energy to need to move forward and the water (blue) is representative of emotions, strong sensitivity, empathy, and compassion. Even though the woman is trying to ground herself on land with one foot, she willingly puts her other foot in the water and empties water from two jugs in her hands. One jug on each side of her denotes an emotional imbalance issue. Notice the water jug in the future making many more rivers of water, indicating that emotions will be a bigger part of her future unless she deals with the concerns at hand now. The white stars represent spiritual guidance and her many options; the large yellow star indicates the one priority issue she must make with her intelligence, rather than emotions. In making the major decision, the other concerns in her life will just start falling into place. The green grass of abundance and prosperity is there for her to grab if she makes a commitment to herself about progressing towards a decision or goal one step at a time each and every day. Notice the bird in the tree towards the future connoting taking a risk. "What risk?" you may ask. Only the Querent would know that. The mountains in the left or the past still indicate that there are procrastination issues that must be dealt with in order to proceed forward. Notice her yellow hair - she is an intelligent woman who is also methodical, analytical, has common sense and reasoning ability; however, confusion over issues is not letting her favorably proceed. Of course, looking in the past does not help her get on the path she needs to follow. Your advice would be to tell her to turn around, look towards the future, take her foot out of the water, take the risk, and get on with her life. Otherwise, she will be involved in this emotional drama for some time to come.

THE MESSAGE OF THIS CARD is to try to prioritize your decisions. Make the most important decision and the others will fall into place. If you do nothing, your future will be more emotional and unfocused than the present. You are too innocent, naïve, vulnerable and gullible, so everyone can take advantage of you and when they do, you become upset and overly emotional by their actions. When you feel like this, it is hard for you to continue towards your future in a positive or optimistic way.

TEENAGER MEANING: You have so many decisions to make and you will do that by picking the priority issue and dealing with it logically, intelligently, analytically and with reason. Once your life is prioritized and you take a step towards the appropriate risk, you will be on a much more positive path which will lead you to your goals, aspirations and dreams.

KARMIC LESSON: The Karmic Lesson of The Star is that you must make choices even if it is confusing or painful. Pick the most important issue or choice and take one step towards resolving it. Once you do this, your life will be much easier to deal with. Procrastination has to stop as it is only attracting more negativity. You should look into your future to fulfill the rest of your life. Emotions hold you back, so use some of the intelligence the universe has given you and make good choices.

ASTROLOGICAL CONNECTION: Aquarius

MEDITATION/AFFIRMATION: I need to focus on my priority issues so that I can attract positive energy into my life. Although I may be perplexed at times as to what direction I should go, I will handle the most important issue first and then the ones that follow will be easy to resolve.

TRADITIONAL MEANING: This is the card of inspiration, insight and hope. Dreams for the future will come true. Contact with someone who will dramatically change your life. Strong love between two people. Entering a period of serenity and satisfaction. Enjoy this calm period. Emotional needs are filled. Share your good fortune.

XVIII
The Moon
(Major Arcana – 18/9)

The card represents the basic needs of everyone, imagination, fantasy, and security. It also is a creative card indicating an artist, writer, actor, singers or musician. This is a card where you never quite get to your goals because you feel more comfortable in the emotional water where you may even hide some secrets from those you love. Your fear of reality and illusion keep you paralyzed. Get over your fears and move towards wonderful opportunities and blessings that God and Goddess will bestow upon you.

ILLUSION, DELUSION AND CREATIVITY CARD

Whenever there is a sun/moon combination in a card, it denotes that there is deceit, treachery, hidden secrets, or lies. It also means the lobster in the card sees what he wants to see and hears what he wants to hear. Illusions or delusions confuse his life. Things are not always as they seem to be, yet you are willing to accept them at face value. The blue sky and the Yods, blessings from God and Goddess, push you in the proper direction. There are twin towers (castles) indicating that love, happiness, prosperity, and joy are at hand; however, you are the lobster in the water. The lobster tries very hard to get out of the sea (emotional issues) and would logically like to take the yellow road to a new life (new path or path to the unknown future). Each time he tries to get out of the water, he openly faces the large beige dog of reality, but blows things out of proportion instead of dealing with it. Then he sees the coyote or ghost dog in the future as all the fears, doubts and worries he must deal with. He is so scared to proceed that he retreats into the water yet again. The coyote and dog are indistinguishable to you. The little lobster must face his fears, doubts, and anxieties by using his intelligence and get on the yellow road of intelligence to the mountains and in between the twin towers. Then and only then will he be blessed with the Yods from Above. The green grass is helpful because harmony, security and peace of mind is wanted and needed, but you are not sure how to get to it. You are seeing things in an unrealistic light from a fear base or foundation. You must face your fears, but must also face the dog from the past to know what is real and fantasy. Both energies need to be balanced and quickly dealt with. Once realized, the lobster can get out of the water and onto the yellow road leading towards the mountains. All it has to do is grab the opportunity and it will be his. The clear blue sky shows you that once you take a positive step towards a brighter tomorrow, there will be only happiness, harmony, wisdom, and inner peace; however, all the negativity and anxieties need to be left behind.

THE MESSAGE OF THIS CARD is to stop letting your fears stop you from pursuing your future goals. You imagine things to be worse than they are and continually wind up back at the beginning. Gain confidence and plan your future goals. Continue on an intellectual road where blessings from God and Goddess, happiness and good fortune will help you get what you want in life.

TEENAGER MEANING: Stop living in fantasy land and see reality for what it is. Once you decide to stop living in fear and/or take control of your life, everything will be much more positive and in your best interest. Decisions need to be made, so it is about time you make them.

KARMIC LESSON: The Karmic Lesson of The Moon is to live in reality. Even though fantasy through acting, writing, singing, dancing, the arts, etc., may be a wonderful place to live and create, it is not the real world. You need to see reality, deal with it and not be afraid of all the unknowns around you. You must take control of your life and plan to start taking the opportunities that life has to offer. If you do not, you will never get those opportunities offered to you again.

ASTROLOGICAL CONNECTION: Pisces

MEDITATION/AFFIRMATION: I must learn the difference between reality and fantasy and balance both of them. Reality will help me deal with any issues that I must resolve. In this way, I will reach my full potential in this lifetime. Negativity can only damage my progress, so I reject any negative issues, people or things that try to pull me down onto their level.

TRADITIONAL MEANING: This card stands for your personal faith and ethics will be tested. It's hard to think clearly. You're confused and easily distracted. Fear and anxiety haunt your thoughts. Paranoia. Secret enemies. Deception. Your security is at risk. Your friends or family may be in danger. Bad luck for those you love.

XIX
The Sun
(Major Arcana – 19/10/1)

This card represents pure happiness and seeing the world through the eyes of a child. Nothing can go wrong. The sun represents your Spirit, the human energy that makes you who you are. Applied properly, this energy is unstoppable. This card indicates a positive and spiritual outlook while leaving the negative past behind.

NEW BEGINNING CARD

This lucky card is one of the best cards in the deck. The sun takes up almost half of the card. The radiant yellow rays shine on the baby boy that are full of energy, vitality, strength, optimism, direction, goals, and new beginnings. He feels as if he is now coming into the world like a newborn baby. One particular concern might be that although he is going in the proper direction, he seems, innocent, vulnerable and perhaps a bit naive, as indicated by his lack of clothing. He should prepare for the unexpected and try not to believe in those who seem to have all of the answers. New situations and circumstances will abound. He should be open to the opportunities that will be put before him. The clear blue sky indicates a happy and problem-free time. The red/ orange flag waving in the wind indicates strength, assertiveness, passion and determination as well as a desire for change and new experiences to become part of his life. It will also help focus and balance his ambitions and keep his goals for that new experience on track. The gray horse indicates that he has now overcome his fears, doubts, worries, anxieties, procrastination and stress. The gray wall indicates that problems are now in the past and are being held behind him or out of his present life. None of that negativity will follow him to the future. The sunflowers indicate new growth, new adventures, new career, new journeys, new beginnings and the sprouting of logic and intelligence that will get him far in his new ventures. He should expect and plan for a wonderful new part of life to open up in the near future.

THE MESSAGE OF THIS CARD is that all new beginnings are starting for you from this moment on. You seem to still be a bit vulnerable; however, you have the ability to ground and protect yourself if needed. The problems and concerns of the past are behind you now and will not resurface. You are going in to the proper direction where spirituality and enlightenment will guide you. The negativity which surrounded you in the past will not follow you in to your future. All new beginnings, new journeys, new growth, adventures and a new path to follow are before you – enjoy!

TEENAGER MEANING: You are going in a much better direction in all areas of life and just need to move forward in a very confident manner. All negativity and concerns are left behind you and not following you into your future. Make better decisions and stick with them. Be open for new adventures to come your way.

KARMIC LESSON: The Karmic Lesson of The Sun is that you should move forward to the new beginnings you want in life and just keep looking towards the future. Everything that could possibly hurt you is in your past now and not following you into the future. You are safe, but only if you believe it. Doubts and anxieties may mar your future goals, aspirations, dreams and ambitions, so be sure they are kept in check and see all of the good that can be attained by being positive.

ASTROLOGICAL CONNECTION: Sun

MEDITATION/AFFIRMATION: All new beginnings are here for me. All I need to do is grab those opportunities to find my new path and start over again. The world is an open book for me and I have the pen with which to fill the pages with positive energy, good deeds and all of my unbelievably great accomplishments.

TRADITIONAL MEANING: This card indicates that your personal magnetism is high. Success in good health. High self-esteem and confidence in love and career. Improve physical condition, overall energy level, mental alertness. Optimism and happiness. A period of contentment and joy. Doubtful ventures now have a great future. Education or study will be successfully completed.

XX
Judgement
(Major Arcana – 20/11/2)

This is a strange card because I do not use it as a Judgement card per se. It lets you know that even if you do not do one more good deed in your life, you have already learned your karmic lesson of giving and now, you must learn your karmic lesson of receiving (something that you find extremely hard to do). You must accept help or gifts of any kind from those around you so that you get some reciprocal energy back for all the good deeds you have done. You need a balance of energy. Once this is done, you will find that you real refreshed, confident and looking forward to moving in to the future with positive energy and new hope.

RECIPROCAL ENERGY CARD

I believe that this is the card that tells someone who is a sucker (too giving, too caring, too loving, too kind, too generous, too honest, too trustworthy, etc.) that even if he did not do one more good deed in their life that they have already learned the lesson of giving. From now on, he should learn the lesson of receiving or of getting reciprocal energy. He should practice saying "Thank you," or "That is so kind of you," every time someone wants to do something for him. A cup of coffee, lunch, making a copy, going to the grocery store or post office, etc., can get one chore off of your list of things to do and the person helping you feels as if they have helped you in some way to repay the debt of all of your kindnesses to them throughout your life.

If you feel depressed, nervous, stressed out and overwhelmed, this card explains that you are suffering from doing way too much for others and have not learned that you are supposed to be getting something in return for everything you have done.

I believe that we have a task before us. Our task is to ask assistance from our own kind (humans) before the angels can come in and help us further. Angels can protect you, but your first karmic lesson is to count on your fellow man for help. Once this is accomplished, not only would you feel that protection from the angels is infinite, but now you can ask for your wishes for your best interest or the good of all involved to be granted. The more you trust in the entities that protect us, the more protection and good results occur.

Do not be gullible and vulnerable any longer; take control of your life, let others help you and continue the fine work you have been doing for others only with more limitations and boundaries. However, your life is just as important as the people you are helping so learn to understand that.

THE MESSAGE OF THIS CARD is that it is about time that you get reciprocal energy for all the good you have done for others. It is a card that demands that you accept the gifts or help from others who you have been helping throughout the years with nothing in return. You should now say, "Thank you," when someone wants to help you in some way because this energy will assist you to get more grounded and focused, centered and stable each and every day.

TEENAGER MEANING: Be positive that you will start getting or asking help from others. You have given out all of the help, compassion and joy that you can and now the universe demands that you accept whichever gifts or favors that others want to do for you. You need to receive energy and good deeds so you can become more balanced in all things. You have learned your lesson of giving and now you must learn your lesson of receiving. A simple, "Thank you," will suffice.

KARMIC LESSON: The Karmic Lesson of Judgement is that you have been one of these people who feel that it is your lot in life to help out the world even at the expense of not having enough time to take care of yourself or your family. It is also important to let others help you now. When someone offers to do anything for you, smile and say a resounding, "Thank you!" or "That's so kind of you," and let it go. Did you ever think that they may be trying to thank you for all of the help you have given them throughout the years?

ASTROLOGICAL CONNECTION: Pluto

MEDITATION/AFFIRMATION: I will learn how to accept gifts from others. I will say "thank you" every time someone does something for me because of my past deeds with them. It is a nice feeling to get help from those I have helped in the past and I will gratefully accept all help offered to me.

TRADITIONAL MEANING: This card means initial arguments, legal and contractual issues resolved in your favor. If you have wronged someone, seek reconciliation and forgiveness. Forgive those who have hurt you and move on with your life. Find a new career. If you have been in a low period, this card signifies a turnaround.

To avoid confusion, I have used the spelling of "Judgement" as it is written on the tarot card.

XXI
The World
(Major Arcana – 21/12/3)

This card represents completion and fulfillment. A phase of your life has concluded. Anything you have not completed will now be easily and quickly finished. With learning more wisdom and knowledge, being more persistent and tolerant, calling upon your inner strength and courage, and not being afraid to take risks, you will have everything that you need and want for the time period of the reading. You will be very happy.

EVERYTHING YOU NEED AND WANT TO BE HAPPY CARD

The World is a special completion card that shows great promise for the future. It is a card that finishes projects, concludes adventures, and solves problems. The world has the power to give you anything the woman may need and want if she follows certain rules. It is the completion of a cycle, a way of life, or a new spiritual or optimistic beginning. Getting interested in religion, philosophy, or spirituality is common. The four heads, one in each corner, represent the four fixed astrological signs of the zodiac: Aquarius, Taurus, Leo, and Scorpio. The head in the upper left-hand corner indicates that the woman can get whatever it is she wants with more wisdom and knowledge. This would indicate reading, attending lectures, workshops or seminars, looking at videos, or attending formal education classes or training of some kind. The bull suggests stubbornness, persistence, and tenacity; the lion, indicates strength and calling upon your inner courage; and lastly, the eagle, which can soar to new heights, suggests that a risk must be taken in order to obtain her goal. All are within her grasp. She is encompassed within a green wreath of abundance, prosperity, harmony, and peace, and her efforts will bring financial rewards. The blue sky indicates that whatever she chooses to do will help guide her onto the right path. The two white scepters in the woman's hands indicate bringing spirituality from the Heavens Above to the earth below to help others. She is using them as tools to assist spiritual knowledge and enlightenment being brought down to humanity. She still may be a bit vulnerable, as indicated by her lack of clothing, but in general, she is a very spiritually gifted person who can make dreams come true as the most spiritual vibrational color of purple is starting to cover her body. The red ribbons on the green wreath indicate her desire and passion for all of these options to come together so that she can continue on the path she was supposed to travel.

THE MESSAGE OF THIS CARD is that all the prosperity and abundance that you want can be yours if you gain more wisdom, knowledge or training, become more persistent and tolerant, call upon your inner strength and courage and are not afraid to take appropriate risks.

TEENAGER MEANING: You must gain more knowledge through education, be more adamant about attaining your goals, have true self confidence and inner strength so that you can decide to take appropriate risks. Once this is done, you will have everything that you need and want in your life to be happy and to make the best decisions possible.

KARMIC LESSON: The Karmic Lesson of The World is that it is up to you to find out what you need in life by taking risks, getting more formal education in your field (or if you want to go to another field) or attending seminars, lectures, training or classes in which you may be certified. It is also telling you to be confident enough in yourself to do whatever you feel is right and to be very adamant about your direction. Once you commit to taking an appropriate risk, you will feel as if you were meant to be on this path your whole life. It is a liberating experience.

ASTROLOGICAL CONNECTION: Saturn

MEDITATION/AFFIRMATION: I will surround myself with positive energy, opportunities, and spiritual knowledge to help me get to my goals and dreams. I will have everything that I need and want to enjoy my life here on Earth and will be able to share my good fortune with those I love.

TRADITIONAL MEANING: This card represents you will enter Heaven. Of great happiness and positive events. The pieces fall into place. Goals are achieved. Unexpected sum of money comes your way. Travel or vacation. Possible change of residence or job. Sense of fulfillment in her piece from helping the less fortunate. Whatever you give will be returned to you many times over.

MINOR ARCANA INTERPRETATIONS

T HE MINOR ARCANA are the cards that refer to our everyday or "mundane" life. They are the cards relating to our jobs, finances, conflicts and relationships. These are the cards that tell you how to handle your responsibilities, relationships or partnerships, your concerns, doubts, worries or challenges, and finances. The suits are numbered two through ten and then next come the court cards: Page, Knight, Queen, King and Ace.

As the Major Arcana tells the Reader that the Querent will have much spiritual guidance during the next year (or whatever time period you have chosen), the Minor Arcana reminds us that we are in control of our own destinies and must make the decisions, choices, set goals, and objectives which will lead us into our next adventure in life. Remember that the tarot cards show what will happen if you do nothing to change them. We all have free will and freedom of choice -- use it wisely.

(Even though we have free will and most people think it is a gift, I actually believe it to be a curse. We know what we are supposed to do, but with free will, it seems we are always second guessing ourselves. Many times we make the wrong decision when we know in our gut what the action or inaction should be).

WANDS

Wands represent career, job, school (including higher education, lectures, seminars, workshops or training in some fashion) and health. It also includes the work place, physical labor, spirituality, and crafty ideas. They are also the seeds or conception of ideas and original thought and intention. Wands are extremely creative, artistic and are most happy when they can use their imagination and inventiveness.

Regular Card Suit:	Clubs
Direction:	South
Elemental:	Salamanders
Element:	Fire

Fire Sign Qualities - Aries, Leo and Sagittarius

They are adventurous, aggressiveness, attractive, bold, brave, charming, cheerful, confident, courageous, creative, daring, eager, energetic, enthusiastic, extroverted, forceful, heroic, inspiring, inventive, optimistic, original, outgoing, passionate, self-assured, self-confident, headstrong, hot-tempered, impatient, impulsive, irresponsible, and thoughtless.

A preponderance (see glossary) of Fire sun signs exemplifies high spirits, great faith in self, enthusiasm, and direct honesty. Your fire sign nature projects a radiant, vitalizing energy that seems to glow with warmth and high spirits. You need a good deal of freedom to express yourself naturally, and you will usually display a fairly unyielding insistence on your own point of view; however, you put all of yourself in whatever you do. Wands and Fire Signs are intensely assertive, individualistic, active and self-expressive. Fire sign energies stimulate people who are more lethargic, but often your energies overpower or exhaust the more retiring or sensitive type. Good natured and fun-loving, you have many friends and you are generous with your time, energy, and resources. You place a far greater value on having a good time than on material possessions or financial reward. For all the natural generosity displayed by the fire signs, they are also famous for their big egos which they frequently demonstrate. You may believe so strongly in your own powers and abilities that you overlook and frequently fail to take advantage of the talents and abilities of others. You try to do it all yourself and do not delegate well. Despite this detrimental flaw in your managerial abilities, you belong to a group that is the most daring and capable, inspiring in a management sense; you are the natural leaders. In battle, sports or business, it is usually the fire signs out front leading the charge. You are the type of leader who is very independent and individualistic, rarely consulting with others for advice. You are constantly out front or "on stage" and you need to be recognized and admired for your attainment of goals, dreams, aspirations and accomplishments. Appreciation is more important than money in your pocket. Nothing hurts more than being ignored. The fire signs' sense of honesty is straightforward and often innocent. Thus, you believe everyone is, like yourself, an open book. You may be somewhat gullible and naïve and can get hurt if you do not set good boundaries and are a little wary of others until you get to know them.

You should familiarize yourself with the fire signs' qualities and attributes. This can be particularly helpful if someone asks you, "What type of partner will I attract?" Or better yet, ask the more pertinent question, "What type of partner should I attract for both our best interests?" Then, you can give the qualities of whichever suit comes up.

The Court Cards give double insight to the Numbers two through five, so if you are between these numerology numbers, you have two mundane every day cards with issues that must be dealt with and not just one issue. The people who are a 1, 6, 7, 8, 9 and 10 have only one mundane karmic lesson, the other numbers from 2 through 5 have two every day karmic lessons. Number 1 is represented by the Aces of the suit and element of which you were born. They will have the first one from the regular deck and suit with their birth path number and then add the court cards for their second karmic lesson. For instance, a 2 of Wands would show the first karmic lesson of a 2 Fire person, but the second one would be the Page of Wands as well which comes in as number 11 or broken down to a single digit (1 + 1 = 2). The Knight would be a 12 or 3, the Queen would be a 13 or 4 and the King would be a 14 or 5.

When dealing with Karmic Lessons for the Minor Arcana, remember they represent the mundane or everyday lessons that you will have to learn and deal with for the rest of your life until you learn the lesson.

The Major Arcana are the cosmic Karmic Lessons that are on a higher and more spiritual level.

In all of these mundane suits (wands, pentacles, swords and cups) there will be sections that you can choose to look through for a good interpretation of the card, or its karmic lesson, i's meaning for a teenager, etc. The wands are the only ones that we mainly use for career or job, but I have added an education and health section since wands encompass all these areas.

INTERPRETATION OF THE CARD: This tells you what the card means in detail.

HEALTH: You will get a synopsis of what may be hindering your health since the wands stand for career, education and health.

EDUCATION: Again, the wands represent career, education and health, so the cards may give you some insight into future training, certifications or just knowledge based seminars and workshops.

THE MESSAGE OF THIS CARD: This area will give you a brief description of the card so that you can look at the meanings and move on quickly to the next card and the full reading. It summarizes the meaning of the in-depth card.

TEENAGER MEANING: This is a brief meaning for the teenager.

MUNDANE KARMIC LESSON FOR BIRTH PATH NUMBER 2, ELEMENT FIRE.

KARMIC LESSON: This section explains your karmic lesson for this time in your life. Read the card and study it and then try to accomplish what is needed to push you forward. With much determination and good ol' American know how, I am sure you will learn your lesson well and move onto your next life time without the hang-ups and trappings of this life. In essence, that is your true goal.

ASTROLOGICAL CONNECTION: There will be a planet or sun sign listed here to show which energies are connected to the particular card.

MEDITATION/AFFIRMATION: A brief meditation or affirmation will appear in this section. They were written by me after meditating on each card.

TRADITIONAL MEANING: The explanation was taken off of the Rider Waite deck.

Scans of Wands

Scans of Court Card Wands

II
Two of Wands
(Minor Arcana - 2)

This card signifies that the Querent does not know in which direction to go. Should he stay with his old job or should he look for a new one? Should he stay with his major in college or change it to reflect what he wants to do down the road? Should he stay with his doctor or look for other physicians because his health has not been improving. There are so many questions and he has to balance his energy to be able to make proper decisions for his future.

TAKE A CHANCE CARD

The sky is gray, so he is not completely happy with the circumstances on the job, but will continue to work as if nothing is wrong because he is afraid of the consequences if he decides to leave and work elsewhere. The purple and blue mountains of goals, dreams and aspiration are off to the right side of the card and out of his vision. The mountains to the right indicate that his goals and objectives for his career, health and education will be easily met if he takes the chance. Remember, if you do not see it, you do not get it. He is standing on the sturdy and unwavering cement, so we know he feels very secure, yet still looks unhappy. The ocean's waves seem to make him think of his current situation fluctuating in positive and negative aspects, back and forth. He is so unsure of change, but he needs to know that there is a better opportunity in his future which he does not see now, but he will if he takes the chance. The wand represents another career opportunity or position behind him, but he is so interested in holding on to his current benefits, paycheck and security, that he is not paying attention to anything but his current situation. Look at the green grass in the future showing how prosperous he will be. The house, which in essence is like a castle, indicates love, happiness, prosperity and joy, inner peace, guidance, strength, self-esteem and everything to make him happy in the future. He still needs to look in that direction to get all of that good energy. He has the whole world in his hand and does not even know it. This career change, change of physician and education in some aspect, will make him much happier which implies better productivity, security, and peace of mind.

THE MESSAGE OF THIS CARD is that you are holding onto one particular job, (or it could be a health or school issue) thinking that everything is okay. You have the world in your hand, but it does seem to be helping you now. You are only holding onto the job for security reasons (regular paycheck and benefits), or your education and/or health issues. You are afraid to take a chance or make a change. Look to the future; there is another chance for success available, which will make you happier and bring a better salary, health or educational situation than your current situation. Be open to new opportunities. If we use the future for health and school, it will mean that once he makes up his mind, he will choose the right healthcare professional (and/or medication) and all school concerns will be decided easily. If he does not change anything in his life, it will remain the same.

TEENAGER MEANING: There is an issue with one or all of the meanings of the wands: career, health and school. Being the Querent is a teenager, we can assume it is school; however, do not overrule health and jobs. Looking to the past, we know there is something wrong in one or all of these areas. It could be a decision about a major in college, which college to go to, or even moving away from home for the first time and living in a dorm. The counter balance would be going to school near-by and to continue to live at home. It could be a struggle between doing well in school and getting a part time job. Perhaps the teenager is taking on too many credits and sports activities so he does not have enough time for either. If it is health related, there may be important decisions that need to be made. For example, he could give up sports, extra curricula activities or withdraw from a few classes so that he could rest and concentrate on his studies, etc. There will be a lot of choices for this teen.

HEALTH

If we use the wands for his health or education, it could be that he is contemplating a health related issue and perhaps is going to the wrong doctor. He may have even gotten the wrong diagnosis or medication. He needs to get a second opinion, perhaps change medication or treatment and look to the future where the green grass indicates better health.

EDUCATION

In school, he may be going in the wrong direction or will be changing his major. He is not sure what he wants to be in the future, but all will work out and make him happy. He just needs to check the opportunities presented to him before rejecting them. Once he gets all of the information about each opportunity, he will choose wisely and his family will actually support him one hundred percent.

MUNDANE KARMIC LESSON FOR BIRTH PATH NUMBER 2, ELEMENT FIRE.

KARMIC LESSON: The Karmic Lesson of the Two of Wands is that you need to let go of your career, health or educational path. Times have changed and you know this is no longer in your best interest. Holding onto the security, paycheck or benefits may be fine for now, but you need to look for other opportunities in your future. These new opportunities or changes will bring you the much needed happiness, good fortune and prosperity you have always wanted for your family and you. Be sure to choose the job, health or career path that is right for you in all aspects. You realize money is not everything.

ASTROLOGICAL CONNECTION: Mars in Aries

MEDITATION/AFFIRMATION: I will look into all opportunities presented to me to see if they are in line with my goals and objectives for the future. If I do not see the chance now, I know it will be coming shortly and I will be in a much better place than I am now.

TRADITIONAL MEANING: Indicates growth of personal power and courage. You will command the respect and attention of others. You will embark on a new adventure. Act decisively. Research carefully before making decisions. New, creative ideas needed for success. Commit all of your energy to new projects.

III
Three of Wands
(Minor Arcana - 3)

Here you are in between two wands, so there is an imbalance within your workplace, your health or education. This card has you choosing an important positive decision in your future away from the indecisiveness of the present. You are looking out into the world at the many opportunities before you and you finally choose wisely.

CHOOSE AN OPPORTUNITY CARD
CAREER

The Three of Wands is similar to the two, although there are several opportunities behind him yet unseen or unnoticed. He is busy watching others in their daily lives and is thinking too much about all the possibilities and opportunities around him. It is confusing and overwhelming and the small procrastination mountains to the left keep him from making a quick decision. This decision will be informed. This is a mental activity or intelligence card; he should use his mind to help make a decision about his life. Even the water is yellow which indicates that emotions are not an issue at this time and everything in his life is proceeding in a very logical and methodical way! The mountains of many wonderful opportunities are far away across the sea and he does not even notice them. He is standing on uneven ground splattered with spots of green and brown, indicating growth and grounding. He is trying to be stable and secure as well as figure out how he can be more prosperous. He is in between two wands which means there is an unbalanced situation or perhaps he is the imbalance in whichever situation he finds himself into. It could also be about confusion about his employment. The red garment worn depicts the desire and ability to do a good job no matter what sacrifices must be made; however, the green abundance or prosperity part of the garment indicates that a fair wage for a good day's work is all he needs to be satisfied. He must make a decision about his future or it will stay as uncertain and confusing as it has been for some time. Take charge, go forward, and proceed in the proper direction. Do not be afraid of change, as it can be his ally.

Notice the green on the man indicating that there will be some sort of wealth, prosperity and abundance coming with this decision. He also has to be very persistent, adamant and stubborn to make sure he gets what he wants as indicated by the red. His grounded brown shoes help him stay focused and alert to opportunities while his black hair gives us a clue that he may be somewhat depressed because of not being able to make the decision. The yellow headband gives him hope because he knows with logic everything will make sense and he will be able to move forward with the best decision possible.

THE MESSAGE OF THIS CARD is that there are other careers, health and education choices available to you even though you are not currently pursuing them. Be open to opportunities presented to you. Prosperity and abundance are right around the corner if you allow yourself to see other perspectives. Do not let fear stand in the way of pursuing your goals and dreams in life. It is time for a positive change.

TEENAGER MEANING: There are many decisions to make about career, health and education. So many beneficial opportunities are on the horizon and now he must decide in which direction would be in his best interest. The teenager may be confused and indecisive about any or all of these areas, but once a logical decision is made about the future, everything falls into place. He should choose with confidence.

HEALTH

This is an impasse. He is in between two wands, so there may be some issue with health that he is not quite aware of or his health care professional is not quite sure about a diagnosis. A second opinion is warranted. He is looking out onto the mountains beyond trying to get some clarification about his illness and may be hoping for opportunities to fix whatever the problem is. He is persistent and adamant that he will find out what is wrong. The green on your garment indicates that health will be restored and the issue resolved, but it may take some time. Once he makes a change and claims the positive future being offered, his health and related issues will be resolved.

EDUCATION

This card usually indicates that there may be more than one major he is interested in pursuing and he goes back and forth like a see-saw about which one would be in his best interest. This also indicates that he may just change his major as he is not committed to the major he has have chosen or additional information which came to him has made him rethink his educational future. Whichever decision he makes will be the right one since he is grabbing the wand in the future or the right direction. Seeking help from others is fine; however, do not get too over burdened with others' opinions as it will only confuse him. He must do what feels right to him.

MUNDANE KARMIC LESSON FOR BIRTH PATH NUMBER 3, ELEMENT FIRE.

KARMIC LESSON: The Karmic Lesson of the Three of Wands is that you need to look out onto the world to see what opportunities may be there for you rather than suffering in silence. Your position is no longer stable, as indicated by you standing on the cliff, and you need to venture forth to see what changes you should formulate in order to make your position more secure.

ASTROLOGICAL CONNECTION: Sun in Aries

MEDITATION/AFFIRMATION: I will no longer stand in the middle of my career, health or education issues and will take the best opportunities offered to me and move forward into a positive career path, attain perfect health and pursue a proper education. My future depends on it.

TRADITIONAL MEANING: Through careful planning, a goal or project management long in your dreams will be realized. A new business or ideas assured. Anticipate obstacles and visualize how you will overcome them long before they appear. Develop contacts. Such exceptional leadership skills will be needed; others consider you a visionary. Carefully weigh the risks.

IV
Four of Wands
(Minor Arcana - 4)

Here we are shown a feast, celebration or party. This card also stands for a serious relationship including an engagement or a marriage in the future. Your hard work will soon be rewarded; your efforts are paying off. Happiness and prosperity will come your way. You will be prosperous, abundant and fruitful.

THE ENGAGEMENT OR WEDDING CARD

This is the personal or business celebration card. The background is bright yellow indicating intellectual thought, an inquiring mind, and logic. There is also fruit and foliage draped over the four wands, representing good fortune on the job and abundance. Remember that foliage also indicates growth and fertility, so there would be much room for growth on the job, which may lead to other possibilities. The other meaning would be new growth within a family, as in having a child. This castle is the largest of all castles in the deck. It indicates the love, happiness, prosperity, and joy that accompanies a celebration, as the fruit and greenery above the wands represents fruitfulness and abundance. This card can stand for large gatherings and joyous events such as weddings, engagements, births, baptisms, etc. There are so many things to celebrate and these people are all having a wonderful time. I have usually found this card to mean a wedding or birth is imminent. Occasionally I have noticed it had to do with a celebration of a promotion or new job with a considerable increase in salary and a higher level of management within a company than you previously held. Either way, it will bring much happiness and inner peace to the Querent.

THE MESSAGE OF THIS CARD is that there is a celebration coming soon, whether it is a birth, a wedding, or just a special event in your family or with close friends. It also can be a time of great joy from a promotion or change of job. You will be prosperous and happy in making this change and accepting the fruits of your labor.

TEENAGER MEANING: Life is going well in career (could be part-time jobs), health and education. It is a great time to get life in balance, become more centered and strong. Once determination and persistence is used to get goals, everything will be fortunate, happy, and good luck will surround this teenager. Also, there is a good probability that within the year, there will be many family and friend parties or special events (births, baptisms, engagement parties and weddings) that will need to be attended.

HEALTH

Everything in your life is going well. You feel great and you share your good fortune of good health with everyone, possibly even helping those who are less fortunate. It indicates that you will be with family and friends and will be able to attend parties, weddings, baptisms and general get-togethers. You will feel wonderful and will enjoy the company of those you love. Love and good fortune are here for you now so do whatever makes you happy. If there were to be a health glitch, it will be fleeting. The results would be positive and it would be taken care of immediately and permanently.

EDUCATION

For education, this card represents that everything is going well. You have made friends in school, like to party and now have a firm foundation on which to grow the rest of your life through your strong dedication to your education. This can also indicate you will meet a romantic partner in your place of education which may be quite serious.

MUNDANE KARMIC LESSON FOR BIRTH PATH NUMBER 4, ELEMENT FIRE.

KARMIC LESSON: The Karmic Lesson of the Four of Wands is to accept all the love, happiness, prosperity and joy, inner peace, guidance, strength, wisdom, knowledge and everything to make you happy. Embrace the good luck and the people in your life. Know that abundance is coming to you from your job and your health is good. Just enjoy.

HOW TO BE A TAROT DETECTIVE 189

ASTROLOGICAL CONNECTION: Venus in Aries – strong leadership abilities and keen observation. You can get things done by being kind and in a harmonious way, but by also being strong, self assured and confident.

MEDITATION/AFFIRMATION: My life is getting more stable and enhanced. The prosperity and abundance is all around me. I must grab the opportunities to bring me happiness and joy. Everything is going in the right direction, so I should allow positive energy into my life and let it lead me for a positive future.

TRADITIONAL MEANING: Creative goals and projects will be completed ideas are plentiful. Financial rewards come in from completed work. Money does not necessarily mean happiness. Celebrate life passages. Renew yourself for the success you've achieved. You feel really alive and excited about the future. A period of freedom and new choices begins.

V
Five of Wands
(Minor Arcana - 5)

The Five of Wands represents the different aspects of the self. It determines that you are working against many other aspects. Expect some opposition and competition in your plans. You may find roadblocks that you need to remove. When you handle these obstacles, you will succeed.

THE COMPETITION CARD

Competition is the key to this card. This depicts five figures fighting or competing for the same position. Do not worry if this card comes up in a reading and you are interviewing for a new job because this indicates you will succeed in getting that position. You will win over the other competitors, as you are most suited to the job. You stand out among the rest. Notice the red outfit and cap on the main figure. He is different than the rest of the figures and seems to be in the middle of all the competition and commotion. He is also standing in the center of the group and has complete balance in the situation. He is defending his position and promoting himself well to potential employers. He is standing on uneven ground, but his footing seems to be better than that of the rest of the figures shown. The sky is clear blue showing that nothing will stand in his way. Obstacles will be removed and a clear path will open up ahead of you. Be assured that the Five of Wands will be lucky for you and that you will overcome any obstacles that you may encounter.

THE MESSAGE OF THIS CARD is that you will compete for a job and win the competition. Stand your ground and you will succeed. Use your desire and passion for your profession to make an impression on your employer to show your true abilities.

TEENAGER MEANING: This card usually comes up when there is a competition at school, such as sports or extra curricula activities. It can also mean that there is strong competition for the college or university that the Querent would like to get into. It stands for competition, fighting for what you really want and if you want it bad enough, everything will come your way.

HEALTH

The competition card means that there may be a few different issues that you need to deal with. Make sure you keep good personal records for any health care professional you will see and be ready to make some changes in your life style so that you may live a long and healthy life. You are under a great deal of stress and your lifestyle has to change in order to bring more balance and peace into your life. Your good health depends on you.

EDUCATION

You may wish to go to a particular school, but the competition is fierce. If this is the school that you want to attend without any reservations or doubts, then you will be chosen. If it has one or two things that you wish were different, then this school will not be for you.

MUNDANE KARMIC LESSON FOR BIRTH PATH NUMBER 5, ELEMENT FIRE.

KARMIC LESSON: The Karmic Lesson of the Five of Wands is that you will always be in competition with others for your job. Whether others like or do not like you, whether employees think you are self-righteous or a know-it-all, there will always be others who do not like you for some reason and will do everything they can to keep you off balance and on guard. You must let things go and know that you are doing your best. Even though others are jealous of you, you should not be concerned.

ASTROLOGICAL CONNECTION: Saturn in Leo

MEDITATION/AFFIRMATION: I will strive to be the best in my chosen profession or as a student and will get everything that I am one hundred percent interested in and dedicated to. I will succeed and move on to reach my goals and dreams easily and effortlessly.

TRADITIONAL MEANING: Caution. You may have to resort to underhanded methods to get a project pushed through. Completion. Competition. Greed and lust for power. Obstacles. Secret opposition to your plans. Arrival challenges your authority. There is no easy way to do this-arguments will be part of every day. A frustrating and difficult time ahead. Hospitals, bad luck, and nuisances.

VI
Six of Wands
(Minor Arcana - 6)

This card stands for victory. The laurel wreath on the main figure's head denotes winning or succeeding in a competition, but there may be apprehension. You have overcome struggle and are now victorious. Once a decision has been made, you will be successful. Promotions are likely. You have the ability to get the woman or man of your dreams.

VICTORY ON THE JOB, WITH HEALTH OR EDUCATION CARD

The Six of Wands indicates victory in securing the job you wants or getting the promotion you deserve. Riding on a horse physically seats you above others. This indicates that you will gain a position of authority or will have others reporting to you. You are in control and riding into the future (or right direction) with victory written all over the card. A laurel wreath on your head and wand indicate that you have finally succeeded in obtaining the position you have always wanted. You sit on top of a green blanket depicting the abundance and prosperity you will gain. Remember that anything on the head is very important in an interpretation, so the laurel wreath is extremely important in this card. There is a clear blue sky indicating success, happiness, and nothing to stop your progress. Riding a very spiritual and enlightened horse to the future indicates that you have come a long way in your career and are obtaining everything that you have worked so hard to achieve. Others will follow you and respect your authority and position. Remain fair and just.

THE MESSAGE OF THIS CARD is that there is abundance and success will come your way on the job and a possible promotion or change of job is at hand. You will be extremely successful. Be sure to continually strive towards the future.

TEENAGER MEANING: This most likely stands for a victory at school, being number one in class, doing everything right in testing, studying and homework. The Querent is on the right path and will be very successful in whichever field (s)he has chosen for himself. The other message would be that health issues are improving and good health, resolution of health issues, medications and reactions to them are all in the past. This is a very good year to improve one's health. Also, if one is graduating from college, this could be victory on the job, getting a new job that will be fantastic and going in the right direction.

HEALTH

You are healthy or have just conquered a major illness and are on the road to recovery and good health. This is the victory card, so everything is going well. The only thing you have to do is take care of yourself, rest and take care of yourself You must be your first priority and everything will continue to go well. Be the best you can be and practice good health, exercise and eat right so you can continue to live life the way you would like to.

EDUCATION

You have picked the right school, the right major and the right classes. You will be very successful in all that you do in your new school. You will have friends and followers and you will continue to lead those who need direction and help. You are confident and assured about your life. You see that life only getting better with a formal education which you will have. Everything before you will continue to grow and prosper because you believe in yourself and your ideals.

MUNDANE KARMIC LESSON FOR BIRTH PATH NUMBER 6, ELEMENT FIRE.

KARMIC LESSON: The Karmic Lesson of the Six of Wands is that your hard work is paying off. You are getting the position you want and will move forward with good luck, prosperity, good health and an opportunity to get or give training to your employees. You will use your intelligence to get what you need for your own satisfaction and rise to the level that you feel is appropriate for you. This is a winning card.

ASTROLOGICAL CONNECTION: Jupiter in Leo

MEDITATION/AFFIRMATION: I will continue to be victorious in all areas of my career, helping those who need guidance and mentorship, but most of all, I will be grateful for the opportunities that have been given to me to be as successful in all things as I am.

TRADITIONAL MEANING: Your dreams and plans are finally fulfilled. Hard work and careful planning results in glorious success. Pain, public recognition and honor. Victory over the opposition. Triumphant success how positive effect on your self-esteem. You are bursting with pride. Avoid arrogance. Financial rewards for hard work.

VII
Seven of Wands
(Minor Arcana - 7)

You are competing against a group of people. There are difficulties ahead. Fight for your beliefs, because you have the superior position. Conflict needs to be resolved. Expect to face opposition. You will need all of your inner strength to and deal with your problem(s).

The Seven of Wands represents fighting, arguing or opposition in a particular area of a job or personal life. More often than not, it is a job-related card. You are on top of a green hill, wearing a green tunic, covering yellow. Your good fortune or abundance will come by logically thinking over and dealing with situations from that level. You know there will be some opposition and you are willing to fight it. You will stand your ground, as your feet are firmly planted and you are ready to deal with the competition. If you are persistent, you will be successful. Another issue that will be a little harder to achieve is trying to remain focused and balanced. You are not happy being in the constant position of having to prove your skills and abilities over and over again, but you will do what needs to be done to keep your current status and position. Notice the two different shoes. This may represent other unsettling or unbalanced issues within you that need to be dealt with as well. Keep your guard up and protect what is rightfully yours.

THE MESSAGE OF THIS CARD is that you will be competing on the job and will be victorious. Hold your ground, watch your step, and keep your balance. You will get ahead and be prosperous and abundant; however, it may require a little more positive action than you had originally anticipated.

TEENAGER MEANING: The teen feels on edge, not particularly safe, secure, grounded nor stable. (S)he is trying to protect him/herself by using intelligence, common sense, logic, reasoning abilities and analytical skills. Once the Querent decides in which direction he will go, everything else will follow.

HEALTH

You are holding your own; you are bringing clear sailing, harmony, peace, and going in the right direction in all health related matters. Take care of any issues quickly and they will be resolved.

EDUCATION

You may have some issues at school and feel the need to defend yourself on some level. Are you studying? Are you absorbing your school's knowledge or are you just passing through by partying and having fun? If you apply yourself, you will be very successful and will overcome any obstacles before you. Your logic and intelligence will be the best defense against anything that can hurt you in any way.

MUNDANE KARMIC LESSON FOR BIRTH PATH NUMBER 7, ELEMENT FIRE.

KARMIC LESSON: The Karmic Lesson of the Seven of Wands is that you should hold your ground no matter what. You have a keen sense of fairness and right and wrong and although you have been always on the defensive regarding health, your career and education, you know what you have to do to get the job done correctly. Others try to keep you off-balance, but you continue to strive for calmness, perfection and equality.

ASTROLOGICAL CONNECTION: Mars in Leo

MEDITATION/AFFIRMATION: I will be balanced and centered in all aspects of my career (school/health) so that I may use my intelligence and logic for my greatest good. I will also protect myself and my interests from those seeking to make my life negative and inconsequential.

TRADITIONAL MEANING: You are on the defensive. You have the advantage and will eventually win. Be strong and aggressive. Expect criticism and challenges to your authority. Send up for yourself and for your ideas. You'll never regret your actions, even though they may seem too aggressive at the time. People compete for your energy and resources.

VIII
Eight of Wands
(Minor Arcana - 8)

This card suggests a scattered life or circumstance in a very disorganized or chaotic fashion. Nothing has been decided. It reflects the person's life, which needs order or perhaps different spacing. Order is being sought but more things need to be done to get it right. You may get what you want, but not what you need.

ORGANIZE YOUR LIFE CARD

The Eight of Wands stands for a scattered existence. Things seem to be up in the air. When I see this card, I know that the Querent is usually stressed out because she is simultaneously doing too many things. These types of people have lots of energy, ambition, and drive; however, it tends to be unfocused. This type of person also needs a vacation or rest since they push themselves too hard. This could be a workaholic who thinks everything on their list should get done before someone else does it incorrectly. The clear blue sky is promising because once you realize you are doing too much, it is clear that you should take time off, even if it is just reading a book each day, watching a TV show that relaxes you, or taking a long, refreshing bath or dip in the pool. You need renewal and rest. The green mountain with the house or castle indicates your fruitfulness and prosperity and the calm waters show all other emotional issues are under control. However, the procrastination mountain is in your past, along with family concerns, as indicated by the small house. These issues should be re-examined and dealt with in a better fashion than before. They will not disappear on their own. Your work habits must be addressed or the universe may force you to rest by giving you some health ailment that will require long periods of rest.

THE MESSAGE OF THIS CARD is that you have too much responsibility in your job. This is a good time to start delegating your work. You must prioritize your obligations and take care of yourself. Give yourself time to rest.

TEENAGER MEANING: Life is throwing the Querent everything it has to test your courage, self-confidence, self-esteem and stamina. It could be job, health and school issues here. The very simple message of this card is for the teenager to deal with only a few things at a time finish them and then move on to the next item. Basically, this type of personality wants to handle everything, takes on too much responsibility and then gets very depressed or upset when things are not done on time.

HEALTH

You are too active and doing too many things that are not bringing much satisfaction. You need to take care of yourself and rest. Delegate and put projects on the back burner. No one could possibly handle all the activities you have started. If you do not calm down and reorganize your life now, it will become harder in the future. Take this time to reevaluate the amount of time you have and what you really wish to accomplish. Blend the two and give yourself permission to relax, enjoy life and be around family and friends.

EDUCATION

You have taken on too many activities in school and have a full load of classes. This will not be healthy in the long run because you cannot keep up this workload. You may wish to give up some after school activities or sports until your workload is under control. Even though you feel that you want to do everything now, it will not be in your best interest to continue. Prioritize and see which classes and activities will be in your best interest.

MUNDANE KARMIC LESSON FOR BIRTH PATH NUMBER 8, ELEMENT FIRE.

KARMIC LESSON: The Karmic Lesson of the Eight of Wands is to stop trying to do a million things at once and take the most important issues, deal with them and move forward a little at a time. All finished chores and projects attract positive energy which you so desperately need. Be mindful of your health since you are so weighed down and overwhelmed that you do not seem to have time to take care of yourself. Prioritize your life and your importance in it.

ASTROLOGICAL CONNECTION: Mercury in Sagittarius

MEDITATION/AFFIRMATION: I will consolidate the many areas of life that I juggle so that I can bring projects and issues to a speedy conclusion for the good of all involved.

TRADITIONAL MEANING:

Major crossroad in life. You must take action to resolve events. Move quickly or miss out on an opportunity. Careful planning is important, but be sure that it does not slow you down. A good time to clarify your goals and set new priorities. Situations come to resolution. Be on the lookout for important news or information.

IX
Nine of Wands
(Minor Arcana - 9)

This person has gone through many struggles, obstacles, challenges, or difficulties and wants to be better prepared for the future. Think before you leap and you will succeed.

LET IT GO CARD

The bandage around the man's head in the Nine of Wands suggests he has already been wounded. He is cautious and looking over his shoulder; he is afraid of something or someone on the job. I have found that when there is a break in the suits, as seen in this card with a gaping hole in between the row of wands in the background, there is something missing. In this instance, it is regarding one's career or relating to co-workers. It seems as if he needs to watch his back. Someone may be up to "no good" on the job. It could represent gossip, rumors, or jealousy. The figure in the card does not want to get involved in any of the negative aspects of the work environment again, so he is trying very hard to protect himself. Although he is standing on cement, he is still guarded. He feels secure in the knowledge that he will be watching out for himself. The green mountains are abundant and prosperous, but behind him. He must look at the mountains to reap their benefits. The clear blue sky is another good indication of harmony and everything turning out in his best interests but again, it is behind him. Wands behind you always indicate that better opportunities were not previously considered and turn out to be a blessing in disguise. The wands are sprouting leaves which mean that the new opportunities will flourish once the Querent is unafraid to stand up for himself and explore the possibilities.

THE MESSAGE OF THIS CARD is that it would be wise to watch your back in your place of business. You are holding onto one job for security or monetary reasons. There are many opportunities awaiting you if you are brave enough to turn around, look at the abundant and harmonious background, and take a chance.

TEENAGER MEANING: Again, this card represents career (or job), health and/or education and holding onto one aspect of any or all of those situations and being really afraid to let go of it even though it is dying. Security in all areas is needed to be successful and to finish whichever job/health/education issue has been the most disturbing. The Querent must move on into a new direction since nothing will flourish where you are now whether or not you wish to believe or understand that.

HEALTH

You are holding onto a dying wand which means that your health may be in decline. You are so afraid to go to the doctor or health care professional that you may be the one making your health worse. See what is wrong and get it taken care of. If you don't do it now, you will not be able to completely heal your body in the future. The sooner you go to the doctor, the better. You'll be if you wait any longer. The sooner you handle your medical issue, the sooner the doctor can cure you. There are very healthy, green mountains behind you which mean that there will be many wonderful healthy alternatives from which to choose, but if you do nothing, you will get nothing in return. Get rid of your fears and take care of yourself as soon as possible.

EDUCATION

You may have bitten off more than you can chew. You are upset, confused, overwhelmed and afraid that you will fail. With this attitude, it is certain that you will fail. You need to let go of some of the courses or extra school activities that you have taken on because it seemed like the cool thing to do. Now, it is about handling what you need to do and taking care of your health. Even though this is under the school section, this will definitely affect your health if you do not give yourself the luxury of rest, relaxation, meditation or exercise to release some of this stress. There are plenty of good choices around you, but you must let go of the one that is dying or causing you many problems before the good choices will become visible to you.

MUNDANE KARMIC LESSON FOR BIRTH PATH NUMBER 9, ELEMENT FIRE.

KARMIC LESSON: The Karmic Lesson of the Nine of Wands is that you must let go of situations, people, and environments that are unsafe or dying around you. Just because you are somewhat secure does not mean your life will stay that way. You need to know there are many more wonderful opportunities in your future and trust that the universe will let them unfold before you. Protect yourself from ever getting hurt again.

ASTROLOGICAL CONNECTION: Moon in Sagittarius

MEDITATION/AFFIRMATION: I will protect myself from others who find it necessary to injure or ridicule me in any way. I will let go of anything that is not working in my life and look towards the many opportunities that are in my best interest which are just waiting for me to choose.

TRADITIONAL MEANING: Be on the defensive. Prepare for assault. Keep resources and reserve. You will be surrounded by trouble. You feel emotionally and physically tired from the constant conflict and setbacks in your life. No easy answers, but inner strength and perseverance will see you through. No matter how bad it gets, you must reach the end.

X
Ten of Wands
(Minor Arcana - 10)

This card indicated added intensity. The figure is loaded down; his head is lowered and shoulders are slumped, which denotes overwork and burdens on the job. He seems to be heading home after a rough time. He is taking on more than can be handle at the present time.

WORKAHOLIC CARD

Here is the workaholic card. Notice how the man is burdened with responsibilities on the job. See how hunched over he is, as if barely able to manage all the situations his career or work related issues are causing him. The house is in the background and to the right of the card - the future. He is not looking at it, which means he will not receive the love, happiness, prosperity, and joy that he should. He is concentrating on his job and its responsibilities. There is a clear blue sky filled with hope, serenity, and fulfillment and the green shrubs indicate the potential for abundance or prosperity, but he is not noticing them. With this card, I usually suggest that the Querent try to rest more than usual and take some time off from work. Even an extra half hour of relaxation after work each day will help rejuvenate you. Enjoy family, friends, hobbies, and interests. Go on an extended vacation. If you do not, you run the risk of becoming run down and catching a cold, which could lead to bronchitis, pneumonia, or worse. Then the Universe will force you to rest while you recuperate from the illness. This has happened to me several times in my early twenties when I thought I was invincible and could push myself to the limits. My body pushed back. I had gotten pneumonia three separate times in a short period of time, so I know the truth of this. Rest and take care of yourself. Work can wait while you tend to your health and family. Both are more important than your job.

THE MESSAGE OF THIS CARD is that you are handling too much responsibility on the job. You are burdened and should rest and take care of yourself. You could cause yourself to get ill if you continually push yourself. Look towards the house to bring love, happiness, prosperity, and joy into your life.

TEENAGER MEANING: This is the workaholic card which certainly can cover jobs and education. It may also cover education and working too hard and on too many committees or after school activities. It is also indicating that by doing too much, you will get ill in some way. You then may find yourself with the flu, colds, bronchitis, headaches, migraines, depression and any type of aches and pains.

HEALTH

You are overburdened, stressed and overwhelmed. You feel as if you do not have a choice other than to continue the way in which you are going. However, you need to delegate, put some things on the back burner, and let some things go for now or just forget some of these dreams or wishes at this time. One person could not possibly do this much without a threat to their physical or mental health. Be strong and make sure you do whatever you feel you must and no more. There are others who can help you, but you do have to ask. Your family needs you and if you continue down this overwhelming and burdensome road, you may not be there to spend the rest of your life with them.

EDUCATION

You have taken on too many classes that you do not have time to rest, relax or unwind at all. You are way too serious about school and even though it is wonderful to graduate with a degree, it is not worth your health. Being intelligent and creative, you should figure out how to study smarter and not harder. Attend only the classes that you truly need at this time and let some go for another semester. Whether it is sports and/or after school activities, you would not have the mental or physical stamina to keep up with them on a long term basis. Take care of yourself.

MUNDANE KARMIC LESSON FOR BIRTH PATH NUMBER 1, ELEMENT FIRE.

KARMIC LESSON: The Karmic Lesson of the Ten of Wands is that you must lighten your load. Being the workaholic card, this energy is oppressive, strong, overwhelming and heavy. You feel as if you must continue forward no matter what, but in reality, your family would much rather share time with you than having the things that you are working so hard for them to have. Financial security is a wonderful thing, but sometimes sharing time with your family can be just as rewarding and powerful.

ASTROLOGICAL CONNECTION: Saturn in Sagittarius

MEDITATION/AFFIRMATION: I will make time for my family and me in my future. Money isn't everything and as long as I have my health, time with my family and a plan for our futures, everything will work out in God and Goddess' time.

TRADITIONAL MEANING: Life is a constant battle. You never seem to get a break. Your heart will be happy. You doubt your own worth. You're overextended and overcommitted. You will be tested. No rest from your burdens. Your responsibilities are suffocating you. Look for new, creative solutions to your problems. Make changes in your life.

Page of Wands
(Minor Arcana - 11)
Also used as a Mundane Karmic Lesson 2/Fire
Court Card

This card represents a new prospect or endeavor, infancy, adolescence, new undertakings, and a sense of wonder. It is a new awakening or good news. This can stand for a very enthusiastic, intelligent, and forceful person.

NEW BEGINNINGS IN YOUR CAREER, EDUCATION OR HEALTH

The Page of Wands indicates new endeavors, opportunities, and adventures in your career or job. It is a person who is willing to accept change to make things better. Spirituality is guiding his decision to move forward, as indicated by the white hat with red feather. The feather de*notes* his assertiveness or passion to change his job and many times start a career or business of his own. The yellow outfit suggests he will use his mind to accomplish goals, objectives, and dreams. His yellow boots are firmly planted on the ground so we know he is focused, stable, grounded, and centered. He knows exactly in which direction he needs to go and is taking steps to get to his destination. The red tights indicate his desire to be successful with this new venture and how he is going to handle the new responsibilities associated with the new job: with assertiveness, desire, passion, and a bold attitude. The clear blue sky says it all: he will be successful in his new venture and not let any obstacles interfere with his goals. The brown mountains or objectives in the future confirm that all of his goals, objectives, desires, dreams, and wishes will be easily met soon. The growing leaves on the wand in his hand foretell of an abundant future with his career - one that will continue to grow and prosper.

THE MESSAGE OF THIS CARD is that there will be new beginnings in your career; if you are unemployed, a new opportunity will be presented to you. There is a possibility of promotion of many new responsibilities being given to you for additional competition. Be brave and follow your dreams to start a new business or venture. Do not be afraid to take a chance on that promotion or look for a new job. Many wonderful opportunities await you, but you must grab them.

TEENAGER MEANING: New beginnings in career/health and education will be given to the Querent. Goals and objectives will be easily met and all of your dreams and aspirations are coming to fruition. This is a spiritual quest ready to happen, but it may be that the Querent is somewhat reluctant to start the journey or does not know how to begin. Example of a Page is: starting a new business or being accepted by a new school, etc.

HEALTH

Your health is going in a new positive direction. A new procedure or medicine (or any area of medicine including holistic health) is found and you are feeling so much better. New beginnings in better health start and your stamina will increase; your mental attitude as well as any physical manifestations of illness will start to disappear. Using your logical mind now will help you move forward and continue to get better each and every day. The branch has leaves on it, so holding it in the right hand indicates that your goals and objectives, dreams and aspirations for your health will manifest shortly.

EDUCATION

This Page indicates that you are going to a new beginning in school. It can be as simple as going from grade school to high school, or high school to college, or of course, getting higher degrees. It shows your conviction to learning and improving yourself because you see the value in education and you may want to continue with lectures, seminars, workshops and/or teaching in your field of expertise as time goes on. Every time you move forward in a new adventure in learning, this card is represented.

KARMIC LESSON: The Karmic Lesson of the Page of Wands is to look forward to starting a new life towards your career, school or health. You are on a much more spiritual journey than you could ever realize and your challenges will be handled one by one, so do not let them overwhelm you. Your goals and objectives, aspirations and dreams will be easily met once you decide what they should be.

ASTROLOGICAL CONNECTION: Beginning of Spring - Aries

MEDITATION/AFFIRMATION: I look forward to the future with anticipation and hope that the next position I get will bring me prosperity, new opportunities, growth within my job and a bright new future. Let me be intelligent enough to take the appropriate risks that are given to me for my highest good.

TRADITIONAL MEANING: May signify male under 30, who is self-confident, charming and generous. Nature lover, enthusiastic, active, and involved. Very emotional. Courageous – has strong convictions. Encourages and inspires others to be their best. Outgoing and gregarious personality.

Knight of Wands
(Minor Arcana - 12)
Also used as a Mundane Karmic Lesson 3/Fire
Court Card

This card represents adolescence, working towards understanding yourself or your situation and testing the information you are receiving. It is full of positive energy and can stand for someone who is quickly going places, though perhaps not in the right direction.

LEARNING THE ROPES IN CAREER, EDUCATION OR HEALTH

The Knight of Wands indicates that you are going in the wrong direction in your career. You are not particularly happy in your current position and should start looking into the future - or the opposite direction. Notice the three mountains in the left (or the past) of the card. There are procrastination issues that you have not dealt with. Deal with them quickly so you can proceed in the proper direction. They will not just disappear. You have the intelligence to move ahead, as indicated by the yellow garment. However, the yellow is covering a suit of armor, indicating that you are ready for a fight or confrontation if needed. Armor always indicates that you feel as if you must protect yourself because you were most likely hurt before. In this case, the hurt or betrayal was probably associated with someone on your job. You are seated on a tan horse indicating grounding; however, the horse only has two feet on the earth. The horse is not totally stable or grounded so although you feel as if you are; it may be a false feeling of security. The light blue sky indicates that all can be well with a little more confidence or knowledge of the situation. Everything will fall into place for you once you proceed on the right course. Do not be afraid of handling issues and concerns that trouble you. Turn your horse around and proceed towards a rewarding, new position or career opportunity with confidence.

THE MESSAGE OF THIS CARD is to continue with your new career path in a very deliberate and analytical way. You may have a false sense of security since you are proceeding in the wrong direction - towards the past. Handle your procrastination issues and go after your true goals rather than making excuses why you cannot reach them.

TEENAGER MEANING: This card says that the choices the Querent has made on career, health and education seem to be going in the wrong direction. You can see that the Knight is trying to protect him/herself with the armor which indicates he does not want to be exposed or hurt in any way. This is a redefining of the self type of card with procrastination being your worse trait.

HEALTH

This Knight is a very volatile card. On the health issue, it means you are going in the wrong direction. Are you with a doctor with whom you are not comfortable? Are you not getting better as quickly as you had hoped? The procrastination mountains to the left show that either you have not gone to the proper doctor or are putting it off until you are not so busy. If you keep procrastinating about taking care of this illness, it will get worse as time goes by. You are protecting yourself with armor and think that you are safe from anything that can harm you, but an illness or medical concern will find a way to keep you in bed or at the very least, off of your feet until you feel you should get proper attention from your healthcare professional.

EDUCATION

This is a very difficult card for education. It shows you may have procrastinated too long to get into the school of your dreams. It may also show that you are not taking the appropriate major for you and once you go in the right direction (going right in the card to the future), you will not be happy with your choice. You will always look for something better, or be really bored with your field that you do not pay attention to it and may not get the marks that your parents were truly looking for. If you are an adult, the one you will disappoint will be yourself. The armor seems to protect you, but what are you protecting yourself from in education? If you are taking up your major for someone else, such as a parent, etc., perhaps you should have a talk with them to let them know that this area is not your passion. It is your life and you should do what makes you happy as long as you are not hurting anyone else.

KARMIC LESSON: The Karmic Lesson of the Knight of Wands is that you should protect yourself from those you feel may hurt or challenge you. You clearly have a vision of what is right and how you are going to handle your life, but it would be wise to get grounded and focused before you put all of your energy into a plan, desire, goal, or dream that may not be leading you in the right direction or on the right path.

ASTROLOGICAL CONNECTION: Sagittarius

MEDITATION/AFFIRMATION: When I feel that life is not going in a correct direction, I will be strong enough to see all perspectives of any situation so that I may make the right choices for that particular issue.

TRADITIONAL MEANING: Indicates male under 40. Confident, sexy and seductive. Attractive to women. Full of energy. Always in a rush, with a lot of nervous energy. Excellent at starting a project, not good at maintaining things. Sees constant change. Impatient. Passionate temperament. Enthusiastic, very emotional. Understands others' motivations.

Queen of Wands
(Minor Arcana - 13)
Also used as a Mundane Karmic Lesson 4/Fire
Court Card

This card represents the mature aspects of the suit: receptivity and femininity. It can stand for motherhood, dependability, or unconditional love.

How to be a Tarot Detective

BECOMING AN EXPERT IN YOUR FIELD

This Queen is seated on a cement throne. No one is going to sway her without her consent. She is dressed in yellow and white, indicating the logical manner in which she deals with situations. Her generosity accompanies all of her decisions. She is holding onto a wand, indicating that the career/job you have tried so hard to attain is within your grasp. The sunflower might indicate daydreaming or a desire to stop and smell the flowers more in life, but it usually indicates new growth, new beginnings, new ventures, fertility, and cosmic knowledge. The Queen of Wands is not easily swayed, but is fair. This Queen responds well to people asking favors of her, rather than demanding she does something for them. The yellow mountains off to the left of the card indicate that you will your dreams and wish would come to be if you use common sense and good planning and stop procrastinating. The light blue-sky means that things will come together after you start to push your ideas about your new job into motion. There will be happiness, clear sailing, harmony and peace with no concerns related to your decision in this area. Now we come to something very interesting: the black cat. I have noticed when there are black cats, trees, or birds in a card; it usually means there are secrets that need to be addressed. Notice this secret or concern is right in front of the Queen, indicating that she knows about it and chooses to ignore it, believing the concern is not a major issue at this time. Be aware of and deal with it in a forthright manner so it will have no power over you.

THE MESSAGE OF THIS CARD is to stand your ground. You can proceed favorably on the job if you use your intellect above your emotions. Be ready to discover secrets, which will be revealed to you if you are open to them. Handle yourself with dignity and fairness and all you want will be yours.

TEENAGER MEANING: This card represents new beginnings, new ventures, new journeys and looking toward the future in career, health and education, even though you are not quite comfortable yet in figuring out what that might be. The procrastination is the worst energy field in metaphysics because the negativity attracted to the Querent by the procrastination will make the Querent's life much more difficult. If there is an idea about your future, now is the time to grab it.

HEALTH

There is still procrastination around you. You are looking towards the future and new beginnings, new ventures, new journeys, a new direction in life, but you are still seated on the throne and find it very difficult to get up and move. You are tired of the way you are feeling and are thinking about making a change. With your free will, you can certainly make the change that will bring you the best health possible, but you are afraid of what you will find out. Use the intelligence that you have and make yourself do the right thing. You should find out how to help yourself with the help of a healthcare professional and get on the speedy road of recovery.

EDUCATION

You are not very happy with the way things have turned out at school, so you are looking for a change. You are hesitant to make the change because of "starting over" or the feeling that you will disappoint someone, but you must take a step forward. The procrastination mountains to the left of the card are pressuring you to be worried, fearful and have anxieties about changing your path or direction. Be sensible and know that whatever you do to move forward will help those little blobs, in the right of the card which are showing you that your future is not written yet, turn into mountains. Those mountains will be your goals and objectives that you have wanted from the start, but were afraid to pursue. Go after your dreams!

KARMIC LESSON: The Karmic Lesson of the Queen of Wands is that even though you may have done well, know your stuff, and have a good handle on your life, there are many other areas that need your attention. The most important areas in your life are daunted with procrastination, dreams that are unfulfilled and holding onto the familiar because you are afraid of changing the security or paycheck and benefits for the unknown. Take the risk and your life will be much more rewarding. Opportunities abound, so take them while you can.

ASTROLOGICAL CONNECTION: Aries

MEDITATION/AFFIRMATION: I will look towards the future for new positions or opportunities before I decide to leave the job that has been my main source of revenue for the last (how many) years. I am looking forward to having new opportunities to come into my life, but as long as I am comfortable and secure, I will not make any rash moves that may not be in my best interest.

TRADITIONAL MEANING: Signifies a popular an outgoing woman. Attractive, healthy, fit, and fashionable. Competent. Decisive and intelligent. Methodical planner. Creative and full of new ideas. Practical with money. Kind, emotional, cheerful and easy-going. Protective and supportive of others.

King of Wands
(Minor Arcana - 14)
Also used as a Mundane Karmic Lesson 5/Fire
Court Card

This card represents masculinity, decisiveness, and assertion. This card represents honesty, sincerity, and a very down to earth way of thinking. One must concentrate on old-fashioned values. It also represents a good career and possibly being ready to leave it by retiring.

ACHIEVING YOUR GOAL IN YOUR
CAREER, EDUCATION OR HEALTH

The King of Wands is shown sitting on a throne with his feet firmly planted on the cement, so we know that he is firm in his beliefs, set in his ways, and not easily swayed. He is facing into the past, or the wrong direction. This may indicate that the Querent has done everything he could to get a job and follow through with it, but then discovers it is not what he had wanted in the first place. He is a traditional man in that he expects admiration, respect, and loyalty. He represents the conclusion of a journey from the beginning of a search through the conclusion of a new job or career. He expects that you would use your intellect to get what you need and follow through in a very analytical manner. The red robe indicates the assertion or aggression that this man is trying to control under the cape of intellect, as shown through the yellow; the green color of prosperity and abundance is now the top covering of his robe. Notice the yellow crown on his red hair. This combination is asking the Querent to balance his assertion and intelligence to get to his goal. The clear blue sky shows the promise of the conclusion being the one that was expected. The black salamander on the lower right hand side of the card may indicate that problems and concerns have transformed themselves into very small obstacles, which can now be handled. Being a little cautious about any aspect of the job that makes you uncomfortable would be in your best interest.

THE MESSAGE OF THIS CARD is to be assertive, stand by your convictions, and balance your desire for abundance with intellectual thought, reason, wisdom, and honesty. Most of all, you should look towards the future. Try to turn around and set your sights on a more meaningful position or to start a new direction in life.

TEENAGER MEANING: This card represents that everything is on course and almost completed. Life may get a little boring, but the Querent is in much more control than usual. (S)he has to decide to go apply for a very important or prestigious job, continue to deal with health problems and figure out after graduation what will he do as a profession.

HEALTH

You are now at the end of the issue with your health. It seems that you have been through an ordeal and are now on the mend; however, it does not look like you are taking your condition seriously and may do some foolish things to undo everything that has been accomplished regarding your health. Be sure to take your medicine, keep up with doctor appointments and take care of yourself. Just because you are feeling better now does not mean that you can automatically take over all the issues and concerns you had before you were ill. Take on things slowly. Rest when you are supposed to and just do not do anything that will make you relapse.

EDUCATION

This King represents that you have gone as far as you are going to go. Whether is it an undergraduate degree or advanced degree, or whatever you choose, you are where you are supposed to be. You are accomplished at this point and know what you are doing in every sense of the word. You may also know your area of expertise so well that it may have bored you a little bit. This also can be a card which would suggest leaving your field and perhaps getting into another new and exciting field to adjunct this one. You are confident, strong-willed, logical and prosperous now (or you will be prosperous as soon as you get a job in your field) and you feel very self assured and persistent about your new path.

KARMIC LESSON: The Karmic Lesson of the King of Wands is to be somewhat flexible in your life and know that change is the only constant in the universe. Doing things the same old way, year after year, will not push you into a peaceful future, but will give you thoughts of anxiety, fear, and doubt and worry because you are afraid to take risks or change from the norm. If you have the chance to start again or to start over, this is the time to do it. A new life direction, such as a retirement, would be the best thing that could possibly happen to you.

ASTROLOGICAL CONNECTION: Leo

MEDITATION/AFFIRMATION: Is it time for me to pass the torch onto someone else? I am secure and confident with my abilities and can only make the decision for myself as to whether I should retire or stay in a position that has become too routine and boring for me.

TRADITIONAL MEANING: Denotes a handsome, charismatic, and bold man over 40, who has a commanding presence and strong convictions. Strong leadership skills. Attracts attention wherever he goes. Takes action and gets results. An innovative, creative man who is open to new concepts.

The Court Cards give more depth and insight to the Numbers 2-5, so if you are between these numbers, you have two mundane every day cards with issues that must be dealt with frequently.

~214~   REV. VIKKI ANDERSON

Ace of Wands
(Minor Arcana - Gift from God and Goddess – 1/Fire)

This card shows the hand of God and Goddess reaching out, giving you new beginnings and opportunities in your career, job, and all relating to it. Your desires are about to be put into action. Your thoughts will soon become a reality with the help of God and Goddess.

BLESSINGS FROM GOD AND GODDESS
IN EDUCATION, CAREER AND HEALTH

Be certain that this represents a gift from God and Goddess and, as such, cannot be the wrong opportunity. Even though there is a cloud in the sky, I believe it is just the way the hand of God and Goddess is portrayed in these cards. There are leaves on the wand, so we know that the new or upcoming venture in your business will be blossoming. Since it is a God/Goddess-sent, it will be a very positive and revitalizing experience. You will be able to handle the new job or career with ease and will be happy in your new adventure in the business world. This may also indicate a promotion on your job. The gray sky will cause some uncertainty as to whether or not you will take the opportunity offered. It also indicates that you are unsure and things are cloudy or uncertain about your new position. You may associate fear, doubt, concern, and anxiety about taking a step in this direction, but that is expected since you do not know how this opportunity will be given to you. The blue creek is calm and meanders gently throughout the card, indicating that your emotions about this decision will be serene and calm. There is a castle in the background, depicting that love; happiness, prosperity, and joy are within your reach. It is in your past, which could indicate that you should keep your family in mind for the future. The green hills of abundance show that prosperity is around you and the mountains from the center to the right of the card show that there are so many objectives and opportunities to choose from. Just take the necessary steps to make your dreams come true.

THE MESSAGE OF THIS CARD is that this is a gift from God and Goddess in your career. Opportunities in your career will come to you.

This is the luckiest card in this suit, so feel honored and blessed that you have received it and make the most of it.

TEENAGER MEANING: Everything that you need to be happy and successful in your career, with your health and in school will be blessed and push you into a happier future where many of your dreams will come true.

HEALTH: This is a blessing from God and Goddess in your health, career and educational pursuits. If you have an illness or something that needs to be identified by a health care professional, this card will bless you during the examination, treatment and recovery. One person told me that her friend found out she had breast cancer and did not understand since this card came out in a reading she had done for her. Shortly afterwards, her friend was diagnosed with cancer. I told her that it was a good thing because it was found early enough to be rectified and her friend is now healthy because of the cancer's early discovery and the blessings of this card.

EDUCATION: No matter which direction in school you venture into, you will be successful. The Wands always bless you no matter which discipline you decide to study. Remember, this can be formal education, or you may attend lectures, seminars, workshops, classes or training in one or more subjects. No matter what you do during this Ace grace period, it will be for your best interest. Take as many courses as you think you should because it is a time of learning exploration and fun.

KARMIC LESSON: The Karmic Lesson of the Ace of Wands is that everything will work out even though you have your own fears, doubts, worries, anxieties, indecision and procrastination about particular issues in your life. God and Goddess can do anything and can change your life in an instant. Be open to all of the possibilities and be thankful and grateful for all that you have already been given.

ASTROLOGICAL CONNECTION: Sagittarius

MEDITATION/AFFIRMATION: I am blessed in my career, health, and higher education. I will use this knowledge to better myself and move forward to all the things I have wanted to accomplish. God and Goddess are with me and showing me that everything I may want is right there before me.

TRADITIONAL MEANING: Anything is possible. Good time to begin a new project. Personal power and intellect is at a high point. Into your creativity. High energy and enthusiasm. Good time to start a family. Fertility assured. Warm, wonderful family life.

This card may also be used as a "one" in any of the suits.

PENTACLES

Pentacles represent money, possessions, home, prosperity, security, property, abundance and real estate. It also represents skills, artistic ability, manifestation, the end result, and realization of an idea or project. In many instances, it affirms that one can make a living or extra money from a hobby or interest that can turn into a part time or full time career.

Regular Card Suit:	Diamonds
Direction:	East
Elemental Fairy:	Gnomes
Element:	Earth
Astrological Signs:	Taurus, Virgo, Capricorn

Additional qualities of Pentacles are being capable, cautious, competent, conscientious, dependable, determined, efficient, generous, hard working, industrious, loyal, meticulous may not be quite responsible, if a bit rigid, methodical and detail-conscious. The term "down to earth" may suit you quite well. It might be said that you are one of those people who is very well adjusted to life on this planet. A concern for the physical or material world makes you very much the realist. You are an organizer, a builder, and a hard-worker. The earth sign traits provide you with the skills and attitude necessary to succeed readily in the world of business. So pragmatic, you do not often gamble or take unnecessary chances. You understand the reality of a situation and you understand value, both in a material and in a human sense. Your approach to people is much the same as your approach to life. You are reliable and steadfast. You are predictable and you do not like surprises. Dependability, diligence and a pragmatic, no-nonsense approach to life are your greatest strengths. Lack of ideas or imagination, dullness, rigid conservatism, extreme materialism, and blind adherence to rules and regulations are your potential faults.

The Court Cards give more depth and insight to the Numbers two through five, so if you are between these numbers, you have two mundane everyday cards with issues that must be dealt with frequently.

Scans of Pentacles

Scan of Pentacle Court Cards

II
Two of Pentacles
(Minor Arcana - 2)

This card is about the balance of two different aspects. There is turmoil because of indecision and lack of committing yourself to one side. One must also balance functionality with creativity or security with risk. Look at your plans from all aspects so that the forthcoming change will be a pleasant one without surprises.

BUDGET YOUR MONEY CARD

Just looking at this card brings to mind the image of juggling or a balancing act. Notice how the man is desperately trying to balance his money and skills, or tradition and the modern way, etc., and could be in search of grounding and security in all things. He is dressed in red and beige with green shoes. His red hat de*notes* the desire to achieve his goal of balance. He wants and needs to know that he will have the freedom and ability to do what he must to attain his goals. The beige tunic represents his being centered, focused, and grounded as he tries to balance his world. The clear blue sky indicates that things will work out in a very positive manner if he truly tries to balance at this time. Notice the water. There are rolling waves, which can indicate an emotional roller coaster at the time period of the reading. The ships are not sinking, but floating on the water, continuously up and down indicating riding out the emotional turmoil. He is alternating feet on the solid cement ground, which can put him temporarily off balance. He must have both feet on the ground simultaneously for things to work out as he had hoped. The infinity sign is green, showing that the outcome of balancing his life, finances, and important issues will bring prosperity, abundance, and new growth in whatever area is most important to him.

THE MESSAGE OF THIS CARD is that balance in your financial affairs is very important, as well as in your emotional life. Intellectual pursuits should be sought. Try to be a bit more focused and grounded.

TEENAGER MEANING: This is a great time to learn to balance and budget your money. You seem to be spending too much on things you want but do not necessarily need. This spending will cause problems at home as well as some unnecessary drama. If this is not corrected by trying to save more money in the bank or putting some aside for a rainy day, this will set up a template for the rest of your life.

MUNDANE KARMIC LESSON FOR BIRTH PATH NUMBER 2, ELEMENT EARTH.

KARMIC LESSON: The Karmic Lesson of the Two of Pentacles is that you should buy what you need and not what you want at this time. You need to pay down your debt and perhaps only pay cash for the items you need. Buying what you desire will bring you debt, upset, confusion, and many negative feelings regarding your debt. Save for a rainy day and make sure that the purchase you want can wait for another time when you have your finances in better shape.

ASTROLOGICAL CONNECTION: Jupiter in Capricorn

MEDITATION/AFFIRMATION: I will spend money wisely and stick to a budget. I am intelligent enough to deal with any issues that come my way. I have complete control of my life and no one can stand in my way. I need to get a better grip on the issue and look towards the clear blue sky. Research the attention to the details. Be patient and wait for all the elements to fall into place. Pick up a project that has been put aside.

TRADITIONAL MEANING: This card has one central meaning that can manifest in several different ways: At best it reveals clever accounting and tricky cash flow to keep everything afloat, even against the stormy seas of volatile economic times.

III
Three of Pentacles
(Minor Arcana – 3)

This card can stand for entering a new job, getting a promotion, or professional activities. Working within a structure or as a team player will help you obtain your goals. Plans are about to be carried out, as it is a good time for business transactions and new opportunities. Use your skills and abilities well and you may find yourself in a new, better position.

COOPERATION CARD

It is a good time to work with others and combine your knowledge. The architect, priest, and mason seem to be cooperating nicely and the end result will be a job well done due to their teamwork. However, look at the black background. The black garment worn by the priest usually indicates negativity and conflict, however; in this case I feel it stands for hidden knowledge. The architect is wearing red and gold, indicating his desire to be helpful and aid in the building of this Church, and perhaps his flamboyant nature. But notice that he is totally covered with robes, so things may not be as they appear. The mason, or worker (Querent), is dressed in black to conceal himself, gold to receive higher knowledge and logical thought, and blue for serenity and calm. He wants things to go smoothly. However, he is standing on a bench and does not seem too concerned about his safety. If he takes one step without looking, he may fall and get hurt. If he pays attention to details and works closely with others in a concerted effort for positive results, the outcome he seeks will be positive, enduring, and abundant. Most beginners do not see the pentacles in this card. They are in gray at the top of the card, hidden as part of the building. Perhaps balance of the money in this situation is also a concern of all involved.

THE MESSAGE OF THIS CARD is that to be sure to work within a framework, in a team and be part of the whole. This is not a time to try to accomplish anything alone, since you will find it easier to do much more with the help or guidance of others. Knowledge from many sources will get you to your goal sooner than trying to do anything by yourself.

TEENAGER MEANING: This card represents someone who is trying to work together with others, but there is little cooperation from those around him. There can be others trying to tell you what to do even though you may know that your way is better. Give suggestions and recommendations, but do not demand that your way should be followed or it would backfire. Suggest that working together would mean a quick result. If you have a great idea, introduce it to the group as a unit so that you may all work to get that idea going in the right direction and it will finish on a high note.

MUNDANE KARMIC LESSON FOR BIRTH PATH NUMBER 3, ELEMENT EARTH.

ASTROLOGICAL CONNECTION: Mars in Capricorn

MEDITATION/AFFIRMATION: I will follow through with all projects as given to me by my employer to the best of my ability. I will be ready to give my opinion, only if asked, and be a valuable part of my organization. I will learn to set boundaries and not work too many long hours without recognition.

TRADITIONAL MEANING: This is the card of the master; whether that is a master artist, or any other occupation, this card shows great skill and achievement. This may indicate the master himself, his masterpiece work, his studio, or even a visit from clients. Similarly it can represent artistic criticism, or a critique of one's work, an employee evaluation, quality assessment, even a promotion or a raise.

IV
Four of Pentacles
(Minor Arcana - 4)

This figure is literally holding onto his money, thinking about his money and stepping on it so that it does not leave him. This man is very greedy, but that is because he has security issues. Money is the only security known to him and he is unwilling to let anything happen to it. Stability and security are important now. Without money, he feels like a failure.

EBENEZER SCROOGE CARD

You are thinking of abundance, money, prosperity, security, and even what skills may be left in your life. You are holding onto your material possessions and even standing on them for fear they may elude you if you are not "on top of them." You are dressed in black and red with a small amount of blue. The red shows your desire to have a great deal of wealth and not to squander your money. The black is keeping the wealth "under wraps," or there may be some hidden secrets to your wealth. The blue stripe indicates the joy and happiness that will come when you feel emotionally safe. The gray sky in the background makes the future unclear, foggy, or beyond your understanding or reach. You feel safer holding onto your money during this period. All the houses of the city are behind you. Houses or castles represent love, happiness, prosperity, and joy, but only if you are facing them. Turn around and find all the happiness and security you desire. Do not be so self-absorbed. This is a skinflint card, a cheapskate, and a miser like Ebenezer Scrooge. You have the money, so buy what you need or you may die with lots of money in the bank and no satisfaction from getting the things you deserved from it. The cement grounding your feet is interrupted by the pentacles under them. You may not be as grounded or centered as you think. You think you are being thrifty and penny smarts while others see you as stingy.

THE MESSAGE OF THIS CARD is that even though you are guarding and watching your money carefully, it is okay to buy things that you need. You feel you are simply being cautious at this time due to a particular goal you wish to achieve, but others will see you as miserly.

TEENAGER MEANING: Stop worrying about money all of the time. If you constantly worry about it that is what you will attract . . . a lot of money problems. There will be no money for school, for extra-curricular activities or to save for a car or anything else that you truly want. Buy what you need and not the things that you want right now (you can always get them for Christmas or your birthday), and you can concentrate on thinking about money in a positive way because you will have savings to withdraw if you need to.

MUNDANE KARMIC LESSON FOR BIRTH PATH NUMBER 4, ELEMENT EARTH.

KARMIC LESSON: The Karmic Lesson of the Four of Pentacles is that you have everything you need, but you are afraid to spend money even though it is there for you. Buy what you need and not what you want and you will do well. If you are too cheap, you will push people away and live a miserly life filled with fear of not ever having enough. Once you realize you do have what you need, or can buy what you need, more prosperity and abundance in all things comes to you.

ASTROLOGICAL CONNECTION: Sun in Capricorn

MEDITATION/AFFIRMATION: I will use my money for the good of all involved. I will purchase items that I truly need and stop repeating that I do not have enough money or abundance in my life. I have enough to purchase what I need and live comfortably.

TRADITIONAL MEANING: An inheritance, gift or large sum of money leads to arguments, possessive this and selfishness. You tried to keep all the money for yourself. It is foolish to try to control others' actions or the situations around you. Resistance to change is affecting your judgment. A contract to sign or agreement is reached. You will be in a position of authority.

V
Five of Pentacles
(Minor Arcana - 5)

The beggars or homeless are outside of a Church, looking in and feeling extremely sorry for themselves. Expect competition and opposition in your business dealings. A project or event could leave you emotionally drained.

THE LEECH CARD

These poor souls are walking through the snow in bare feet and tattered clothing. They look depressed, lonely, and abandoned. They are trudging through the white snow of spirituality and enlightenment. The black background denotes the hopelessness, conflict, and negativity of their situation, but the falling snow of hope is bringing the vision of better times to come. This seems to be another balance issue card. The stained glass window of the Church suggests that prayer, MEDITATION/AFFIRMATION, or getting back to your God and Goddess and realigning yourself with their energies will bring happiness and peace of mind. Prosperity will come if you follow the positive and energies around you. The woman is covering her green abundant garb and the small blue sash, which represents her emotional happiness, and good fortune that she feels was stolen from her. The beige color is a very grounding color, and she is walking in the right direction. The man can hardly stand on his own two feet; one is covered with a shoe, the other is bare. He tries to cover himself with happiness, but his black negative pants show that he has a hard time keeping his focus. He may also be an energy leech; she must be strong enough to continue to reach the enlightenment that is needed at this time. This card reminds you that you have taken care of others for a long time, and now it is time for you to take care of yourself, leave others behind, and assure them that they can take care of themselves from now on.

THE MESSAGE OF THIS CARD is that you should not feel sorry for yourself. Pick yourself up and pray to whomever you believe in. Help is on the way. There is plenty of hope in your future; do not give up. You are headed towards a future of spirituality and enlightenment so now seems to be the time to take care of yourself, not others.

TEENAGER MEANING: This card recommends that you stop helping all of your friends. If they are continually coming to you for help, advice, opinions or even money, this is a good time to start on a different path. You can say, "I would love to help you out, but I was just going to ask to borrow some money from you!" A more spiritual (religious) life is suggested whether it is through going to church, prayer or even general meditation.

MUNDANE KARMIC LESSON FOR BIRTH PATH NUMBER 5, ELEMENT EARTH.

KARMIC LESSON: The Karmic Lesson of the Five of Pentacles is that you must get rid of all the leaches in your life – you know, the blood suckers who need every spare minute of your time, your opinions, your advice and even your money. This is a card where you must decide which people to leave behind and which to help. It is a spiritual card moving forward to find out what type of spirituality or spiritual path is there for you and you must now cover up your compassion, empathy, sympathy, emotion and sensitivity – you must be strong and empower others to help themselves. You have done all you can do and now others must fill in the gap created by your absence.

ASTROLOGICAL CONNECTION: Mercury in Taurus

MEDITATION/AFFIRMATION: I will start moving forward without guilt when I think of myself first. My compassion is being balanced with my intelligence so that I too can be an important part in this journey of life. I seek the spiritual path and know that I have done what I could to help others. Now I must help myself.

TRADITIONAL MEANING: All aspects of your life are open to disaster – physical emotional, and financial. Worry, stress and insecurity. Possible unemployment, loss of home, health problems, weight gain or loss, and financial room. Support lost. You're at the bottom. Seek support from religion or spiritual institutions from friends and family. You are at the bottom. Seek support from religion or spiritual institutions.

VI
Six of Pentacles
(Minor Arcana - 6)

This card deals with equity or the scales of justice and helping others or someone who desperately needs help. This can indicate accomplishment. You will succeed in your business and all aspects of life in general.

PATIENCE CARD

This card can be used as a balance card. Here we have a very generous and rich gentleman giving out money (prosperity) to the poor. He may also represent your boss, authority figure, job, corporation, or anyone who has control in your finances in some way. He is standing on solid ground with his feet planted firmly on it. Notice the green boots of abundance and the red cloak of desire, assertiveness, and an optimistic, positive attitude. The red is covering the white stripes of honor, trust, and reliability in his undergarment, as well as the happiness, focus, and clarity of the blue in the tunic. He holds a scale in one hand, representing justice and fairness, while giving away money with his other hand. The gray sky adds to the uncertainty of the situation. The one beggar is happy to get the riches; more recognition, time, or honor while the other seems to be forgotten. Even though there are castles in the background (the place where the gentleman obviously lives), neither of the beggars are looking in that direction. One is covering himself in a gold cape; the other in blue. One is grounded and happy at the moment, while the other will be happy and have a sense of purpose IF he is patient, waits his turn, and does not display emotional upset. Do not be greedy or impatient and the money, abundance, and prosperity you desire will come to you. The other person needs the added attention or financial gain at the moment, and by being patient you will certainly get what you deserve in a short while.

THE MESSAGE OF THIS CARD is that others may seem to be getting things that you feel you deserve. Be more patient with your financial gain, time, responsibilities, and promotions, since all will come to you in due course and will be better than you thought possible.

TEENAGER MEANING: This card shows that others get the extra credit or appreciation of a father, coach, teacher or classmate. You feel as if you have done a lot and even helped many friends or co-workers (if you have a job); however, you do not seem to be getting any of the praises or raises. If you are patient, you will get what you deserve. So be happy for the other person who is getting all the kudos and just know that more will be coming your way with just a little patience.

MUNDANE KARMIC LESSON FOR BIRTH PATH NUMBER 6, ELEMENT EARTH.

KARMIC LESSON: The Karmic Lesson of the Six of Pentacles is that you must be patient. Do not think that just because others are getting their just rewards now, that you will not get yours. Others are looking at you to see if you are acting in a professional manner. You will be given more than the person getting the raise, new office, new assignment or promotion if you just hold on a little while longer. Be gracious and wish them well. Your time is coming soon.

ASTROLOGICAL CONNECTION: Moon in Taurus

MEDITATION/AFFIRMATION: I must be patient and remember all things come to those who wait. I will rejoice in others' successes and know that my time will come to be abundant, prosperous in all things, happy and healthy.

TRADITIONAL MEANING: you gain control over your financial life. It will become easier to meet payments. Concerns over yourself worth. Success in business or sales. Increase personal power at work. You develop an understanding of financial success and how to manage it. You must give to others in order to keep money flowing through your life.

VII
Seven of Pentacles
(Minor Arcana - 7)

Plant good seeds and watch them come to harvest. You must be patient during this time. Do not think too much about the past and how it used to be. The figure is not attending to the future. You will reap the rewards of your hard work, but be careful how you use those rewards. Carefully consider how to multiply your money.

RECALLING THE PAST CARD

This is a card of nostalgia. Here we have a farmer daydreaming towards his green foliage underneath a gray sky full of questions, uncertainty, and fogginess. He looks as if he has decided not to tend his garden because his daydreams are very important to him. Remembering the past or when things were better, bigger, calmer, or more prosperous may be taking his focus away from present and future opportunities. He seems centered and grounded with his beige tunic covering his past desires and thoughts of being happy, secure, and serene. He regrets not being in that time now and is not paying too much attention to the lone pentacle below him. The green bush beside him seems abundant and alive, but on further study, we see that it is starting to wither and die. The mountains in the right background indicate that he is very close to his goal, but he has refused to take advantage of it. He is standing on serenity at the moment and not paying particular attention to the ground beneath him, which has a little green in it. Although he is facing the past or in the wrong direction, with very little effort he can focus on his future and what needs to be done to put the past to rest and move on with life.

THE MESSAGE OF THIS CARD is that if you do not set your sights on the future, it will not be as prosperous and abundant as you need it to be. You must forget the past, and plan your future, as there are many goals and opportunities awaiting you. You must deliberately grab them to make them come true.

TEENAGER MEANING: If you have to think of the past, think of happy times. The past is gone and if it was upsetting or unpleasant in any way, you should not recall those circumstances. There is nothing positive about remembering terrible times; it would be so much more positive to learn from your mistakes or past heartaches and move forward to a bright, better future. There are so many wonderful opportunities waiting for you, but not if you are stuck in the past.

MUNDANE KARMIC LESSON FOR BIRTH PATH NUMBER 7, ELEMENT EARTH.

KARMIC LESSON: The Karmic Lesson of the Seven of Pentacles is that living in the past will keep you from moving forward to the future and your goals and dreams. If you constantly think about when you had more money, a better life, a good relationship, better health or whatever the image is in your head, your future is not formed. Stop being the sucker and make sure you are working towards your dreams, goals and aspirations. Stop thinking in a depressed or saddened manner and get grounded and focused and move forward to bring about the life you really want.

ASTROLOGICAL CONNECTION: Saturn in Taurus

MEDITATION/AFFIRMATION: I must remember that I cannot change past events and will now look towards my future with hope and anticipation. I can only change my attitude about what happened and will move forward with a happy heart. I will make a move towards unfulfilled goals and objectives and make them as financially viable as possible.

TRADITIONAL MEANING: Indicates a major turning point in your finances. Take a complete financial inventory. Money comes in from investments. Use this time to assess progress towards career goals and financial plans. If there is little profit, radically change your direction on money issues. Choose low-risk investments and plan carefully.

VIII
Eight of Pentacles
(Minor Arcana - 8)

This is a card that shows that you can always make money and have made money from so many different businesses or skills. A craft/hobby can be used to supplement income. Skill and wisdom and perseverance are necessary to make your work pay off.

SKILLED ARTISAN CARD
(Exception Card)

Here is an artisan who is talented and able to make money from many different skills or interests. He has lined up his pentacles on a mighty oak tree in the hopes of seeing all of his accomplishments before him. He is currently focused on only one job or situation and is not paying particular attention to anything else at the moment, including the castle behind him. That could indicate that he is ignoring his family and home life and putting all of his concentration into his career. His red shoes are not planted firmly on the ground and show aggressiveness or the ability to be a leader and do what he feels is correct. He may even do things that others disapprove of, since he feels he is the best judge of his own future. The gray sky confuses the situation and may cause some fear, doubt, worries, and concerns over financial issues. The black tattered jacket over his blue shirt is adding confusion, negativity, and despair to the situation. The gold earth is grounding for him, but he has to learn how to accept another's point of view or listen to Nature. He is not seeing his happiness and needs time away from his current position or job to get his life in order or on the path that he was destined to live. If he is looking to make extra money during this time, the pentacle under him indicates that there may be a new or part-time position in the near future if he stops to look at and consider it. Taking on this new job would be most beneficial.

THE MESSAGE OF THIS CARD is that there is another skill or job you can do which you are currently not realizing. It may make you happier and give you more money. This may also be a part-time job in addition to your full-time employment. Concentrate on family matters so that your home life does not suffer from your lack of attention and workaholic tendencies.

TEENAGER MEANING: Whatever you do, you do well. You are a hard worker in business and in your educational studies. You want to be the best. This is also a card that shows many interests, perhaps in sports or after school activities. Be sure that you do not spend too much time away from home. Balance in school, a job and home life should be a priority.

MUNDANE KARMIC LESSON FOR BIRTH PATH NUMBER 8, ELEMENT EARTH.

KARMIC LESSON: The Karmic Lesson of the Eight of Pentacles is the skilled artisan card which means that you were blessed with many talents and can do many things at an expert level. You have always worked hard and are working very hard on one job at the moment, but do not see the other job related opportunity in your future. (I call this an exception card because the Pentacle with the new business opportunity or job actually is in the past – or left – of the card which usually means that it had already happened in the past). Be sure that home life is balanced and that you are there just enough to make yourself and your family happy, but also that you can bring prosperity and abundance by doing your job well.

ASTROLOGICAL CONNECTION: Sun in Virgo

MEDITATION/AFFIRMATION: I can do many things to make money; however, I will focus on the skill that I feel is my best and concentrate on moving myself forward in that field. I will balance my life more so that I can share my life with my partner and family so that all of us will be happy.

TRADITIONAL MEANING: Pay attention to details. Errors in sloppiness may be your undoing. Double check work for accuracy. Hard work will be satisfying and successful. There is no get rich quick path for you. Apply yourself. Work smart. Learn a new trade or profession, or upgrade your skills. Be very cautious with money. This is good time to begin a profitable venture.

IX
Nine of Pentacles
(Minor Arcana - 9)

This card indicates great abundance and wanting to keep it. You are making good money and are satisfied that things are going well. Examine your priorities and use your resources carefully to plan for the future. Keep yourself emotionally and financially in control. Inheritance or other material gain is probable, but do not lose your sense of reality.

FINANCIAL RISK CARD

The yellow sky indicates use of your intelligence and common sense when dealing with money. You have enough money, but you are afraid to lose it. You are holding it down in the lush green orchard of grapes bearing fruit (prosperity). The green leaves represent abundance and prosperity. You are surrounded by it. The two green trees on either side of the woman show a need for balance in monetary issues and concerns; the mountains stretching across the whole background of the card indicate that things will go exactly as she has planned. The mountains across a whole card indicate many wonderful opportunities ahead of her, but she must grab one of them. She is also standing on golden, level ground, indicating that she has the ability to be logical and analytical in her financial dealings; she also has much wisdom. Notice the yellow house in the card. Houses or castles always indicate love, happiness, prosperity, and joy. Unfortunately, the mistress is not looking at the house at this moment, but concerned about her financial situation. She should send the bird off on an adventure to see what he can bring back to her. Remember that birds indicate that it would be in your best interests to take a risk. In this card, it seems as if that would be a financial risk. If she is careless, her future will not hold as much prosperity as her past.

THE MESSAGE OF THIS CARD is to turn around and look at the house. You must stop worrying about your finances and think logically about all of your options. Make the decision that seems to be based on the most common sense. Taking a risk that you feel is appropriate will be in your best interest.

TEENAGER MEANING: This is a card which shows that you may be having financial issues at this time. You feel as if there is never enough money, but you are unsure of how to solve the financial issue. You are surrounded by money decisions; however, it will never really change in a positive way unless you take an appropriate risk. Once the risk it taken, everything falls into place.

MUNDANE KARMIC LESSON FOR BIRTH PATH NUMBER 9, ELEMENT EARTH.

KARMIC LESSON: The Karmic Lesson of the Nine of Pentacles is that throughout life you must take a financial risk to keep all of your wealth or to ensure its continuation. There is so much love, happiness, prosperity and joy ahead of you that your life is going in a very good direction. The money being spent needs to be watched so that there will be enough money in your future to take care of you as there was in your past. Being assertive and going after what you want is paramount to your happiness and bliss.

ASTROLOGICAL CONNECTION: Venus in Virgo

MEDITATION/AFFIRMATION: I must balance my finances and keep a close eye on my money. I will buy what is necessary, but will keep money in the bank for a rainy day. There are many possibilities for me in the future, and if I take appropriate risks, everything will fall into place easily and effortlessly.

TRADITIONAL MEANING: Money and possessions are safe if you are cautious and disciplined. Watch out for your financial interests. Rely on your own instincts and research. Cannot trust financial advisors. You come into a large sum of money. Possible inheritance or lottery winnings. Investments pay off.

X
Ten of Pentacles
(Minor Arcana - 10)

This man represents old age and wisdom. There is great abundance, material and financial success around him and in his life. Everything you planned and worked for will bring you rewards.

PROSPERITY IN ALL THINGS CARD

There is half of a bridge, indicating that things are not yet resolved or completed. You may also only know half of the story. The bridge is gray, indicating that there are unclear matters to be resolved or the situation is "foggy" at best. Fears, doubts, anxieties, and worries surround all in this card. We have a couple looking in opposite directions. The two have totally different opinions about many things; this is obviously the issue. The man is looking at the houses in the city and wants to be there. He wants a better or happier home life. The woman is looking away from the city for her contentment and desires. She is venturing out of her familiar surroundings. She feels there will be more money or opportunity beyond home life. The dogs represent fidelity. The little child is greatly attached to the older person and is attracted to older people in general. An embellished cape of green and red covers the older person, representing abundance and prosperity. It may also represent his opinion of money and how to wisely invest it. He is usually a close family member or friend who would be there for the couple to lend them money and help them out of a financial bind. Appropriately, the woman is all in red, as she desires to get out of the city and make a mark on the world. She wants excitement and new adventures. The man is grounded by his beige tunic and feels a sense of security and stability with his point of view. Things go unresolved unless both are willing to face their differences and compromise for the good of all concerned.

THE MESSAGE OF THIS CARD is that things are better than they seem. Know the facts before jumping into a new situation. An older or wiser person may give you the guidance or money you need to reach your goal. Use that wisdom, for it will make your decisions much easier and clearer.

TEENAGER MEANING: Money seems to be around you. Your job is going well. Your parents are paying for just about everything that you need, but you may not be seeing the money that is being given to you in the same light as your parents or family members. Just remember to thank whomever is giving you this money and if you need any more in the future, they will be there again bailing you out or helping you with school costs. Try not to be on opposite sides with those who help you out. Be appreciative of all the help you are receiving.

MUNDANE KARMIC LESSON FOR BIRTH PATH NUMBER 1, ELEMENT EARTH.

KARMIC LESSON: The Karmic Lesson of the Ten of Pentacles is that you have done enough in your life to make a financial difference and may even be able to assist family and close friends with their financial issues. You are now in control of your own finances and should share the wealth with those you love.

ASTROLOGICAL CONNECTION: Mercury in Virgo

MEDITATION/AFFIRMATION: I have enough money for my purposes. I can help out family and friends if I so choose and lighten their burdens. I will notice how I think about money and try to be a valuable member of the family by offering help whenever I can even though I do not see eye-to-eye about their spending habits.

TRADITIONAL MEANING: Inheritance or gift of money. Affluence and importance. Material success-security achieve through conventional wealth-building methods. Invest in the stock market. Buy real estate. Plan for long-term gain, not quick returns. Seek a permanent job that will serve your ultimate career goals.

Page of Pentacles
(Minor Arcana -11)
Also used as a Mundane Karmic Lesson 2/Earth
Court Card

You have a down to earth attitude about most things in life - perhaps a master of common sense and practicality. This card is usually indicates a workable solution or can be seen as the giver of messages and reflection.

NEW BEGINNING IN FINANCIAL SECURITY

Here we have a young man who is intently looking upon a pentacle (material possessions and financial security). He is wondering how to make more, how to keep what he has and what fate money holds for him in the future. He is dressed in green, red, and beige. The green tunic represents his prosperity and abundance. The beige indicates that he is grounded, focused, and stable in his dealings with and views of money. His red hat shows that he has a sincere desire to succeed in his new business venture or adventures with finances. The yellow sky dominates most of the card, indicating that he is thinking about his financial future in a very logical and analytical manner. The trees to the left of the card and the luscious green grass he is standing in reflect his prosperity. The (blue) mountains on the right indicate that he is coming to the realization of his goals and wishes after much preparation. This card usually comes up in a spread when someone is about to inherit money or get a new job or a promotion with greater compensation or possible lottery winnings.

THE MESSAGE OF THIS CARD is to be sure you have all the background information required to get on with this financial venture. You do not want secrets looming in the background. Be smart and use your brain in these dealings. Do not take unwarranted risks. Prosperity and abundance is at hand. You are going in the right direction, so continue to look ahead for all of your opportunities and when it feels appropriate, grab them before they disappear.

TEENAGER MEANING: This is a brand new start in financial security, prosperity and abundance. You may be getting a scholarship, a grant or having others pay your way. You may be getting a new job which will bring more money into your life so that you can save for that car (or whatever it is you are saving for) and help with the costs of college.

KARMIC LESSON: The Karmic Lesson of the Page of Pentacles is that you are going on the new path of financial security, opportunities and gain. You should be assertive enough to know in which direction you must go, take the risk and move forward. Your goals will be accomplished with little effort, but you must make an effort. Your passion and persistence will make you victorious in any financial venture that you go on.

ASTROLOGICAL CONNECTION: Beginning of Winter - Capricorn

MEDITATION/AFFIRMATION: Now that I am going in the right direction with my finances through good luck and motivation, I will use all my energy in accomplishing what I feel is right for me to attract a positive financial future.

TRADITIONAL MEANING: Signifies a male under 30, who is high-spirited, engaging and optimistic. Makes friends easily. Sociable and charming. Intelligent. Educated with good common sense. Loyal, honest, trustworthy. Thinks before he speaks. This person trusts you and looks out for your best interests. He will have an effect on your life.

Knight of Pentacles
(Minor Arcana - 12)
Also used as a Mundane Karmic Lesson 3/Earth
Court Card

This card represents hard work or a hard worker riding a very steady and enduring course. Dependability and honesty are above reproach. Reward for your hard work is due and will be coming to you shortly. Be patient.

LEARNING THE ROPES IN FINANCES

Here is a knight surveying his land (or his hard work), concentrating on his financial issues, and taking the time to reflect on them. His workhorse has stopped in his unsowed pasture and the knight is trying to figure out which seeds to plant. The yellow sky indicates he is very intellectual and logical about his financial future. He could be thinking of how the money can help his dreams come true. He can sow anything he wishes with the right attitude and foresight. His armor shows that he is ready for a fight and willing to protect himself if needed, but his demeanor on the horse indicates that he is not in a fighting mode. He is relaxed, laid back, and contemplating his options. The black horse might indicate negativity or forces that stand in his way, but his harness is red, so the horse is as anxious as he to get on to his next pasture and on the way to a positive conclusion. When someone is riding a horse, I find that it means the rider has overcome the negative quality of that color. In this case, the rider has won over depression, sadness, negativity, limitations, responsibilities, and gloom. Notice the small mountains on the left; there may be some procrastination issues that he still must deal with. Things have not come to fruition yet. In fact, things are still in the planning stages. Procrastination needs to be handled.

THE MESSAGE OF THIS CARD is to think things through carefully before starting any new venture. Your detailed analysis will be the key to success even if others do not believe so. You are now in control of the situation, so plan wisely and do your best to achieve your goals.

TEENAGER MEANING: You are definitely trying to figure out how to make your money grow as well as how to save more of it for your future expenses in school or in a dorm. This is a good card because it says that you look at all alternatives relating to your finances and then make a good decision. If you feel you need to talk to your parents or see their accountant or financial planner, feel free to help yourself make good decisions.

KARMIC LESSON: The Karmic Lesson of the Knight of Pentacles is that you must be very cautious when making financial decisions so you must sow the financial seeds of security before you. Make a plan, think of the future and move forward slowly and deliberately with determination, pride and honesty. You want to protect yourself, but you have already done a wonderful job on that front. Now is all about your procrastination turning into action and your logic making your dreams come true?

ASTROLOGICAL CONNECTION: Gemini

MEDITATION/AFFIRMATION: Wisdom makes me know the difference between procrastination and surmising the situation. When I am confident that I am going in the right direction, nothing will be able to stop me from attaining my financial goals.

TRADITIONAL MEANING: Signifies a male under 40. Works hard. His job is the center of his life. Financially successful, patient, and extremely focused. Traditional values of hard work in public service. Ethical. Conservative. Realistic and down to earth. Follows through and keeps his word. Underestimated by most people.

Queen of Pentacles
(Minor Arcana – 13)
Also used as a Mundane Karmic Lesson 4/Earth
Court Card

This card represents the ultimate mother, reliability, dependability, and trust. Motherhood and family values are very important. Stability, security, and trust will surround any issue. This is a card of generosity and intelligence.

WORRYING ABOUT FINANCES

Here we see the Queen (or Querent) is sitting on a cement throne. This is a stable position, since no one will be able to get her out of the cement throne. Her feet are firmly planted on the ground.

You are seriously contemplating your financial situation, which is already very good or improving. You are a very generous person and may be thinking of helping your family or friends who need money.

You may also be thinking of your financial future. Do I have enough saved? Should I invest in bonds, stocks or insurance? It is a card that makes you re-evaluate your financial circumstances. The clear yellow sky behind indicates mental abilities and aptitudes. You are a very intelligent person thinking about your options in life. The queen has red rose bushes and green leaves crowning her head which show a rich future with prosperity and abundance and her desire to achieve financial security. The serene, blue mountains that stretch across the background, indicate that there are many goals and objectives ahead of you, but you must pick one of them or they will pass you by. This is an especially nice feeling, since you have planned so well for it. Your feet are in lush multi-colored vegetation, specifying that there is a lot of abundance, grounding, stability, and security in this position. You are dressed in red and green, the colors of desire and abundance. The white blouse indicates purity and being too giving, caring, and the like with friends regarding any financial situation. At least, the red dress is covering the white, taking away its negative aspects. The yellow crown points out that you will be an extremely logical person regarding this matter. Turn around and face the future or the financial concerns will not be resolved as well as you would like them to be.

THE MESSAGE OF THIS CARD is to hold onto your money and use it to buy the things you need, not what you want at the moment. Stop procrastinating in deciding what you must do. Turn around to see the future and grab the opportunities that await you.

TEENAGER MEANING: The more you procrastinate about what you have to do with your finances and how much money you really need to move ahead in a positive way, the more you will be missing out on opportunities to get it. Apply for scholarships, grants and other student loans that will be available to you. If you keep the money, you will wind up losing more than you make. Do what you must do to have a stable financial future.

KARMIC LESSON: The Karmic Lesson of the Queen of Pentacles is that while you worry too much about your future finances, you have enough to get what you need at the moment and to share it with those you love. Do not make yourself paralyzed by the fear of not being able to make proper decisions for your wealth as you always have those you trust to ask or confide in if needed. You need to use your intelligence and reason to know what needs to be done and then start going in that direction a little every day until you feel you have reached your goal.

ASTROLOGICAL CONNECTION: Sagittarius

MEDITATION/AFFIRMATION: I will no longer worry about my financial future and stop procrastinating because of fear of the unknown. I will be successful in all that I do once I make the appropriate choices that are given to me.

TRADITIONAL MEANING: Signifies a nurturing, down-to-earth woman who shows concern for others. Intensely loyal to her friends and family. Stable. Dependable. Help others in need. Organize. No one generous, sympathetic to social and political issues.

King of Pentacles
(Minor Arcana – 14)
Also used as a Mundane Karmic Lesson 5/Earth
Court Card

This card stands for financial success, wealth, and power. It could mean preoccupation with material possessions, money, and the power they bring. The future is well formulated and will play out according to plan.

ACHIEVING YOUR FINANCIAL GOALS

Another throne of cement indicating the King (or Querent) is very courageous, strong, abundant, stable, and wise. You hold the pentacle in one hand. With the other hand, you hold a scepter, focusing the powers of the universe down to the earth through you. You are dressed in a very colorful and fruitful robe of growing grapes and greenery. You are secure, knowledgeable, confident, and have a great deal of integrity and pride in your accomplishments. The castle to the right relays that love, happiness, prosperity, and joy have been accomplished and are assured in your future. The blue waterfall to the left indicates sensitivity and emotions that seem balanced at the present time. This is a considerate king who cares about his family, friends, and co-workers. The black throne may have kept some dark, past secrets; however, you are on top of the situation and are handling it very logically and methodically with the clear, yellow sky above you.

THE MESSAGE OF THIS CARD is that there is success and wisdom ahead. Use your analytical mind to obtain your financial and security objectives. Reap the rewards you have earned through being a devoted family member. You know how to gain respect and power from following your heart.

TEENAGER MEANING: You will be very self sufficient in finances in a very short period of time. This is someone who has what they need to fulfill their dreams, goals, aspirations and objectives. Everything is falling nicely into place. Good luck, happiness and prosperity will be a part of your life shortly. Apply for every resource you can and move forward in a very abundant light.

KARMIC LESSON: The Karmic Lesson of the King of Pentacles is that you have enough to make you happy. You have family life, good health and spirituality coming into your life. However, you sit on a blackened throne. How did you get your money? Was it legal? Are there secrets? Were you happy with the decisions you had to make to get the money? Your arrogance will be your downfall, so be humble, help others and know that you are set for money for life. Do not get greedy.

ASTROLOGICAL CONNECTION: Taurus

MEDITATION/AFFIRMATION: I have all the financial security I can need and will help out family members and close friends with their financial difficulties. I do not only seek money as a source of power and authority, but also for the financial security for my family and all of those that I love.

HOW TO BE A TAROT DETECTIVE

TRADITIONAL MEANING: Indicates a man over 40. Consummate deal-maker and risk-taker. Smooth talker. Sophisticated and successful. Gives generously. Devoted to civic, religious or philanthropic activities. Affectionate. Hard-working. Chases the trappings of success including expensive cars, nice home, toys, nice clothing.

Ace of Pentacles
(Minor Arcana – Gift from God and Goddess – 1/Earth)

This card means new beginnings, coming into money, or getting a new home or new job. A new project or opportunity may emerge. An idea will bring material benefit and compensation.

BLESSINGS FROM GOD AND GODDESS
IN FINANCIAL SECURITY, PROSPERITY AND ABUNDANCE

This is a gift from God and Goddess in money, prosperity, and abundance. The gray sky indicates that you may be unaware of your good fortune at first or how it will be accomplished. The grass and bushes are green with abundance. All you have to do is take the golden road that indicates using your intellect towards financial matters. You must take a small risk and then get on with your life. There are many good opportunities before you on this road, but if you never set out on it, you will never know what is available. The blue mountains to the right represent happiness, joy, serenity, and calmness that are coming into focus. They also represent the vast opportunities ahead of you in reaching all of your dreams, hopes, wishes, and goals. There is much clarity of thought and purpose, especially in your material possessions. Your goals will be fulfilled. Money concerns will be resolved. Accept this gift from God and Goddess in financial gain, material possession, or compensation from a job. Generally, I say that prosperity and abundance will be assured because that takes in finances as well as material possessions.

THE MESSAGE OF THIS CARD is that here we have a gift from God and Goddess in the form of money or material possessions. All you have to do is walk down that golden road towards the mountains ahead of you and you will be led to new beginnings and adventures. Most of your hopes, dreams, and wishes will come true with little effort once you take the first step towards obtaining them.

TEENAGER MEANING: You are being blessed by God and Goddess (or whomever you believe in) with finances, financial loans, grants, scholarships and you may even find that your family is helping you a great deal more than you thought. Everything financial is improving and going in the right direction. This is a very lucky period of time with monetary needs. Do not squander your good fortune.

KARMIC LESSON: The Karmic Lesson of the Ace of Pentacles is that you will be given what you need to survive, live comfortably and pay your bills. This is a lucky period in your life when it is recommended that you play the lottery. (If you do not win during this time period, you really do not ever have to play in the future because this is the luckiest you will ever be). This can be a change of life experience through an inheritance that you never expected. It could also be a large sum of money given to you in some way that can change your life. Be thankful for this gift and do well with the money.

ASTROLOGICAL CONNECTION: Taurus

MEDITATION/AFFIRMATION: Everything I need to survive in this third dimensional world will be given to me by a higher power. I need to release want, fear and worry about my finances, financial security and prosperity and abundance in all things. I have courage to make my ideas become a reality and I will have everything I need to survive and be happy. The road ahead of me is going in the right direction where I can make my plans and dreams come true.

TRADITIONAL MEANING: Good time for diet and exercise, physical self-improvement in beauty. Money and material possessions come easily. Success. Projects will grow and prosper. Trust in your own instincts and ideas. Others will help. Rely on your friends and family for support.

SWORDS

Conflicts, lessons, issues, arguments, obstacles, challenges, arguments, scattered energies, defending one's honor or home, responsibilities, negativity, limitations, upsets, fears, doubts, worries, and the mental realm.

Regular Card Suit:	Spades
Direction:	North
Elemental Fairy:	Sylphs
Element:	Air
Astrological Signs:	Gemini, Libra, Aquarius

Further information about Swords

Capable, cautious, competent, conscientious, dependable, determined, efficient, factual, firm, generous, hard-working, industrious, loyal, meticulous, nurturing, organized, productive, realistic, reliable, resourceful, responsible, sensible, skillful, sturdy, supporting, thorough, and trusting. They can also be hard-headed, humorless, inflexible, materialistic, obsessive, obstinate, over cautious, organized, pessimistic and stubborn.

Air Sign Qualities - Gemini, Libra and Aquarius

A Preponderance of the AIR element.

The preponderance (means a great many of them) of Air signs suggest a strong emphasis on thought, ideas and intellectual pursuits of one sort or another. There is a detachment and a sense of objectivity associated with such a heavy influence in the element of Air. Air signs communicate and express ideas with mental agility. Your Air signs may not, however, always get the job done, and you need to be sure ideas are grounded in reality and put to practical use. You are probably more concerned with theory than with application. Often, individuals having a heavy amount of Air signs become the impractical dreamers, constantly thinking, but not always following through as well as others. Rational and logical, you analyze situations fully, thinking them through and planning carefully before you act. While you may ponder and vacillate, you rarely make foolish mistakes. Detached and not overly emotional, you are almost always objective and fair-minded. You are people-oriented, but more inclined toward the group than the individual. Your interests are varied, and you're apt to be a life-long student.

The Court Cards give more depth and insight to the Numbers two through five, so if you are between these numbers, you have two mundane every day cards with issues that must be dealt with frequently.

Scan of Swords

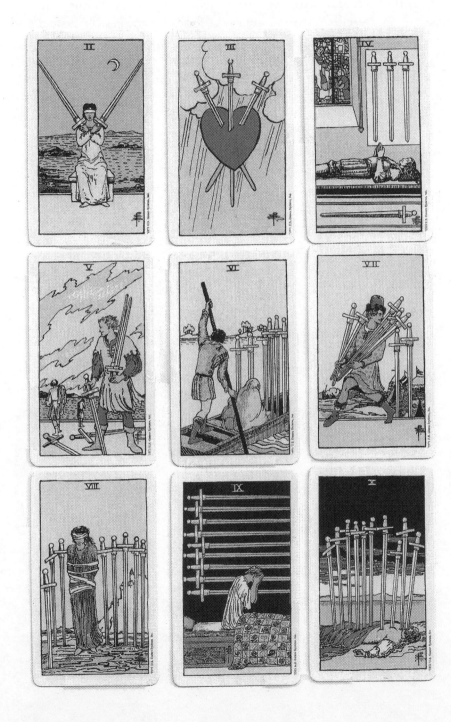

Scan of Sword Court Cards

II
Two of Swords
(Minor Arcana - 2)

This is a duality card. It may stand for a dilemma or difficulty in making a decision. Take the blindfold off to enjoy the beautiful scenery and see reality. A decision has to be made, but only by logical thinking. Do not let emotions guide you on a false path.

DEAL WITH REALITY CARD

The Two of Swords is a fascinating card. The blue sky is cloudless, but sees the crescent moon looming in the background. Whenever a moon appears in a card, it de*notes* illusion or delusion and that you see what you want to see and hear what you want to hear! The woman is seated on a cement bench indicating her feeling of strength and stability and her feet seem to be planted firmly on the cement ground. However, the ground is gray; there is vagueness and uncertainty in her life which she must handle. Her white dress indicates that she has probably been taken advantage of in many situations. She holds two swords, which she assumes will protect her, but with the self-imposed blindfold, she cannot be sure of her defense and cannot figure out how to properly protect herself. The blue water behind her has many ripples, indicating problems, sensitivity, and emotional situations that affect her. The small islands or rocks are stumbling blocks before attaining her goal (the hills beyond, shown at the right of the card). When mountains or islands are present, it indicates that there are new beginnings ahead of her if she will just turn around and look at the wonderful, blue sky. Perhaps letting her know that the sky will bring many exciting opportunities will help give her some of the strength she needs to take control over her life. She must take off the blindfold, hold the swords appropriately to defend herself, and get on with her life. She has to take more positive action.

THE MESSAGE OF THIS CARD is to take off your blindfold, handle the situation, and get on with your life. Things are not as they seem, so deal only in reality. A new beginning is forming for you, but you must be strong enough to let go of fantasy and live in reality.

TEENAGER MEANING: This card means that you should stop trying to live in a fantasy land and protect yourself better than you currently are. With the blindfold on, you see what you want to see, and hear what you want to hear and it may not be the truth. Deal with your feelings in a realistic way, express yourself (or communicate your inner feelings to those you trust) and move on from this depressed and negative world.

MUNDANE KARMIC LESSON FOR BIRTH PATH NUMBER 2, ELEMENT AIR.

KARMIC LESSON: The Karmic Lesson of the Two of Swords is that you are not protecting yourself as well as you may think you are. You are protecting your heart from being hurt again, but you really do not want to see any other issues going on. You are comfortable not knowing the truth. Living in fantasy land may be nice upon occasion, especially if you are a writer or artist, but in the real world, it is always wise to know who you can and cannot trust, who has your back and who is in your corner. Open up to the possibilities of the nurturing moon and know that you will be protected if you desire it.

ASTROLOGICAL CONNECTION: Moon in Libra

MEDITATION/AFFIRMATION: I trust the universe to help me make the proper decisions for my best interest. I will be strong, brave and have faith to make strides forward to get to my goals and objectives with confidence and poise. Being afraid of life will hinder me, so I am ready to see what the world has to offer. I will keep myself balanced and centered which will bring me peace of mind, body and spirit.

TRADITIONAL MEANING: No major changes and fewer events. Your heart is closed off to avoid the possibility of pain. Emotional barriers protect you from love. You're basically in denial. Inability to accept the reality of your problems keeps the situations from changing. Take action and compromise to resolve issues.

III
Three of Swords
(Minor Arcana - 3)

This card symbolizes a broken heart. Prioritize and take care of your top three conflicts. It can represent difficulties in relationships, (personal or business), disappointment, trouble, and opposition. Use logic to resolve issues.

BETRAYAL CARD

This card looks more menacing than it is. There are clouds in the gray sky that indicates anxieties, worries, and growing concerns. Things seem unclear, foggy, or hidden at the current time. It is raining, indicating tears, crying, depression, or emotional upset. The heart, the center of our emotional life, has three swords piercing through it. This can indicate problems and conflicts that will make you feel as if you were "stabbed in the heart." It may also indicate that there are, were, or will be three circumstances or separate events in which you feel betrayed. In my experience, it also can mean a child hurting a parent in a way that only they can. You will come to terms with the conflict or struggle, which gives you this heavy heart or pain. This in no way represents a physical heart attack, as some have asked. The lesson of this card is that if someone lies about you, you must not ignore the incident but rather deal with it so it will end. In standing up for yourself, the other two swords will never hurt you. If you ignore the hurt, the other two will surely follow.

THE MESSAGE OF THIS CARD is that to handle your problems or conflicts one at a time. Things will work out if you give yourself time to heal. You must deal very strongly with the particular child, family member, friend, co-worker, or acquaintance that is lying about you, gossiping, or spreading rumors so that they are assured that this continued behavior will not be tolerated. The other two injuries or insults will then not materialize.

TEENAGER MEANING: This is a betrayal card from people you trust. It could be just gossip behind your back or something else that may hurt you. Someone may say a careless word or spread a rumor about you; if you do not stand up for yourself and deal with it (for instance, you can say: *I know you are spreading a rumor about me and I would like it to stop*), then the other two times do not happen. If you do not stand up for yourself, you are put into a situation where you will be hurt or betrayed three times within whichever time period you asked about.

MUNDANE KARMIC LESSON FOR BIRTH PATH NUMBER 3, ELEMENT AIR.

KARMIC LESSON: The Karmic Lesson of the Three of Swords is that you will be betrayed at least three times. If you ignore the betrayals, you will get hurt at least three times. If you stand up for yourself and take a stand, the other two times never happen and the one that happened would be of minimal effect to me. I will take stock in myself and my abilities to stand up for my beliefs and for the people that I love. I will be good at setting boundaries and keeping all out of my life that are not in my best interest.

ASTROLOGICAL CONNECTION: Saturn in Libra

MEDITATION/AFFIRMATION: I will let old wounds heal and will be looking at life from a different point of view. Though life is full of heartache and negative people, I will overcome the disappointment, betrayal and pain by looking forward with a happy heart. Whatever I give out into the world is bound to come back to me three-fold. I am open to receiving all of the love and happiness I have spread around the world.

TRADITIONAL MEANING: Sorrow and loss. Arguments with a lover. Match its mad-bridge separation. Incompatible lovers. Cruelty, abuse and separation cause emotional upheaval. Someone will betray you. Mistakes are made. Accept blame for your part.

IV
Four of Swords
(Minor Arcana - 4)

This card represents that is it time to rest and think logically about your concerns. Analyze the situation. Perhaps a break is needed before making a decision. Take some time off before reviewing your position or situation.

TAKE YOUR TIME TO MAKE A DECISION CARD

Each sword stands for a particular problem or issue. Here, we have a man lying on a coffin in a Church. Both are yellow, indicating that there is a lot of thinking going on. Intelligence must be used to handle this issue. A sword, his most important decision/concern, is displayed on the coffin's side. He has to decide his priority issue in a logical and analytical manner so the other issues will take care of themselves or start being resolved on their own. There are three other concerns/issues above him, all in gray. The stained glass window with the words PAX ("peace" in Latin) to the top left indicate peace of mind will come as soon as he makes a decision. There is always hope, as only he has true control over his destiny. The other three swords are shrouded in conflict, negativity, and mistrust or are not seen clearly at this time. This card also represents not jumping to any conclusions. You must think about an issue before dealing with it. He looks as if he is praying for assistance or guidance from above. The man will find peace after his meditation and will know in which direction he should proceed.

THE MESSAGE OF THIS CARD is that this is not the time to make your decision. You must think about your alternatives and choose the most logical choice to handle the situation. Handle the priority issue and the other concerns will take care of themselves.

TEENAGER MEANING: With all the decisions you have to make, pick the most important one and once you have made a final decision, you should not change it or it will be wrong. Also, swords are the easiest to handle in the cards. Once you slow down, think about your issues, make an informed decision and try to get more centered in your life, your life will start moving in a much more positive direction because you made the decision and will do something about it.

MUNDANE KARMIC LESSON FOR BIRTH PATH NUMBER 4, ELEMENT AIR.

KARMIC LESSON: The Karmic Lesson of the Four of Swords is that even though I have many decisions to make, I need to rest, contemplate and pray for an answer. I must not make a rash decision, but should take my time in making the right decision for me. If I deal with the priority issue, the other issues over my head will disappear. Once I make a decision, I will not change it or it will be wrong. I will weigh the pros and cons carefully and come up with a logical and reasonable decision for all involved.

ASTROLOGICAL CONNECTION: Jupiter in Libra

MEDITATION/AFFIRMATION: I will not rush my decision. It will be in a time that is right for the universe and me. I will think my plans or decisions through carefully and meditate (or pray) on them and when I feel I have made a decision, I will follow through with confidence and certainty. All the issues will disappear once I take care of my priority issue.

TRADITIONAL MEANING: a personal battle ends. Choose a break in the fighting. Anxious feelings diminish. You let your guard down. Peace and quiet follow stress. You are alone with your thoughts. Stockpile resources and mentally prepare for the next battle. This is just one battle in a long war.

V
Five of Swords
(Minor Arcana - 5)

A battle may be brewing. This card can represent an inner conflict, a battle, or possible arbitration. Things will not come easily. Proceed with caution.

GRACIOUS WINNER CARD

We first notice the streaking clouds in the blue sky, which depict stress, trouble, problems, conflicts, disagreements, arguments, disharmony, friction, and strife. The water in the background is not calm, denoting emotional issues, outbursts, and sensitivity. All the figures are standing on cement that is very fortifying, strong, grounding, and stable. However, the two figures in the background look as if they have been defeated and are leaving the scene. The man in the foreground dressed in green and red with gold boots has a smirk on his face. Obviously, he has won the battle. He has knocked two swords out of his enemies' hands and now holds three. He is confident and assured of his position as the victor. His green tunic represents his abundance and prosperity in the situation. The red hair and shirt beneath the tunic represent his desire to win, get on with his life, and be able to handle all of his problems as easily as he had this one. He may also have a temper. Notice that two of the swords are up and one is down on the ground. Maybe the one touching the ground may symbolize an issue not totally resolved or you might view the one sword as the only one that is grounded. This card means you need to be a gracious winner. If the man is not a gracious winner, he may wind up being the loser instead. He must stop concentrating on the past and get on with his future. Although the gold grounds him on the cement, he is feeling superior at the moment since he is the victor.

THE MESSAGE OF THIS CARD is that even though you win the situation or issue, be a gracious winner or all the troubles and challenges that made you fight others in the first place will come back to haunt you. It would be surprising if you were to win against these opponents again. Do not be too over-confident.

TEENAGER MEANING: This is an argument or disagreement card in which you win most of the issues. It asks you to be a gracious winner or you will eventually lose everything you have gained. You win the swords that are up in the air, the swords on the ground were easily defeated and the one stabbing into the ground is the one that still needs to be determined. Stay strong, but not arrogant and everything will come your way.

MUNDANE KARMIC LESSON FOR BIRTH PATH NUMBER 5, ELEMENT AIR.

KARMIC LESSON: The Karmic Lesson of the Five of Swords is that I know I can win at anything I try, but will be kind and considerate of those who have lost some of the argument or disagreements. I will be a gracious winner so that I will keep the victories I have won, or lose them by being hostile and self-righteous.

ASTROLOGICAL CONNECTION: Venus in Aquarius

MEDITATION/AFFIRMATION: Even though there may be obstacles ahead of me, I am patient and know in my heart that right will win. I will be a gracious winner so that no one is a loser in any arguments or disagreements I may have with family or friends. I will move forward stronger and more positive because I did the right thing.

TRADITIONAL MEANING: Put self-interest in self-preservation first. You can't be of use to anyone else if you do not look out for yourself. Conflict and hostility defeat and destroy important projects. The outcome may seem and feel it unfair. This of course time will provide insight and growth. Possible illegal or immoral conduct. Public shame and dishonor.

VI
Six of Swords
(Minor Arcana - 6)
(Exception Card)

This card indicates guiding someone going through rough times to a Promised Land, better times, or serenity. This means proceeding towards the unknown, but it is your destiny. A new opportunity awaits you, but you have to grab it. A journey over water is possible.

MOVING TOWARDS A NEW DIRECTION CARD

This card represents starting anew, getting on with your life, and leaving your problems and concerns behind. You will notice immediately that the water on the lower right (usually indicating the future) is wavy, rough, and disturbing. The water represents troubles and obstacles this person had to endure. However, if you look at the calm water on the other side of the boat, it extends well into the future. A woman is in a boat, a cape protecting her whole body from further harm. There is a child next to the seated figure. Many times this represents a single parent with responsibility for their children. The man steering the boat is helping the person get to a new life (new island) so they can start fresh, leaving all the problems behind. This can represent any helpful family member or friend who wishes to help you on your journey. Notice the pole is black, so there continues to be some negativity that needs to be handled, but it is now being shared with others who may be stronger than the Querent at this time. This does not mean that you are without problems in your new life on the distant shore. The sky is still gray in the background. You are taking your problems (swords) with you, but you must handle them one at a time for if you pulled the swords out of the boat simultaneously, the boat would instantly sink. They are intermingled and depend on each other to stand. Handle your most important concern first and the others will be easy to deal with.

THE MESSAGE OF THIS CARD is that you are going to a new beginning, although bringing some concerns from your previous life. Do not try to handle everything at once. Pick your most important issue or concern and deal with it. Your new beginning will be full of hope, clarity, direction, and a sense of purpose.

TEENAGER MEANING: This card represents someone who has had enough and wants to start a new life or a new beginning. A friend or family member helps you move on to a new life; however, you are still taking your issues with you. Now you can handle them one at a time. The emotional stress you have been through is turning into quiet solitude and inner peace. You are going in a much better direction once you realize that you may not be able to handle everything on your own. Accept the help that is offered to you.

MUNDANE KARMIC LESSON FOR BIRTH PATH NUMBER 6, ELEMENT AIR.

KARMIC LESSON: The Karmic Lesson of the Six of Swords is that you need to move forward to a new life and new beginnings. Others will want to help you, but will not be as much help as you would have liked. They give it their best effort. It is up to you to figure out in which direction you want to go and which opportunities or challenges you will bring with you or leave behind. You will now be able to take care of your issues one at a time before moving to your new life, but you are on the path towards starting over on a very positive path.

ASTROLOGICAL CONNECTION: Mercury in Aquarius

MEDITATION/AFFIRMATION: I am covering myself up from negativity, problems, concerns and issues as I move to a new part of my life, a new venture, journey, new career or new adventure. My family and friends are welcome to help me get to my destination; however, how I get there is up to me and me alone. I will be happy to walk into a more happy future with nothing but positive opportunities, good health for my family and me and abundance in all things.

TRADITIONAL MEANING: Problems. In favorite favorable judgment a lawsuit. Unwanted marriage proposals. Overwhelmed by crisis. You feel unable to cope with day-to-day problems. Dealing with the aftermath of problems drains your energy. The future will be better than the present. Things will eventually work out. Travel or journey, possibly by water.

VII
Seven of Swords
(Minor Arcana - 7)

This card shows a balancing act. You must put things in order. Someone may steal something from you. This is a game of give and take. You may get only partial success although at first you think you have won it all.

TAKING CARE OF EVERYONE ELSE'S BUSINESS CARD

We have learned throughout this book that yellow represents the intellect, an open mind, and power of the mind. It is the one clue that directs us to handle this situation cleverly and logically. This is not a time for emotional reactions or sentimentality. There are tents to the right that could indicate a town, a group of people, an ethnic group, or a culmination of friends and family. The main character seems as if he is sneaking away with problems and obstacles. Although the man seems confused, as represented by his head going towards the future while his legs are in the past, he really is a decent man who wants to be helpful and responsible. He seems very sure of himself and is also very happy that he has handled the situation well. He is unaware that he has left two swords (problems) behind. He feels grounded by his beige tunic and has the desire for calmness, serenity, and harmony, shown by his blue tights. There is also a desire to put these troubles behind him, as represented by his red boots and hat. The hat may also indicate that his desire has been on his mind for some time. He does not want others to know that he is handling the situation or helping out, but is quite pleased with himself for being altruistic.

THE MESSAGE OF THIS CARD is that no matter how hard you try or how much you are able to handle, there are some unforeseen obstacles or concerns left behind. Be aware that other situations will eventually make themselves apparent to you. Some issue you thought was over will come back to haunt you. You may be trying to handle too much at one time, and in doing so, overlook some aspect of the overall picture. Be careful not to do this.

TEENAGER MEANING: You seem to think you can continue to handle everyone else's issues and problems. However, if you look at the card, you are holding the swords by the wrong end and you are the only one who will get hurt. This person continuously looks back to the future at the two swords in the ground. These are issues you would like to deal with for yourself, but you have too much to do by helping others that you will never get to finish your goals and dreams. Let some of the responsibilities go and help yourself for a change.

MUNDANE KARMIC LESSON FOR BIRTH PATH NUMBER 7, ELEMENT AIR.

KARMIC LESSON: The Karmic Lesson of the Seven of Swords is that is about time that you take care of your own projects, concerns and responsibilities instead of helping everyone else with theirs. You need to focus on your future and complete the chores that you promised to others, but you need to divorce yourself from ever offering your help again. If you do, you will never reach the future that you were meant to and will be annoyed with those who kept you from being able to accomplish your dreams.

ASTROLOGICAL CONNECTION: Moon in Aquarius

MEDITATION/AFFIRMATION: I am the most important person in my life and I will do whatever I need to do for my best interest. I will help only those who truly need my help and give my projects, chores or opportunities more attention than I ever have. My wishes are also important and should come true.

TRADITIONAL MEANING: Many choices confront you – only one is correct. All others will bring disaster. Running away from decisions, problems and commitments makes things worse. The first instinct will be to try to do everything on your own – back office for sign that this is working. Selfish decisions bring dishonor and shame.

VIII
Eight of Swords
(Minor Arcana - 8)

This card may indicate self-binding limitation or limiting one's own progress. Look inwardly to see how you are causing your own turmoil and obstacles. You are receiving criticism you are not willing or able to handle. You have heavy or burdening thoughts. You must see the big picture, not just the small details.

FEELINGS OF IMPRISONMENT CARD

Uncertainty, cloudiness, and confusion surround the woman in the card. There are many swords surrounding her. Remember when a figure puts herself in between a suit, it means that she may be causing her own problems within that suit and we know that swords are conflicts, problems, responsibilities, obligations and decisions that need to be made. She is dressed in red, indicating she has the desire to be out of this situation and may have been assertive at one time; however, she does not know how to handle her present concerns. She put herself right in the middle of the problems and is standing on wet, uneven ground, representing sensitivity, compassion, and emotions. She may fall in any direction she attempts to take a step without looking at the path ahead. Her eyes and heart are bound. She does not want to see the truth and is very afraid of letting herself love again or be in a position where she can be easily hurt. The castle is behind her to the right of the card, which means the love, happiness, prosperity, and joy, inner peace, guidance, strength, wisdom, self-confidence and everything else you need to make you happy can be reached in the future, but she has a few obstacles ahead of her before reaching her goal. She can do it with determination and turning to face reality, but most importantly by looking ahead at the castle. Taking care of family and home life may resolve many of her issues with dependency and rejection.

THE MESSAGE OF THIS CARD is to take the blindfold off of your eyes and bindings off of your heart and handle your fears, doubts and worries. You must handle the most important issue so all the others will be easily handled. Look at the castle behind you to find loves happiness, prosperity, and joy in your future. It is there for the taking. If you do not see it, you do not get all of the goodness waiting for you.

TEENAGER MEANING: You feel as if you are in jail. The eight of swords is a card where it makes the person feel out of control and helpless. The Querent feels as if it is easier and safer to do nothing else so that things cannot get worse. This is not a positive attitude to adopt. You must take the blindfold and bindings across your heart off and deal with the most important issue decisively and quickly. You will then be pushed into a positive energy field where you will find love, happiness, prosperity and joy, inner peace, guidance, strength, wisdom and knowledge and everything to make you happy.

MUNDANE KARMIC LESSON FOR BIRTH PATH NUMBER 8, ELEMENT AIR.

KARMIC LESSON: The Karmic Lesson of the Eight of Swords is like an imprisonment card. You feel stifled in your life and cannot do exactly what it is you want to because of your own self-doubt and fears. Be careful not to be the martyr with this card since you are stuck between many swords with bindings and a blindfold so at this point you are not empowered to help yourself or anyone else. Stop being your own worst enemy; get out of the water and move to more solid ground where you can make a positive difference.

ASTROLOGICAL CONNECTION: Jupiter in Gemini

MEDITATION/AFFIRMATION: I will break free of my environment and stand tall and strong. I will see the truth and no longer see what I want to see and hear what I want to hear. There is so much love, happiness, prosperity, and joy, inner peace, guidance, strength, wisdom, self-confidence and everything else you need to make you happy in my future if I open myself to it. I am ready to be more confident and positive by looking to the future as a gift from Spirit and know that Spirit does not make a mistake.

TRADITIONAL MEANING: You are overwhelmed by problems and personal issues. Domination. Restriction. Forced into living by others' rules. You feel trapped and think there is no way out. Your own fear, indecision or priorities may be causing this. Solutions do exist. Answers require clear thinking and compromise.

IX
Nine of Swords
(Minor Arcana - 9)

This card denotes nightmares and needless worry. The situation is better than you think. Do not give it a life of its own by putting negative thoughts in the universe. You may be confused because emotions got in the way. You must clear your mind and make the right decisions so your future can change for the better.

INSOMNIA CARD

This is the insomnia card. This person is worrying too much about the obstacles, challenges, and troubles hanging over her head. The swords are all intermingled, so each builds on the others. They can be handled by taking the priority issue and dealing with it as directly as possible. Only then will the others fall apart. The black background indicates feelings of helplessness, despair, negativity, and conflict surrounding the figure. She sits up in bed not able to sleep. She covers her face in despair and wonders how she will handle all of these problems. Many times she is worrying for family and friends as well. Dressed in white, she is very giving, caring, honest, pure, and a bit too trusting. We know that she will always be a doormat or be taken advantage of if she does not change her attitude about herself. In the long run, she will be able to deal with her concerns in a positive manner. When she discovers that only one major decision has to be made, she will find her life to be much more manageable and in control. She is covered with a blanket depicting that the power of the universe is at her disposal. The desire for her control of the situation is shown by the red roses in the blanket, the need for her use of intelligence is shown by the yellow, and the blue indicates that through her spirituality or use of universal knowledge, she will overcome her obstacles.

THE MESSAGE OF THIS CARD is to not waste time worrying about your problems. Handle the main concern and all the other problems will take care of themselves one at a time and give you the control you had lost. Rest, relax, and sleep. You should concentrate on your own issues and let others handle their life. It is not your responsibility any longer. Help whom you truly have to help, but at some point you need to empower yourself to have the life you truly want.

TEENAGER MEANING: Stop worrying about everyone and everything else in your life because your mind keeps racing and it will affect your sleep. This is the insomnia card; not because you are ill, but because you think about all the troubles, problems, responsibilities and worries that are around you and most of these troubles are not even yours. Deal with the most important issue first and the rest will fall into place. If it is another person, deal with them in a positive way by talking with them or explaining that you have too much on your plate and cannot always be there if you are needed. Stop being a sucker and move on with your life on your terms.

MUNDANE KARMIC LESSON FOR BIRTH PATH NUMBER 9, ELEMENT AIR.

KARMIC LESSON: The Karmic Lesson of the Nine of Swords is that you waste too much time worrying and being concerned about others. It will take its toll on you through keeping your mind busy so that you can't rest or relax. It is an insomnia card which is not caused by an illness, but rather by your worries of others and if they are okay. At some point, you must let everyone take care of themselves and you have to know that you can only help a few people in this lifetime. Others have to take care of themselves because you cannot do it all.

ASTROLOGICAL CONNECTION: Mars in Gemini

MEDITATION/AFFIRMATION: I will not worry about everyone else's problems and concerns. I will concentrate on my life and get things in order. I will sleep through the night now in a peaceful and restful sleep. If anyone's problems haunt my dreams, I will get up and get a glass of water (and use the bathroom, if necessary) and think of my future, my life and that of my family's before all others. My life will not be the center of my attention. I will get clarity and courage to release anything or anyone who does not serve my highest good for my future.

TRADITIONAL MEANING: Grief. Emotional pain and depression. Guilt and deep regret over something you've done. Sleepless nights rehashing past actions. You've cause someone misery in great pain. Anguish and worry. Fear and self-doubt cloud your thinking. Only time will heal the pain.

X
Ten of Swords
(Minor Arcana - 10)

You can take a sigh of relief, the worst is over. A new dawn is rising. If you see problems arising, you can positively change the outcome. You have gambled and lost, perhaps making a very large mistake. Analyze what you have done wrong and do it better next time.

THE "WORST IS OVER" CARD

When my daughter was approximately three and a half years old, she looked at this particular card and said, "Mommy, that looks like a Swiss cheese card." She was so right. This card indicates that you feel as if you were stabbed in the back on numerous occasions, leaving lots of holes in your trust and belief in others. You cannot get on with your life; you feel defeated and that everyone and everything is against you. But be assured that now nothing else can hurt you. The yellow (intellectual) dawn is pushing away the negativity of the black sky and all new possibilities exist in the new dawn. The worst is over so you must be more optimistic for a bright future. The man is wearing a very grounding color, beige, which is covering a white shirt which may have made him too giving, caring, loving, etc., (likely leading to his downfall) and his red cape indicates that his desire for assertion and control may still be in the works. He is grounded by lying on the even earth and his hand is in an old traditional blessing. This is saying that everything negative in your life is now over and you will triumph as you start again. The water is calm and clear showing emotions are now on an even keel. The mountains across the whole card in the distance show that the opportunities for you are endless, but you have to grab one of them to make them come true.

THE MESSAGE OF THIS CARD is that the worst is over; nothing else that is negative can happen to you. The yellow, intellectual dawn is pushing the black night away, taking with it all the negativity and conflicts that has surrounded you. There are better days coming, so just be patient.

TEENAGER MEANING: This card says that the worst is over card and new beginnings and opportunities are at hand. You must use your intelligence "like the dawn" to push away the negativity, fears, doubts, anxieties and worries away from you so that you can start over again in a much more positive way. So many wonderful opportunities are coming your way, but if you do not choose any of them, they will never be offered again.

MUNDANE KARMIC LESSON FOR BIRTH PATH NUMBER 1, ELEMENT AIR.

KARMIC LESSON: The Karmic Lesson of the Ten of Swords is that the worst is over and although it seems as if things are upset, blown apart and going in directions you may not have wished, when the dust cloud clears, you will find that it is a bright new day with many opportunities for you to move forward and start over. A new life is on the horizon. All you have to do is grab it.

ASTROLOGICAL CONNECTION: Sun in Gemini

MEDITATION/AFFIRMATION: The worst is over and I can look forward to a new beginning with great joy. The negative thoughts, confusion and conflicts will no longer hinder my journey to the future. I will get more centered and focused, more stable and secure so that I may take the opportunities presented to me. I will use my intellect like the dawn and push anything negative in my life out of my mind and out of my sight forever.

TRADITIONAL MEANING: Bottoming out. Trouble is on the way. Thinking like a victim or martyr will keep your life in a downward spiral. Plans and projects are in jeopardy. Your home life may be disrupted. Any area of your life is open to conflict. No matter how powerful and safe you are – trouble will find you.

Page of Swords
(Minor Arcana - 11)
Also used as a Mundane Karmic Lesson 2/Air
Court Card

The Page represents new adventures or beginnings. Swords stand for conflicts, arguments, and mental agility.

NEW BEGINNING IN CONFLICTS, PROBLEMS, AND RESPONSIBILITIES

Here we have a page standing on a grassy mound in a position ready to defend himself. He is looking towards the left of the card or the past, so we know he is not going in the proper direction with this particular issue. The page should also be careful on the uneven ground even though it is green, representing prosperity and abundance. There are clouds in the sky behind him, which indicate things are brewing behind him. Notice the mountains to the right of the card, or in the future, which denote that his goals, dreams and wishes will come true shortly if they have not already recently come true. There are many black birds in the sky; denoting negativity and secrets are all around him. A black bird, tree, lizard, cat, etc., in a card, usually de*notes* secrets, but perhaps you just do not have time to see them. The page's tunic is a shade of purple, indicating spiritual changes and purification covering up the gold and yellow in his tights and shirt. This means he must use his intellect to handle this situation even though his desire to finish this dilemma or obligation is strong. His red boots indicate that his foundation may be a little more volatile than normal and he must remain calm in order to achieve his goals. Obviously, he feels he needs to defend himself or a situation close to him. His integrity or honor has been challenged. He must use patience and caution in dealing with all issues.

THE MESSAGE OF THIS CARD is that you will be able to defend your beliefs and integrity quite well; however, take notice what is going on around you, for there may be things in the background that are unknown to you and might cause some concern. Deal with issues in an intellectual rather than volatile nature, as clarity of thought will help achieve everything that is important to you.

TEENAGER MEANING: You will have to stand up for yourself as new argument, disagreements, conflicts and issues start. This is the worst it is going to be; however, if you start looking towards the future, life will fall into place much more easily. If you keep fighting phantoms from the past, you may stay in the past and find it very hard to live in the present or future. Take control of your life, your issues and your future by being pro-active about decisions and move forward on a positive note.

KARMIC LESSON: The Karmic Lesson of the Page of Swords is that no matter what life throws your way, you have the wherewithal to handle problems, issues, concerns and negative circumstances. This is the worst it will be so stand tall, handle what has to be done and stop fearing the past. The future is positive and good, so why not concentrate on your prospects that are before you.

ASTROLOGICAL CONNECTION: Beginning of Autumn - Libra

MEDITATION/AFFIRMATION: I am stronger than I think and can handle anything that comes my way. I am open to new ways of thinking and will see my life from a new perspective. My self-image is strong, direct, assertive and in control. No one will be able to keep me thinking in old patterns. I am moving forward and no one can stop me now.

TRADITIONAL MEANING: Signifies a male who is under 30. Intelligent, competent and responsible. Intimidates others and challenges them to keep up. Extreme sports and outdoor activities. It represents designers, artists, builders, is many factors – those who work with their hands or create physical objects. Listen to his words and heed his advice.

Knight of Swords
(Minor Arcana - 12)
Also used as a Mundane Karmic Lesson 3/Air
Court Card

This card denotes bravery, skill, defense of one's rights and honor, and being ready to charge ahead without clearly or carefully thinking through a situation.

LEARNING THE ROPES IN CONFLICTS, PROBLEMS, AND RESPONSIBILITIES

This knight is dressed in armor, so we know he is ready to fight or protect himself. Suits of armor usually mean that the Querent has been hurt before and is afraid of being hurt again. His sword is held upright and ready to strike whoever gets in his way. The horse is charging, but has a questioning look on his face, as he sees the knight is hastily rushing into the past. Yes, they are going in the wrong direction - to the left of the card, the past. This knight also has a red cape and a red feather in his helmet, indicating that he is very assertive and aggressive and wants things to happen quickly. His desire or intention is to set things right, handle any challenges, and get on with his life. He also is showing the aggression that red can represent and looks very determined to pursue his enemy. The streaking clouds in the blue sky indicate that problems are full blown at the moment and he is trying to continue the battle. The swaying black trees in the background indicate definite secrets or hidden elements that have contributed to this conflict. The golden, earthen mound to the left indicates that he is following through to conquer this problem; however, it will not be completed at this time without proper knowledge and contemplation of the situation in a calm and unemotional manner. This person is too scattered and unfocused to concentrate on one outcome or particular issue. He desperately needs to focus on one thing at a time.

THE MESSAGE OF THIS CARD is not to go charging forward without knowing your boundaries. An intelligent resolution can be negotiated if you think first and react later. You must stop being so scattered, unfocused, and ungrounded. Prioritize your agenda, hopes, dreams, goals, and objectives and start going after them in an orderly fashion.

TEENAGER MEANING: You are very scattered and running around like a chicken without your head. You feel you can handle just about everything, but you are not being cautious or careful about your actions or decisions. The Knight feels protected with the armor, but it is a false protection. You cannot keep charging towards everything or be disorganized. It will only make your life more confusing and overwhelming in the end if you do not straighten it up now.

KARMIC LESSON: The Karmic Lesson of the Knight of Swords is that you should be less scattered and disorganized and try to find out how to be focused, secure, grounded and organized. You need to look at each situation carefully before making a decision rather than running willy-nilly into the future. Yes, protect yourself at all costs, but at some point you will need to rest, relax and figure out in which direction you really need to be going for your own best interest.

ASTROLOGICAL CONNECTION: Gemini

MEDITATION/AFFIRMATION: I will direct my energy to only one or two projects or chores at a time. I need to calm down and realize that good health is very important. I need time for myself, whether it is with family and friends, or alone time to finish projects by myself. I no longer need to start a million projects which continue to remain unfinished or incomplete. My goal is to start a few new projects each (day, week, month, or year, etc.) and finish as many as I can in a reasonable amount of time so that positive energy follows me wherever I go.

TRADITIONAL MEANING: Man under 40 is about to enter your life. And seals his emotions. Has a military demeanor. Disciplined. Supremely confident. Has courage and a good heart. Responsible, shrewd and alert. Planner, engineer, designer, builder or architect.

Queen of Swords
(Minor Arcana - 13)
Also used as a Mundane Karmic Lesson 4/Air
Court Card

This Queen is full of determination, secrecy, and sadness. She represents female depression, embarrassment, widowhood, and separation.

HANDLING EVERYTHING THAT COMES YOUR WAY

The Queen of Swords is very solid and stable. Here we have a queen sitting on a throne of cement, so no one will easily change her point of view. She is centered, grounded, and fixed. The clouds brewing in the blue sky depict some problem or conflict starting to form. The black bird and trees to the left of the card show that there are things going on behind her back (secrets) that could harm her if she does not pay attention to details, or she might even change her present opinion if these facts were known. She is ready to fight as shown with her sword drawn; however, she is carefully holding it on the throne's arm, while her other hand is inviting friends, family, and situations to present themselves to her in an open and fair manner. The friendship bracelet on her left hand shows that she is more comfortable dealing with people in a trusting and loving manner. She was probably taken advantage of in the past, indicated by her white gown. The blue and white cape over the white gown indicates her compassion, empathy, sympathy, and sensitivity towards others and her efforts in trying to help everyone. The sculpture of a cherub or angel on the side of the throne indicates that she gets spiritual guidance when she requires it. The blue sky indicates that things will turn out for the best when she understands what or whom she is dealing with. Her red hair indicates a fiery temper when pushed to the limit and the yellow crown indicates intelligence and her ability to see all sides of a situation.

THE MESSAGE OF THIS CARD is saying that you will be fair, but ready to defend your honor, family, friends, or loved ones when needed. Things are going on behind your back, but if you are careful to examine all possibilities of a situation in an intellectual manner and do not let your temper get the better of you, you will be able to make a positive, accurate, and quick decision.

TEENAGER MEANING: You are a gracious person who feels as if she has to help everyone. This card says that your life is calming down and you are looking in the right direction; however, it also advises that you start standing up for yourself and limit the help you give to everyone. The help you give out continuously drains you of your energy. You must learn to form boundaries and limitations so that you have enough energy to do what you need to handle for your own life. Intelligence is the key in this card. Emotional decisions will be wrong.

KARMIC LESSON: The Karmic Lesson of the Queen of Swords is to treat people well as you always have, but it is time to think of yourself for a change. It is time to stand up for your beliefs and do whatever you feel is right. Your intelligence and logic will pull you through any hardships, but boundaries and limitations are imperative so that you will no longer be taken advantage of.

ASTROLOGICAL CONNECTION: Libra

MEDITATION/AFFIRMATION: I will make good decisions that benefit me as I set boundaries and limitations of others. I will help whom I truly feel I should help, but will limit my energy expended on them and keep some for myself. I will continue to make friends, but at some point, when the time is right, I will stand up for myself and handle everything that I am supposed to in an assertive and unyielding manner.

TRADITIONAL MEANING: An emotionally balanced woman. She is wise from life's experiences. Can find humor in most situations, no matter how bad. There has been a lot of conflict and sorrow in her life. Extremely intelligent. Analytical mind, logical with a great deal of common sense. Natural leadership abilities. Will be honest and direct with you.

King of Swords
(Minor Arcana - 14)
Also used as a Mundane Karmic Lesson 5/Air
Court Card

This king is full of determination and ready for any type of action needed to handle the situation at hand. He has total power, authority, intelligence, and the knowledge of law on his side.

ACHIEVING OR RESOLVING YOUR GOALS IN CONFLICTS, PROBLEMS, AND RESPONSIBILITIES

Even though the king looks like a very stern individual, he is mostly dressed in blue and the background sky has a similar color. There is a lot of emotion around him. There are things going on behind his back, as indicated by the brewing clouds and black birds in his future. The black trees on both sides of him indicate that balance should be a priority in deciding issues or that he is in the middle of much negativity. This figure has the capacity to be a gentle, kind, and honorable man. He is fair, just, and optimistic in all of his decisions; however, if he has to fight, he will not hesitate to take control over any person or situation. He is seated on a solid throne of cement and is very determined in his beliefs and objectives. His purplish robe indicates his purification and spirituality. His red and yellow head gear indicates his intelligence and desire to get things done quickly and efficiently and he tries to accomplish these things with logic or analytical thought. His feet are on the abundant, green earth scattered with beige and yellow throughout, but the ground is not totally level or stable. It is uneven ground, indicating that his abundance, intelligence, and grounding may waiver at times, but his conviction is pure and clear and will be followed in a very direct manner. He is not dealing with the past or future, but is in the present and doing whatever he can to resolve situations to the best of his ability.

THE MESSAGE OF THIS CARD is to know what is going on around you. Be compassionate but know that many admire your strength of conviction and integrity. Think about your solutions logically and come to an intelligent answer for the benefit of all.

TEENAGER MEANING: You are very secure, stable, centered and grounded, but you still feel as if you have to protect yourself. You are in between negativity and problems and holding your own, but your compassionate heart will get you into trouble. Help whom you truly have to help and let others go that are using you for your advice, opinions, your time and possibly even money. Be careful about how you speak to others since you are very angry over recent happenings and will tell people off in a flash. Use the intelligence you have to get things done properly.

KARMIC LESSON: The Karmic Lesson of the King of Swords is that you must continually balance negativity and challenges during this lifetime. You need to be strong and call upon your passionate personality and assertive nature to stand your ground. Life is getting easier and things are calming down, but you are always on alert that something else will happen. Speak your mind and use your intelligence to get to the bottom of any issue. Once you realize that you are in control, you lighten up a bit.

ASTROLOGICAL CONNECTION: Aquarius

MEDITATION/AFFIRMATION: I am balanced. I am centered. I command respect, and intelligence. I am the master of creative thought and can share my thoughts with others, if they wish. I will stand up for myself and deal with any negativity around me in a very logical, analytical and intellectual manner. If necessary, I will speak my mind without hesitation until everyone realizes that I do control my own destiny.

TRADITIONAL MEANING: Man over 40. Usually conceals his emotions. Does not make small talk. Sharp intellect. Analytical and organized. Abrupt and judgmental. Natural leadership abilities. Highly ethical. Speaks with authority. Good instincts and common sense. Great ideas. High moral standards.

Ace of Swords
(Minor Arcana – Gift from God and Goddess – 1/Air)

Remove stumbling blocks to growth, dreams and objectives. Goals are satisfactorily completed. Your honor and integrity will be won back.

BLESSINGS FROM GOD AND GODDESS IN RESOLVING YOUR CONFLICTS, PROBLEMS, AND RESPONSIBILITIES

Aces are always gifts from God and Goddess, so you immediately know that this card is a gift in resolving all of your concerns, worries, responsibilities, limitations, and conflicts. The gray sky foretells of fear, anxieties, negativity, fogginess, or confusion about a situation. You may have to get to the heart of the matter or deal with a situation. The sword in the hand of God and Goddess depicts a crown and laurel wreath, indicating winning and becoming the victor in your challenge or conflict. The Yods (blessings from God and Goddess) are found above the hand. All will be well and blessed. The yellow crown indicates mental activity in your handling of the situation, so think it through well. The green, laurel wreath will bring success, prosperity, and happiness. The mountains stretching across the card indicate all the goals and plans before you, but you have to be strong enough to choose an opportunity or it will pass you by. There will be new beginnings after a particular conflict, struggle, or negative situation has been handled. Be assured all will be settled, fixed, or rectified within a short period of time.

THE MESSAGE OF THIS CARD is that you should not worry about the arguments and conflicts that surround you. You will be triumphant in your dealings with them. God and Goddess is protecting and blessing you to end the conflicts in your life and to get on the proper path for a harmonious existence with all.

TEENAGER MEANING: This gift from God and Goddess is helping you resolve your problems, issues, responsibilities, troubles, anxieties, procrastination, decision making and overall worries. If you use your intelligence and not your emotions to make your future decisions, you will be on a blessed path with many opportunities to choose from. If you make emotional decisions, you will be making the wrong decision.

Do not let your own doubts about dealing with your future keep you from attaining what you truly want.

KARMIC LESSON: The Karmic Lesson of the Ace of Swords is that you will always have lots of lessons in conflicts, responsibilities, obligations, disagreements and issues. This is a victory card in resolving all of your problems with intelligence, logical and methodical thought and with reasoning power. If you use your intelligence, there is nothing you cannot accomplish. Blessings from God and Goddess help move the positive energy forward, but all in all, the greenery protects you from all ills of the world.

ASTROLOGICAL CONNECTION: Aries

MEDITATION/AFFIRMATION: I am a firm believer in whatever I do will help me resolve my conflicts, problems, worries and concerns. With God and Goddess's help, I will become victorious and abundant in all things. I will use my intelligence to deal with the issues at hand and never make an emotional decision because it will be wrong. Once I accept the opportunity that Spirit has bestowed upon me, I will be going in the right direction and will reach any goal or dream I have planned.

TRADITIONAL MEANING: An excellent time for work in intellectual pursuits – a breakthrough is possible. Your life's mission or career direction will become clear. The ability to persevere will be crucial during this period. Decision should be guided by what is just, true and honorable. Think of problems as opportunities for change.

CUPS

Love, happiness, prosperity, and joy, inner peace, guidance, strength, wisdom, knowledge, self-confidence, self-esteem and everything else you need to make you happy. This also represents endings of a cycle, project or path in life and completions, family, relationships, and emotions. Cups represent action, inner sensitivity, inner courage and strength, wisdom, emotional experiences, and Spirit.

Regular Card Suit: Hearts
Direction: West

Elemental Fairy:	Undines
Element:	Water
Astrological Signs:	Cancer, Scorpio, Pisces

Some General Additional Terms to Describe CUPS.

Affectionate, agreeable, compassionate, concerned, considerate, emotional, empathetic, gentle, good-hearted, gracious, healing, imaginative, introspective, intuitive, joyful, kind, loving, fanciful, fragile, frail, hypersensitive, hysterical, impressionable, introverted, lazy, moody, morose, narcissistic, overemotional, temperamental, patient, peaceful, perceptive, psychic, quiet, refined, romantic, sensitive, spiritual, sweet, sympathetic, and understanding.

| Water Element Qualities: | Cancer, Scorpio, Pisces |

A heavy water emphasis, or preponderance of water, makes you very emotional and in touch with your feelings. It keeps you in tune with nature and your environment in general.

Water signs feel and understand everything through their emotions. They are very intuitive and do not intellectualize things. They respond exactly how they feel. Water people are attuned to their emotions and feelings. Being extremely emotional and sensitive, they can reach very high highs and very low lows. Creativity, innovation, artistic ability and vision are a few of their astonishing traits. If they are lucky enough to lead an artistic or creative life, you would never find a happier star sign. These people are nurturing although sometimes smothering of children, but all in all, they are one of the best parents of the zodiac if there are no negative surprises in their chart. These water signs communicate almost on a non-verbal basis; they would rather communicate emotionally, psychically, or through poetry, photography, artwork, music, dance or any other form of expression they can use. They seem to change their mind often because they are fluid like the water element itself.

The Court Cards give more depth and insight to the Numbers two through five, so if you are between these numbers, you have two mundane every day cards with issues that must be dealt with frequently.

Scan of Cups

Scan of Cups Court Cards

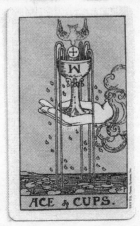

II
Two of Cups
(Minor Arcana - 2)

This card denotes a forthcoming marriage or significant romantic relationship. It can also stand for a partnership, reunion, or a business connection.

THE PERFECT LOVER'S CARD

Cups are wonderful, as they relate to love and relationships. Here are two people on equal footing looking lovingly at each other. They are exchanging love and commitment with each other. Located on a very prosperous and abundant hill, the house in the background denotes happiness, good health, prosperity, love, and joy. This is the only card where the figures are halfway turned towards the house. The lion's head, angel wings, and Caduceus of Hermes bring strength, courage, blessings, and good health to the relationship. The woman is wearing white, which normally stands for purity and goodness; however, it also indicates that the person is too giving, caring, loving, kind, generous, etc. The blue tunic of compassion, sensitivity, femininity, and emotion may add a little stability to her personality and emotional well being. She also has a laurel wreath on her head, indicating that she may have wanted this type of situation for a very long time. Now she has finally won her desires. The man has a wreath of red roses, indicating lasting love and dedication. He is also wearing the yellow of logical thinking. The black may be construed as trying to balance or handle any problems or concerns that enter their relationship. One of his legs is ahead of the other, so he may be impatient and anxious to get this relationship moving in the right direction. This is a happy and joyous card for a couple. Notice she is looking towards the future while he is looking to the past. They can meet somewhere in the middle.

THE MESSAGE OF THIS CARD is that there is a couple on even ground, holding cups filled with love and happiness, sharing everything equally, happily, and lovingly. Once they make their plans final, they will have love, happiness, prosperity, joy, inner peace, guidance, strength, and courage. Wisdom should guide them to a very happy and healthy future as a couple.

TEENAGER MEANING: A serious relationship will blossom during the year. This is someone who is a perfect match for you and who is on your same wavelength. You will keep no secrets from one another, have open communication and will be one of the first most serious relationships you have. Angels are blessing you; it is a healthy and confident relationship filled with love, happiness, good luck and fun.

MUNDANE KARMIC LESSON FOR BIRTH PATH NUMBER 2, ELEMENT WATER.

KARMIC LESSON: The Karmic Lesson of the Two of Cups is to accept the love that feels so right and experience the blessings, confidence, good health and positive energy between the two of you. There is nothing wrong with the relationship so stop looking for issues and concerns between the two of you. Accept that you have finally found the true love of your life and hold onto and treasure it.

ASTROLOGICAL CONNECTION: Venus in Cancer

MEDITATION/AFFIRMATION: I am with my perfect romantic significant other and will allow our differences to make us stronger. Everything that we have, we share with each other and know that our future is bright, positive and abundant in all ways.

TRADITIONAL MEANING: A new love affair. You'll be in sync with one another. Two people finally come together after a long flirtation. A broken relationship is healed through forgiveness. Connections are made in business. The start of a new relationship that will have a dramatic effect on your life.

III
Three of Cups
(Minor Arcana - 3)

In this card there is abundance, a toast, a harvest, eating, drinking, and celebrating. Things are working out well on the emotional level. There is a big celebration with lots of fun, laughter, and camaraderie.

CELEBRATION CARD

The Three of Cups is a celebration card. It could indicate a wedding or a new love. Something wonderful has happened with such a positive outcome that there was the need for celebration. The fruit scattered on the ground indicates fruitfulness and abundance surrounding you. The women's feet are not planted firmly on the ground, so it is as if nothing but the event or circumstance is important to them. Perhaps just the celebrating and having a good time is important to them. The blue sky shows the happiness, clear thinking, and positive future that awaits them. Another viewpoint is that this is the scattered energy of one individual who has finally developed into the person she is today. It was a hard transformation, but now she is celebrating the outcome of her efforts. The ever-giving nature, the side of her that is always being taken advantage of could be construed as being part of her past, as is indicated by the figure draped in white to the left of the card. The one in the future or the right of the card shows that intelligence and analytical thought covers up the white; now in the present, a woman is totally covered by a dominant, aggressive, and passionate red to handle any concerns, issues, or troubles that may come her way. She is also filled with desires and dreams, which she will take steps to make come true. They are celebrating the three stages of development in her personality: naiveté, intelligence, and passion. She has come full circle.

THE MESSAGE OF THIS CARD is that this is a celebration in love is on the horizon. A fruitful, happy, and rewarding time is just ahead. This may also indicate that the Querent has had some issues with consolidating all her positive and negative thoughts and attitudes and has recently become the person she has always wanted to be.

TEENAGER MEANING: This card is self-explanatory. It is a celebration with family and friends. It could be celebrating a wedding, birth, bar/bas mitzvah, graduation, engagement, baby shower or anything. It is a fun time in your life and everything is going well. On the other hand, it could symbolize the journey you have taken from being self conscious, having low self esteem and low self-confidence as well. Now is the time where you are transitioning into someone more centered and focused, secure and stable and getting on with your life in a very positive way. In the future, you will be more spiritual (or religious) and never go back to being the anxious, stressed out and worried person you were.

MUNDANE KARMIC LESSON FOR BIRTH PATH NUMBER 3, ELEMENT WATER.

KARMIC LESSON: The Karmic Lesson of the Three of Cups is that this is a time in your life to celebrate, so be with family and friends and let yourself enjoy the people closest to you. It can also be a lesson about you learning from past experiences, getting more grounded, centered and focused now and then becoming more spiritual. It is also about setting boundaries and limitation so that people do not take advantage of you any longer.

ASTROLOGICAL CONNECTION: Mercury in Cancer

MEDITATION/AFFIRMATION: I celebrate life and all of its joys as well as all of the people in my life. I am able to grow and become a stronger person by experiencing all that life has to offer and to learn from my experiences. My burdens from the past no longer affect me in any way because I am moving towards a brighter tomorrow with confidence, pride and assertiveness.

TRADITIONAL MEANING: Good harvests. Abundance. An active period marked by fun and successful relationships. A new understanding of what makes you happy. You feel energized and in high spirits. Strong friendships are very important at this time. Strong sense of community. Team spirit at work and in leisure activities. Popularity. Invitations to social events.

IV
Four of Cups
(Minor Arcana - 4)

In this card, a man is looking intently on three cups, but does not see the cup (or gift in the air) being offered by the hand of God and Goddess. You need to place attention on unusual and positive opportunities and keep your eyes open for upcoming miracles. A spiritual need remains unfulfilled.

IT'S TOO GOOD TO BE TRUE CARD

Here we notice a glorious clear blue sky and green grass. The blue sky has God and Goddess's hand reaching out giving you a gift in love, relationships, happiness, peace, wisdom, and strength. If you look at the figure under the tree, it is as though he is crossing his arms in an attempt to refuse the gift. There are three other cups in the lower left-hand corner of the card so he knows what he has and is afraid of taking a blind risk. The figure will then reject the gift at first glance, but after much consideration and reflection, will eventually accept it. I always tell my students to think about the gift carefully. They will eventually accept the gift that is being offered. The figure in the card is wearing many colors: the green of prosperity, the blue of compassion, emotion and sensitivity, and the red of desire and aggressiveness. The man is also leaning on a tan tree, which helps to ground him. Notice the leaves of the tree, which start in the present or the middle of the card, but seem to get more abundant in the future. Perhaps this gift also has something to do with finances as well. The man's black hair de*notes* some concerns or issues on his mind, as well as negativity that may be around him. However, that small bit of black does not detract from the happy nature of this card. It is positive and adventurous. The man is unsure of his next move, but after weighing his options carefully, he will make the right decision and take the gift.

THE MESSAGE OF THIS CARD is that at first you may not accept the gift which is offered to you through unusual circumstances, but after careful consideration, you will accept the opportunity and know it was the right decision. Procrastination has to stop and you have to plan for a better and more prosperous tomorrow.

TEENAGER MEANING: This is a great card meaning that life is going well, the choices you have made were correct and now God and Goddess is giving you another choice or gift. You seem hesitant to take it because at first because everything is going too well, but once you use your intellect or logic to get past your fears, you make the right choice and accept the gift from Above. You have made the right choice and are happy with your decision.

MUNDANE KARMIC LESSON FOR BIRTH PATH NUMBER 4, ELEMENT WATER.

KARMIC LESSON: The Karmic Lesson of the four of Cups is that even if you are skeptical in life about good things that are offered to you or given to you, do yourself a favor and just accept the good energy. Thinking of every reason why you should not take the gift from God and Goddess will only hinder you and then make you disappointed that you were not strong enough to make a logical decision about your future.

ASTROLOGICAL CONNECTION: Moon in Cancer

MEDITATION/AFFIRMATION: I will welcome all gifts that Spirit gives to me and will accept them as positive and for my best interest. I will continue to remain grounded, focused, and abundant, but will also let the universe give me a nudge onto the right path for my well being.

TRADITIONAL MEANING: You become increasingly dissatisfied with a focus on material possessions. You need something more in your life. Emotional exhaustion. Loss of interest in normal activities. Depression. Self-absorption. You must take action if you are going to find the answer to happiness.

V
Five of Cups
(Minor Arcana - 5)

The Querent has lost a lot, but you must encourage him to look around and be thankful for what he still has. All is not lost, but you are not thinking clearly and should reflect on your life and the recent happenings that have you in this depressed state of mind. This card indicates some unhappiness and emotional depression, perhaps feeling life is sad and empty with little joy.

WIDOW(ER) OR LOSS CARD

The Five of Cups looks like a very depressed and sad card, and indeed it is. It is a card that represents a widow(er) at times, but most often represents someone who feels very depressed and lonely. The man in the card is wrapping himself in a black cape of despair and negativity. This cape may also keep all of the negativity in this person's life hidden or buried deep inside his soul. The gray sky adds to the desperation and sadness. Things are unclear, cloudy, foggy, and uncertain. The gray color also brings about anxiety, confusion, and doubt. The wavy river flows to an unknown destination. There is a castle in the background, but it is in the distance and in the past. The man is focusing on the fallen cups, which are spilling their love out into nothingness. You must assure the Querent that there is still much love in his future. There are family and friends who care about him very much. All he needs to do is look behind him or to the future for the answer. Getting to any castle or house in a card is a goal. Going through the wavy water will cause more emotional upsets, so his best bet would be to cross the bridge to get to the castle of love, happiness, prosperity, joy, and hope. If he looks around him with hope and optimism, his negative experiences will be able to be handled.

THE MESSAGE OF THIS CARD is to try not to concentrate on the love that has hurt you in the past or those who have left you; instead, turn around to see that there is still plenty of love left in your life. Look towards the castle. Go over the bridge to get to your love, happiness, prosperity, and joy.

TEENAGER MEANING: This card is considered a "mourning" card. You can mourn the death of a person, pet or relationship. You can mourn the breaking up of a partnership or terrible fight you had with a family member. It is a time where you are depressed and sad. You do not think there is any hope in your life because you feel so emotional at the moment. Look to the future and find that there is still an abundance of love and prosperity around you waiting for you to welcome the new day (or new situations) before you.

MUNDANE KARMIC LESSON FOR BIRTH PATH NUMBER 5, ELEMENT WATER.

KARMIC LESSON: The Karmic Lesson of the Five of Cups is that even though life makes you go through so many hardships, losses and disappointments, you need to know that your life will improve in the future. You will get over the loss and become stronger for having gone through it. You cannot wallow in pity and sorrow forever. You must find strength of character, a spiritual path and perhaps a new direction so that you can continue to lead the good life you were experiencing before the upset.

ASTROLOGICAL CONNECTION: Mars in Scorpio

MEDITATION/AFFIRMATION: I will see through these desperate times and come out better for it. I will learn to look to the future and not continually concentrate on the past. I need to take a spiritual path towards my happiness and understand that this too will pass.

TRADITIONAL MEANING: Grief. Loss. Many regrets. Setbacks. Loss of a relationship. Friend, or valued possession. Disappointment in love and friendship. And of the marriage or love relationship. Here strength of spirit to endure. Hope for better future. Choose a creative solution to your problems. This is a temporary and will pass.

VI
Six of Cups
(Minor Arcana - 6)

Flowers and a cup are being given to a love or a wife. This card can denote things are not as they appear to be. It indicates deceit, secrets, or lies. Also, this card can mean that someone from your past will unexpectedly show up.

GOSSIP CARD

The Six of Cups can be a confusing card, since there is obviously some sort of exchange of love and emotion going on. If you notice, the little girl is wearing a white glove covering her hand, which usually indicates deceit, lies, or hidden truths. The next thing you will notice is that the young lady's yellow hair has facial features, indicating that she may be two faced or not showing her true self or motives. The light blue sky de*notes* that the situation can be one of happiness and clarity, while all the yellow buildings imply that logic and intelligence should be used in this situation. Each figure is wearing red, denoting desire, assertiveness, and longing for some type of trust in this relationship. The man is wearing more blue than the woman, which indicates that he is the more compassionate and emotional person in this couple. The upright cups are holding white lilies, denoting honesty, purity, and naiveté. The greenery indicates that this relationship could grow with proper attention to minute details. There is a cement path off to the left of the card. A man is walking that path, away from the situation. It seems as if he has already been defeated and is escaping from negativity. This card usually indicates that you should be friendly with your closest friends and family as usual, but if someone new comes into your life, do not tell them things that you do not want the rest of the world to know in the next five minutes. Be a little more particular about whom you trust.

THE MESSAGE OF THIS CARD is that you may be hearing from or seeing someone from your past. Someone is not being honest with you, so only give your trust to those friends and family that are very special to you or who have proved their loyalty or your secrets may be revealed.

TEENAGER MEANING: This is the gossip or another betrayal card. Do not trust everyone. Just because someone says something is the truth does not mean it truly is. Double check what people tell you and be sure that you do not tell anyone any secrets that you do not want spread around the world in the next five minutes unless you trust them one hundred percent. This is a two-faced person so try to see him/her as they truly are.

MUNDANE KARMIC LESSON FOR BIRTH PATH NUMBER 6, ELEMENT WATER.

KARMIC LESSON: The Karmic Lesson of the Six of Cups is that you should not trust everyone in the world. Your trusted family and friends are fine, but when new people are introduced into your life, be wary of them until they prove themselves 100%. You think that everyone is as good-hearted, kind and trustworthy as you, but this is not the case. Others want to get information from you to injure you in some way. Jealousy or envy may be their reason. You have to hold back, not share everything with strangers and be a little more aloof in new relationships of all kinds.

ASTROLOGICAL CONNECTION: Sun in Scorpio

MEDITATION/AFFIRMATION: I will not divulge my inner secrets to those I've just met. Once I trust someone one hundred percent, I may share my life with them. Otherwise, I will be wary of those who want to be my best friend shortly after meeting me. I will learn to give friendships time to grow and time to understand that trust and loyalty are the basis for true friendships.

TRADITIONAL MEANING: Concentrate on pleasant, happy memories of good times to come for you in times of trouble. Remember the good times and let go of the bad. Someone or something from the past brings you happiness. Emotional relief and healing from grief or loss.

VII
Seven of Cups
(Minor Arcana - 7)

This is a card of illusion. Things are not going as well as they appear to be. There are too many opportunities before you and it is time to make a decision. This card may also represent unfulfilled promises or deception.

MAKE A DECISION CARD

The Seven of Cups indicates many choices that need to be made. As with many choices, you are overwhelmed. Prioritize the major concern or issue so that you only have one choice to make and the other concerns will take care of themselves. It is your inaction or procrastination that is making you depressed, upset, or ineffective. The gray clouds are adding uncertainty, negativity and indecision, but the clear blue sky behind the clouds indicates that once you make that priority decision, all will turn out for the best. The black figure (you) stands for the negativity, fears, doubts, worries, anxieties and uncertainty you have in all the choices put before you. Some of the probable choices you must make are regarding your life path, wisdom, knowledge, higher education, home life, fame and money. The decisions could be any or all of these things as well as other more mundane issues. Remember, once you take a step at controlling your destiny by making the most important decision, the rest will start falling into place on their own. Take control of your life and avoid procrastinating any longer. Try not to listen to others in deciding your priority issue because only your choice counts at this time.

THE MESSAGE OF THIS CARD is that there are many choices before you. Do not be overwhelmed by all of the choices ahead of you. Instead, choose the most important issue in your life and sort it out. Everything else will fall into place.

TEENAGER MEANING: You have so many decisions and choices to make, but you are not dealing with them and this is making you feel overwhelmed. You need to make the most important decision you have, take a step at resolving the issue moving forward in a very positive way. Otherwise, you will continuously be stuck in a confused world where you feel that your life is beyond hope because you cannot make a good decision.

MUNDANE KARMIC LESSON FOR BIRTH PATH NUMBER 7, ELEMENT WATER.

KARMIC LESSON: The Karmic Lesson of the Seven of Cups is that you will continue to be in a negative place and attract more negative energy unless you make a decision. Even though there are many things you need to decide, if you just pick the priority issue, make a positive decision on only that one thing, then you will be putting yourself in a much more positive energy field attracting new energy, positive results and new beginnings.

ASTROLOGICAL CONNECTION: Venus in Scorpio

MEDITATION/AFFIRMATION: Once I make an informed decision, my life will get better and move in a much more positive direction. I will make the most important decision first and then when I am ready, make the next choice and then the next until all are determined. Procrastination will not keep me from getting the blessings of the universe. I am proactive and confident in my decisive abilities.

TRADITIONAL MEANING: Indicates the need for structure and discipline in your life. You are not seeing things clearly. Cloudy judgment. You may be misrepresenting reality. Wishing for something does not make it happen. Risky ventures will fail. There are many more options open then you recognize. Possible religious, psychic or unexplainable events.

VIII
Eight of Cups
(Minor Arcana - 8)

This card indicates gained understanding and moving on, inner level comprehension and work. You need more patience and tolerance. Your emotions might get you into trouble. Do not get overly upset and walk away from a good thing.

THE DIVORCE CARD and MID-LIFE CRISIS CARD

The Eight of Cups is another one of those cards where the figure is in between the suit. The male figure is the one who is filling in the hole or void this time. It frequently indicates that the person for whom you are doing the reading is usually the one who is causing his own love or relationship problems. He is walking away from his current situation and into the future. His red cape and shoes indicate that he desires something else or more in his life. He is looking for something that is probably unattainable or completely unrealistic. This is also called the divorce or mid-life crisis card. He may be looking for an affair, a new sports car, or anything that will define who he really is at this moment in time. He may also be trying to decide whether or not to remain married. He is looking for an unrealistic, illusionary life as indicated by the sun/moon combination in the sky. He is walking on a small cliff and could possibly lose his footing and fall into the water, which would make his life a bit more emotional. The water has rocks strewn across it and the black mountains appear in the right and left of the card indicating that he needs balance on the path ahead of him. The larger black mountain in the future indicates that the problems or negativity may be more of an issue then than in the past. The sun is resting with its eyes closed showing that he is not adding vitality or energy to this situation. The figure is on a quest and has to decide his path from his own life experiences.

THE MESSAGE OF THIS CARD is that you feel there is something missing in your life, so you are going off on an unrealistic journey (whether physical or mental) to find the answers. Many times this is considered the divorce card. Be sure of what you want before you give up what you have.

TEENAGER MEANING: This is the stereotypical divorce card; however, for a teen, I would use it as a break-up card or a moving-on card. You wish to find something more exciting, more fun and more in line with what you think you should be doing in your life now. Do not do anything stupid because if you do, it will all come back to you and you will feel what it is like to make continual mistakes.

MUNDANE KARMIC LESSON FOR BIRTH PATH NUMBER 8, ELEMENT WATER.

KARMIC LESSON: The Karmic Lesson of the Eight of Cups is that even though you may feel that something is missing in your life, you should be grateful for what you already have. Re-examine your life and figure out if there is something you can do to make it more positive for your family and you. Leaving is not always the best answer. Sometimes, it is harder to face problems, but once they are resolved, your life will feel more important and blessed.

ASTROLOGICAL CONNECTION: Saturn in Pisces

MEDITATION/AFFIRMATION: I will thank the universe for what I have and try not to compare myself to others or what they possess. If I feel as if something is missing in my life, I will discuss it with my partner so that I can handle the situation with integrity and honesty. I will be open with my partner at all times and discuss things that are on my mind. In turn, I will listen to my partner's point of view and insights.

TRADITIONAL MEANING: Disappointment. Dissatisfaction. Tired of the current situation. You have a bad attitude. Take action. Leave your current relationship or job. Indicates travel or relocation. Look elsewhere for happiness. Make dramatic changes in your life. Carry through with plans.

IX
Nine of Cups
(Minor Arcana - 9)

This is a wish fulfillment card; you must select one of nine paths. You have many decisions to make. You are likely the center of attention and will receive satisfaction from a job well done. Accomplishment is yours. Vanity and conceit may be at work, so be careful not to let them hinder your plans.

SATISFACTION CARD

The Nine of Cups shows that you are satisfied with your life and the decisions you have made. You feel content because you have reached a period in your life when you are satisfied with your accomplishments. All the Cups are upright and filled with love and happiness behind you. The man is dressed in white and wearing a red cap. The desire for happiness is very real to him and at this point, he has attained it. The white shows that he received his happiness in an honest, pure, and truthful manner; however, he seems to still be a pushover for others to take advantage of him. The red hat may denote that he will only be pushed so far before he will stand up for himself. His feet are planted firmly on the yellow ground, so basically, all his triumphs and results came from his intellect and analytical, logical thought. The blue tablecloth represents his emotional and inner sensitivity. There is a good balance of mind and Spirit (yellow and blue) in this card. He is seated on a wooden bench, so he feels secure and stable. The figure is also dealing with the completion of his plans in a very loving and sincere way. He is generous and wants to share all his wealth, happiness, and good fortune with family and close friends.

THE MESSAGE OF THIS CARD is that you feel as if everything is going well. You have worked hard during your life and now you have reaped the rewards. You are there to help others, but will not allow anyone to take advantage of you. You are secure, stable, and grounded in all your pursuits and want to protect your property or interests at this time.

TEENAGER MEANING: You are very happy about everything in your life. School, work and your extra-curricular activities are going well. You will protect what you have achieved and gained in life as long as you balance your emotional and mental energies; you will be able to continue loving all that you have.

MUNDANE KARMIC LESSON FOR BIRTH PATH NUMBER 9, ELEMENT WATER.

KARMIC LESSON: The Karmic Lesson of the Nine of Cups is that your emotions and intellect are now balanced. You should strive to become more grounded and even though you will continue to be a sucker on some level, you now have limits. You should protect all that you have and speak up when you feel that you are being taken advantage of. No one can let others take advantage of them without their knowledge. Do not let this happen to you any longer.

ASTROLOGICAL CONNECTION: Jupiter in Pisces

MEDITATION/AFFIRMATION: I am satisfied with everything I have and will protect it to the best of my ability. I will no longer be the sucker that gives in to everyone, but will be more selective about whom I will help and not let others take advantage of my good nature. I am resolute and confident that I will keep all that I have and share what I want with whom I want.

TRADITIONAL MEANING: This is the wish card – your deepest desire is granted. A problem is solved. Satisfying sexual relationships. Emotional piece. Goals are achieved. Dreams come true. Take time to enjoy your success and revel in its rewards. Material possessions or attains. Physical fitness and beauty.

X
Ten of Cups
(Minor Arcana - 10)

This is a card that indicates a great home and family life. The house indicates love, happiness, joy, abundance, prosperity, long life, and a happy time. Dreams will be fulfilled. Lasting success and happiness are yours and all your dreams will come true.

HAPPINESS EVER AFTER CARD

I like to call the Ten of Cups the "happiness ever after" card. Everything is going well. This is the only card where the figures are facing the house in the green abundance fields. The blue sky is cloudless, bringing happiness and dreams come true. The happy family is standing on the firm, balanced ground. The river is flowing through their property calmly, without ripples or waves, so things are going smoothly in their emotional lives as well. The children are playing and having a good time. They are celebrating with their parents after a long road of hard work and responsibilities to get to this point. All will be well worth the effort. A well-deserved ending or completion of a cycle is at hand. If your Querent is too old to have small children, ask questions. It could represent grandchildren, children in the neighborhood, or as one client told me, she got her greatest joy from teaching at a day care center around many children whom she considered like her own. This card came up when a woman in one of my classes wanted to know if she were going to have a child. Apparently she was trying for some time and this would have completed her life dreams. I told her it looked very promising and in my next semester, she was pregnant and ecstatic.

THE MESSAGE OF THIS CARD is that this is the "happiness ever after" card representing the love, happiness, peace of mind, and clarity that you need for a wonderful future. Everything you need to make your life fulfilling and satisfying will come to you.

TEENAGER MEANING: When you get the "happiness ever after card," everything falls into place for you. You are happy, and if you are in a relationship, it could not get better than this. Go after your dreams and wishes since whatever your *happiness ever after* is seems to be formulating in front of you.

MUNDANE KARMIC LESSON FOR BIRTH PATH NUMBER 1, ELEMENT WATER.

ASTROLOGICAL CONNECTION: Mars in Pisces

MUNDANE KARMIC LESSON FOR BIRTH PATH NUMBER 2, ELEMENT WATER.

KARMIC LESSON: The Karmic Lesson of the Ten of Cups is that once you achieve your *happiness ever after*, you are now able to enjoy it and trust in the process that everything is working for your best interest. You must decide what your *happiness ever after* is so that you can recognize that your prayers have finally been answered. Do not question the process. Everything in your life is going well, so enjoy the fruits of your labor.

MEDITATION/AFFIRMATION: I will enjoy my *happiness ever after* and be grateful to Spirit that my family and life is going in such a positive direction. I thank the universe for my abundance, good health, and for laughter and adventure. Life will continue on this harmonious path as long as I want it.

TRADITIONAL MEANING: Entering a period of peace and contentment. Supportive family. Great friends. A special of relationship. Commitments made and kept. Joy and happiness. Forgiveness and reconciliation. You have all the material possessions you need. Purchase a home.

Page of Cups
(Minor Arcana - 11)
Also used as a Mundane Karmic Lesson 2/Water
Court Card

Emotions are about to bear fruit. A new mate or addition to the family is possible. This card may represent a loving, gentle, kind, emotional, giving person you have recently met or will meet; this is a fair young man with whom the Querent will have some relationship. It can represent news or a message.

BRAND NEW BEGINNINGS IN EVERYTHING YOU NEED TO MAKE YOU HAPPY.

The Page of Cups represents a new relationship. Cups are love, so it most likely would be a romantic relationship. He is facing the past or the wrong direction, which can mean that he is looking for love, but may only be dreaming about it, never taking a chance to go out to get it. He should look towards the future with happiness, trust, and conviction, as love will definitely come into his life if he takes a step in that direction. The sky is gray which de*notes* uncertainty, doubt, or anxiety surrounding this relationship and the rolling waves indicate a great deal of emotion and sensitivity, but not to worry. The blues in both the ocean behind him and in his clothing show tenderness, emotion, and compassion. He is looking at a fish, which lives in the water (again amplifying the compassion), and it could also indicate the beginning of a spiritual journey or inner knowledge coming your way. The fish in both the cups, and seemingly on his head, may also indicate that Jesus is blessing this union. Jesus was born in the Age of Pisces, represented by the fish. He will multiply this love which is pure, just, and unconditional. The young man is standing on golden, solid earth, which infers he needs to think things through logically. He is also dressed in the red of desire and conviction to get what he wants and golden boots which are trying to ground him in his search. Nevertheless, it is a new adventure in the journey of life towards love.

THE MESSAGE OF THIS CARD is that there is a chance at an adventure in love and romance. Uncertainty or confusion may be present - you may feel like you are on an emotional roller coaster. However, this is an unconditional love relationship with the best of outcomes for both partners.

TEENAGER MEANING: New love is on the way. This is a special person to love because you are both on the same wavelength and you feel you are supposed to be together. This will be one of the best times you will have in a relationship since it is a wonderful partner – so enjoy it.

KARMIC LESSON: The Karmic Lesson of the Page of Cups is know that the person you are totally and uncontrollably attracted to is supposed to be the person you are with. You will also learn many karmic lessons about love, relationships, sharing and honesty. Everything will work out in love even with you sabotaging it. Let love into your life and trust that the universe knows with whom you should spend it with.

ASTROLOGICAL CONNECTION: Pisces

MEDITATION/AFFIRMATION: I am willing to share my life with a new partner. I know that this relationship will be in both our best interests. I will be compassionate, loving, caring and ethical and will treat my partner with love, honesty, loyalty and generosity in all things.

TRADITIONAL MEANING: Signifies a male under 30. Direct and brutally honest, works in a creative or artistic field. This man can be Moody and very emotional. Sympathizes with others troubles. Passionate about life. Outgoing and charismatic. They lack social skills or education. This man enters your life without long-term effects.

Knight of Cups
(Minor Arcana - 12)
Also used as a Mundane Karmic Lesson 3/Water
Court Card

A message is coming to you. You must think clearly, but should take advantage of all opportunities presented to you. You should definitely trust this person's judgment.

LOVE, HAPPINESS, PROSPERITY AND JOY

Even though the Knight of Cups is dressed in armor, his disposition and posture do not show that he is in a war-like state. It is almost as though the armor is protecting him from being hurt again. He is offering love or the opportunity of love to the Querent, whom must make a short metaphorical journey across the stream of indecision and sensitivity to the other side of the mountain (or cliff) of goals and aspirations ahead of him. The mountain shows that all his goals and aspirations will be easily met if he proceeds in a steady and focused manner. The blue sky, although light blue, shows that things will turn out well. Also indicating a good outcome is the knight's horse, taking careful, deliberate steps. Whenever someone is riding a horse, it indicates that the person now has control over the emotions or situations indicated by the color of that horse. In this case, the horse is gray, indicating that this knight has control over his doubts, fears, worries, and anxieties. The knight is proceeding cautiously and carefully into the future. The clear blue sky, taking up three-quarters of the card, indicates that there is smooth sailing ahead without any apparent concerns. Notice the wings on the helmet, almost like Mercury who delivered messages from the God and Goddess. There are many possibilities, but the situation involves love and being able to allow it into your life.

THE MESSAGE OF THIS CARD is to continue to reach your goals in love and happiness. Take your time in a slow, steady relationship. Be patient and tolerant. Be very trusting and compassionate, but still protect your emotions.

HOW TO BE A TAROT DETECTIVE   ~303~

TEENAGER MEANING: This is the best love card you can have. The problem is that the person you love (or you) may be moving too slowly and one of you would demand that things change. On the other hand, it is indicating that if you are in a relationship, it continues to move in a much more secure and focused direction and adding you into his/her life as well.

KARMIC LESSON: The Karmic Lesson of the Knight of Cups is if things are moving too slowly in your life, it is up to you to light a fire under your butt and get moving in the right direction. Being cautious is a good thing, but if you experience procrastination and cannot make decisions about your life or your future, it is time to break that pattern and take control of your future in a timely manner. Set timetables and deadlines for important issues.

ASTROLOGICAL CONNECTION: Pisces

MEDITATION/AFFIRMATION: I continue to move forth in a very positive direction with my cup filled with love, happiness, prosperity, and joy, inner peace, guidance, strength, wisdom, self-confidence and everything else I need to make me happy; although my journey is a long and slow one, I am steady, focused, centered, grounded and ready to make a commitment to the one I love.

TRADITIONAL MEANING: Signifies a male under 40. Romantic and calm nature. Makes decisions with his heart. Thinks carefully before acting and speaking. Sensitive to others. Well-educated. Idealistic. Persuasive. Possible invitation or proposition. In love, he is considerate and generous.

Queen of Cups
(Minor Arcana - 13)
Also used as a Mundane Karmic Lesson 4/Water
Court Card

This queen is good, fair, and an extremely devoted and honest person. She is a very strong person with a deep sense of family and strong maternal instincts. This card represents love in its highest form, as well as beauty and femininity. It also represents a high level of concentration and receptivity.

BEING IN LOVE WITH LOVE

This is the card of "being in love with love" and not doing the best things for yourself regarding your relationship. The Queen of Cups is sitting on a throne of cement, which means obstinate or fixed behavior and a very difficult time trying to convince her of anything other than her own opinion. However, she is slipping off the throne and her foot is now in the water. She is putting herself on an emotional and unnerving path by having a body part in water, causing her own problems. Her other foot is on rocks, so it is not resting on solid ground. Notice how she is facing the past as well. She is daydreaming into a covered cup of love and perhaps even sees visions of the future that she imagines. She may be trying to contain her love in hopes that it will not disappear. She is dressed in white, denoting her honesty and purity of heart and deed. However, remember that white also indicates being too giving, caring, loving, etc. The clear sky indicates the outcome will go well, but perhaps the Querent must take action and get on with her life. The throne is on the multi-colored ground possibly denoting confusion or lack of direction. The cliffs in the background are indicative of an upcoming challenge.

THE MESSAGE OF THIS CARD is that you are thinking too much of romance and causing your own emotional obstacles and challenges. You may be thinking or worrying too much about your circumstances, but not taking any action. Cloudy indecision is surrounding you.

TEENAGER MEANING: This is someone who has set no boundaries and limitations in a love relationship. Usually she is someone who is very devoted to the relationship, but will continue to go above and beyond for everyone and not take her health or life into consideration. Balance and boundaries are desperately needed.

KARMIC LESSON: The Karmic Lesson of the Queen of Cups is that you cannot control who loves you and who does not. You are too involved in a relationship and afraid to let it go. You feel that if you let this relationship go, you will be alone in the world. The only thing that holding onto a relationship that is not meant to be can bring you is the feelings of drowning in sorrow or sensitivity. You are a smart person, so think logically and not emotionally about any love related decisions. Only your intellect and logic will help you make the right decisions.

ASTROLOGICAL CONNECTION: Cancer

MEDITATION/AFFIRMATION: Even though I care too much for other people in my life, I will learn to care for myself just as much. Being intelligent and logical, I can change my life and relationships in any way I choose. I want positive and loving relationships and will release any negative thoughts and people who are in my life. I welcome the universe to bring me someone who loves me as much as I love him (or her).

TRADITIONAL MEANING: Female. Attractive, practical, romantic, emotional, honest, devoted. Careful with money. The perfect wife and loving mother. A nurturing personality. Kind, sympathetic to the feelings of others. She has a positive effect on your life.

King of Cups
(Minor Arcana - 14)
Also used as a Mundane Karmic Lesson 5/Water
Court Card

This card is indicative of being confined and needing more freedom. It represents male emotions and a male way of thinking and shows someone who is well balanced and emotionally stable. You are very much in control of a situation and a very wise and extremely creative person.

RESOLVING YOUR GOALS
IN LOVE, HAPPINESS, PROSPERITY AND JOY

The King of Cups is sitting on a throne of cement floating in the middle of the ocean. How long do you think that cement throne will float? He displays much knowledge, power, and resolve and is determined in his attitudes and opinions, yet he unwisely picked this location to sit. He is dressed in blue and yellow with a sash of red. The blue has a serene, calming effect, while the yellow is representative of his use of intellect. This person needs a balance between the two. His red sash and crown indicate his desire for peace, harmony, and balance. The gray sky de*notes* fogginess, mystery, the unknown, and surprises. The water is rough, denoting problems or emotional turmoil. There are things going on beneath the surface that must be brought to the king's attention. I conclude the fish or serpent on the left side of the card to be a negative force or event that will come into this person's life. Perhaps the only way to escape from these confused and upsetting waters would be to flee on the red sailboat into the future. The king's foot looks as if it is slipping into the water, which would also be negative. More balance is desired and needed in many areas of this love relationship.

THE MESSAGE OF THIS CARD is that balance is needed between emotional and intellectual matters. Situations are going on behind your back. Try to notice what is going on around you or it may wind up being a threat that could potentially harm you. Your romantic choices now will help you to either sink or swim.

TEENAGER MEANING: You feel on top of the world, but your cement throne is temporarily floating on a turbulent ocean. Eventually, you will sink in sorrow and emotion. This is a time to run or get out of the relationship; use that little red ship in your future to escape from the overwhelming relationship you are now stuck in. It may not be what you want at the present time, but you do know that things are not going to work out for anyone's best interest. You must let this relationship go and start fresh.

KARMIC LESSON: The Karmic Lesson of the King of Cups is that you continuously put yourself into situation where you feel that you are about to drown in emotion. You may pick emotional rather than intellectual partners and you seem to be your own worst enemy because you do not want to hurt someone else's feelings, so you stay in a loveless or negative relationship for that other person. You need to escape from the negativity and look towards a new, bright future with someone whom you deserve.

ASTROLOGICAL CONNECTION: Scorpio

MEDITATION/AFFIRMATION: If life gives me surprises, I will surprise life by my positive reaction. I know all things happen for a reason and I am willing to make the changes necessary to fulfill my destiny. When life pushes me in another direction, I will go with the flow and see where life leads me. I am grateful for all choices and confident that everything I choose will be for my best interest.

TRADITIONAL MEANING: Refers to men over 40 with a warm, caring personality. Extremely friendly and outgoing. Emotionally balanced and considerate of others. Responsible. Others can count on him. Kiss wise advice. This man is in a position of authority and has the respect of many. In love, he is giving and trustworthy.

Ace of Cups
(Minor Arcana – Gift from God and Goddess – 1/Water)

This is a card of new beginnings, love, and happiness. Deep emotions are about to come to the surface. This could represent love in its beginning stages or finding the love of your life. Sometimes this can suggest business connections, partnerships, reunion, or even marriage.

THE BEST CARD IN THE DECK

BLESSINGS FROM GOD AND GODDESS
IN LOVE, HAPPINESS, PROSPERITY AND JOY

In my opinion, this is the best card you can get in a spread. It represents unconditional love and happiness. Being an Ace, it represents a gift from God and Goddess. The Holy Spirit is bringing the host into a love situation or relationship and is making it a very positive and loving experience. Notice all the Yods, or blessings from God and Goddess, being showered down upon you. The gray sky indicates minor fogginess on your part as you may think "this is too good to be true" or you are not sure how things can work out for the best. You may not even be certain how you will meet this wonderful new romantic partner or how a love situation will work out for your best interests, but be assured it will. The lily pads are float peacefully in the water and will help things grow and bless you with prosperity and abundance. The blue water, although having minor ripples in it, is serene and loving, as the water falling from the Chalice of God and Goddess is causing these ripples.

THE MESSAGE OF THIS CARD is that this is a gift from God and Goddess in love and romantic partnerships. Blessings will accompany this new relationship. It may be the relationship you have waited your entire life for or, at the very least, a special and loving relationship.

TEENAGER MEANING: Everything that you wanted for yourself and more is falling into place. You are being blessed with relationships, happiness, and all your decisions regarding family, home life, love life, and friends will be very positive and make you extremely happy. This is the card that brings the most blessings to the person it represents so use this time wisely and make sure you avail yourself to the resources that Heaven have in mind for you.

KARMIC LESSON: The Karmic Lesson of the Ace of Cups is the best card in the deck and it tells you that you have so much love, happiness, prosperity and joy, inner peace, strength, wisdom and knowledge. You need to use all of these gifts to not only make yourself and your partner (or family) happy, but it is a card that wants you to help others to find what you have. Share your happiness, help others, and listen to those who need assistance or guidance in their relationships. You are blessed now so whatever you do to help others in need will add more blessings to your life.

ASTROLOGICAL CONNECTION: Sun in Leo

MEDITATION/AFFIRMATION: I am blessed in all that I do. Everything will work out for the best and I will feel a sense of relief and joy in knowing that my vibrations coincide with those of the universe. I am filled with Love, happiness, prosperity and joy, inner peace, guidance, strength, self-confidence, self-esteem and everything that will make me (and my family – or my partner) happy in all ways.

TRADITIONAL MEANING: intense friendships. Loving family. Join inner peace. The beginning of a great love. Follow your heart and your instincts. Let your guard down and open your heart. You can trust this person. You will find your soul mate. Count on your friends.

READING THE CARDS

A YOUNG LADY SURPRISED me with an email recently with a question about my first tarot book. "So how do you do read a spread after you lay down the cards?" I was stunned that after reading my book, she did not know to look up each card and give the Querent the basic information on each card. Of course, if the Reader has been working with the cards for some time on her own and had gotten additional intuitive information on them as well, then the Reader would also add her own interpretation. After you lay down a spread, no matter which one you decide upon, start at card number one and read the card and then card number two and so on. By the end of the spread, you have a good indication about what is going on in that person's life for the next year or whichever timeframe you have chosen. Remember, the timing of the cards is simple, especially for a beginner. If the card is upright, the energy of that card will be from now through the next six months. A reversed card brings the energy of the card to seven to twelve months from now. So let us see which spreads I like and the ones I most commonly recommend.

If you are an advanced Reader, you may also read the cards by month. The first card is the month you are doing the reading and not January. So the first card is the current month, and the next card is the next month and so on and so forth until you have gone through one full year. Be sure to tell your client or Querent, that a full year is from today to next year at this same time and not until the actual end of the year unless you did a reading in January through December.

The basic spreads in tarot are the Celtic Cross, the Year-ahead, your own version, the Birthday Spread, the 3 Card Spread, and the variations of the Yes/No Spread. These are the only spreads we will deal with in this book since they are basic and very easy for a beginner to learn.

There are many types of ways to read various spreads. I use my own version of the Celtic Cross or the Astrological Spread as Year-ahead spreads as well. Any spread can give you the same information. Just be comfortable with the spread you use and be consistent in all your readings.

Anyone who has ever taken any of my classes or has been to my lectures knows how important it is to shuffle the cards well. Shuffling helps put the vibrations of the Querent and the Reader into the cards to help give an accurate and objective reading. The person doing the reading relies on the accuracy of the cards, so getting as many strong energy patterns into the cards as you can is always best.

Shuffling the cards completes the circle of energy. You are shuffling the cards and your energy goes into the cards while the energy of the cards goes back into you.

The following is the shuffling method I use and suggest. Even though it is a bit longer to do initially, I truly believe that it gives you a much more precise reading because it gives you ample time to reflect on your question and/or the Querent.

- Shuffle the whole deck of cards until you feel comfortable that you have shuffled them enough. As you are shuffling, you should either say out loud or in your mind, "I seek insight into (name)'s life for the next year." Repeat this as many times as you feel you must. You may want to say it out loud the first time someone is coming to you for a reading so that they will understand how to do the shuffling and what to say when it is their turn. Say it with them a few times to be sure they know what is expected of them.

- Cut the deck into three piles with your left hand. Vibrations come in the left side of your body and leave the right side, so you want to pull the vibrations from the cards through your body and back out into the deck as you are dealing them. By doing that, the cards and your energetic vibrations become one. In essence, you are making a complete circle of energy patterns.

- Shuffle each pile again until you feel comfortable. You do not have to shuffle the cards for a set time period or a number of shuffles, but you will intuitively know when it is time to stop. You should also explain this to your Querent. However, sometimes when there are time constraints such as five-minute readings at corporate parties or holiday events, do not let the client shuffle for three minutes if the total time allotted for the reading is five minutes. Let them shuffle a few times and put your left hand out to receive the cards. (However, if they shuffle the deck only once, I ask them to at least shuffle the cards three times since we do not want to pick up the energy of the last person's reading).

- Hand the cards to your Querent with your left hand into their left hand and explain the above three steps. Shuffle all the cards, make three piles, shuffle each pile, put them back into one pile in any order she wishes and return them to you with her left hand.

- Any order she wishes? She has three piles in front of her (as you did a few minutes ago). Pile 1, 2, and 3. You can pick up Pile 3, 2, and 1, or 3, 1, 2 or 2, 1, 3, etc., and place them back into one pile. Always make sure you are pulling cards for the reading from one pile, not one out of each of the three piles as many students have done. The reading would not be accurate.

Now you are ready to deal the cards into whichever spread you had determined before dealing them. I use the Year Ahead Spread, the Astrological Spread, or the Modified Celtic Cross (I use twelve cards so that if someone has a question regarding a particular month, I can answer without having to do an extra yes/no spread).

If you do not feel comfortable with my suggested way of shuffling, shuffle your own way, but make sure you shuffle for at least a minute or two. Get those energy patterns into the cards. Whichever way you finally choose is fine; however, always BE CONSISTENT! Consistency is very important in tarot so that the universe will know how you are dealing and reading the cards to help with the interpretations of the information you require.

Remember that this book is only one source of knowledge. Take whatever you need from this book and get information from other sources as well. Tarot is an on-going learning experience so learn all you can. If everyone received the same information, then all Tarot Readers would be identical and thus, not needed. All Readers interpret the cards differently, but it is okay to get a firm foundation of the cards' meanings and then adding your own style or flavor into your reading.

Be aware that nothing is written in stone. That is why I was compelled to write this book. I felt there was a different way of reading the cards than all the books I had studied throughout the years. Whatever feels right for you IS right for you. My method of reading the cards is certainly right for me and has helped thousands of students throughout the years learn tarot without being frustrated, overwhelmed, or confused like I was when it took me over ten years to learn this ancient divination tool. It has also helped them read the tarot quickly and easily within twenty hours or so, not the usual years it used to take.

It used to take so much longer to learn any spiritual modality many years ago because no one wanted to share their knowledge freely. The teachers would let you know this or that about a card, and when I asked why it meant that, the answer I regularly received was, "Because it always meant that . . ." so I knew one day I would have to change the way tarot was taught. And I have! I think most of the former teachers I have had or with whom I had taken lectures and workshops may have been threatened that someone else would have their knowledge and business would be taken away from them. I encourage people to learn tarot or any other modality because this world certainly needs ethical and moral people in this field to neutralize the bad effects, anxieties, worries and negative energy given to Querents from the charlatans. I discuss charlatans later on in this book, but if you are going to be a tarot Reader, be someone to help people. You will learn that even though most spiritual tarot Readers and astrologers are not the richest people in the world, it seems their goal is to help others onto a different path and give compassion and options when there were none.

Just remember too that whatever you project into the universe, you will receive. So if you are kind, considerate, empathetic and compassionate, you will be rewarded in so many ways (as I have throughout the years). You will be surprised with people's generosity, their opinion of you (so that they recommend you too many friends and family members) and in countless other ways.

Be truthful, but tactful. Never hide the truth, but ask questions or make suggestions that will help with the Querent's decisions. Remember, if you see something that looks like a medical problem, ask, "When was the last time you had a physical examination?" and be done with it. You are giving the person a proactive role in his or her own life. You cannot worry about that person making the appointment or not. Your job was done by giving the warning or suggestion.

Look at it this way, if you had a serious illness and the doctor told you to rest, eat more organic food, take vitamins and supplements and continue to take your medication and you will get better, you would be a fool not to listen to the doctor. However, if you decided that you know more than the doctor because you "read it on the web" that this works or does not work, then you are choosing your fate. You may never get better and eventually leave this world. If you would have listened, the doctor said you would get better. The doctor cannot follow you around and make you eat right, take your medications and rest. He told you what you need to do to make your health improve. It is up to you if you want better health, right?

The same holds true for tarot. You gave your suggestions, and if people take your advice, fine. If they do not, it is not your fault if they make their lives worse or get into more trouble, confusion, health issues, arguments, etc. You told them what to do; it was their decision to listen to you or not.

Your ethics should be above reproach. Never tell anyone that a loved one is going to die - that is up to God and Goddess, not you. And just imagine if you were wrong! The anguish and anxiety that you had caused would be horrendous. Never take on that responsibility. Never use the cards as a means of spying on anyone or wanting to know something that is none of your business. You may have the Querent ask about family and close friends out of a sincere love and concern for them, but they should never ask about frivolous things. Tarot is a serious study and should be considered as such. Of course, if you have some time left at the end of a session, your client can certainly ask a few more questions than she originally wanted to ask. You can then do yes/no spreads or get answers from the original twelve cards in the year ahead spread such as information by month or perhaps when it would be best to take that vacation, ask for a raise, get married or something like that.

After doing a spread, look at the cards. Notice if there are more wands, pentacles, swords, or cups. Each pertains to a different area of life, but in a spread it is very common for two suits to be dominant. If the spread has mostly wands, a job or career is the real reason they are seeking insight (usually wands represent work before health and education issues); Pentacles mean money-related issues, usually worries, concerns and challenges. Swords pertain to conflicts, arguments, or people attacking your integrity or honor. Cups mean love, happiness, joy, and prosperity in all areas of life. So decide which suit is dominant (which suits has more cards than the rest of the suits) and that will be the main issue for the year.

How many cards are upright? How many are reversed? Even though we do not use reversed cards as negative in the new millennium, I still make note of them because they still can be areas of potential trouble if the Querent is not aware of them. The more upright cards, the easier the next year will be. The more reversed cards, the more challenging the year will be. Word your statements carefully. (For instance, if you have eight reversed cards and four upright, you can always say, "I see you have had many challenges this past year. It does not look as if they are all going to be resolved immediately, but it seems that you will be working on resolving them one at a time." I also like to say, "If you are more proactive about your choices, you will minimize the time frame before your issues will be resolved."

It is much better than saying, "Oh my God, this year looks worse than last year!" Be selective in what words you use and give as much hope as possible to your client, friend or family member. I remember one student pulling the Death card before we actually studied that Major Arcana card and she yelled to the partner she was working with for the evening, "Oh my God and Goddess, you're going to die!" I can tell you, that statement stayed with the student for a very long time, but eventually when we learned the actual meaning of the card, she felt much better and learned how to properly interpret the card.

Notice how many Major Arcana cards are in the spread. See the meanings below:

• NO MAJOR ARCANA CARDS

If you have no Major Arcana cards in your spread, it means that God and Goddess have decided to let you handle your own responsibilities and issues during the next year. This is the time for you to take charge of your own obligations and take control of your life.

• ONE OR TWO MAJOR ARCANA CARDS

When you receive one or two Major Arcana cards, it usually signifies that God and Goddess, Angels, Spirit, The One, The Source, The All, The Universe, or whomever your client believes in, will be there if guidance is needed, but she must ask for that help or pray for assistance. The client may also need to reconnect with her place of worship in some capacity. Be sure to find out if your client believes in God and Goddess, Angels, Spirit, etc., since there is no faster way of losing a client's trust and interest than when you start referring to something in which they do not believe. If you are reading for an atheist or a Pagan, try using, "Universal Energies" as your guiding force.

• THREE OR MORE MAJOR ARCANA CARDS

If you are lucky enough to receive three or more Major Arcana cards, it means that God and Goddess has decided to guide you in the upcoming year since you have already gone through too many challenges during the past year. You will be guided on the right path and given the information or intuitive insight needed to succeed and get on with your life in a positive manner. It is your job to let the Querent know what is going on in her life and what help, if any, will be forthcoming in the way of guidance from God and Goddess.

The more Major Arcana cards that appear in the spread, the more positive this year will be. In essence, it tells you that it will be a great year ahead although yesterday back a year (and sometimes longer than a year), the cards indicate that life was very difficult and overwhelming. The Querent also had to deal with many obligations, hardships, responsibilities and upsets. These people need to know that potential hardships are at an end and wonderful opportunities and positive energy will be forthcoming.

For instance, when pulling 12 cards, note that they can also be used for answering questions for the 12 months of the year instead of asking specific yes/no questions.

Basically, there are three ways to read these cards when answering questions after a year ahead reading.

- • If you have a Major Arcana card regardless of it is upright or reversed position, the answer is yes. The reversed card will represent the second half of the time frame that was used in the question. If it were a month, the second half of the month would be indicated as the time frame.

- If you use the basic upright and reversed positions for the cards, upright means yes; reversed means no.
- Lastly, your intuitive interpretation. What does the card mean to you regarding the question that was asked? This is the most difficult interpretation, but when you feel comfortable with the cards it tends to be very accurate. Do not interpret the cards to tell your Querent what you think she would like to hear. Always tell the truth as compassionately as possible.

The Four Minor Suits

Here are simplified explanations of the four Minor Arcana suits. You will notice that I repeat information from time to time. I believe the more times you read or hear something, the easier it will be to remember.

For instance, I am taking a refresher course in German on audio CDs. This particular method uses repetition and in the following lessons, they repeat many of the phrases from previous lessons. After a while, I was getting annoyed. I said to myself, "Yes, I know how to say . . ., we said that about one hundred times already." As the lessons progressed, I realized that I was fluent in the previous lessons so I went along with the program. I'm sure you will find that repeating information throughout this text will be beneficial.

- Wands represent Fire Signs in astrology, which are: Aries, Leo and Sagittarius. Wands generally represent the fire traits of enthusiasm, adventure, a positive ego, fun loving, travel-oriented, keen interest, and caregivers to many. They take over a situation at the drop of a hat and like to be needed and wanted. Fire signs like to be needed.
- Pentacles represent Earth Signs in astrology, which are: Taurus, Virgo and Capricorn. Pentacles generally represent the earth traits of being grounded and centered, stubborn, persistent, great at detailed or behind the scenes work, education driven, intelligent, nurturing of those they love and family oriented.

- Swords represent Air Signs in astrology, which are: Gemini, Libra and Aquarius. Swords generally represent the air traits of a balancing act, handling too many things at once, being great communicators, lovers of knowledge, interested in the unknown or like to uncover mysteries. Air signs are very people oriented, very adaptable, multitalented and has a kind of go with the flow attitude.
- Cups represent Water Signs in astrology, which are: Cancer, Scorpio and Pisces. Cups generally represent the water traits of being too emotional and empathetic, too compassionate and much too sensitive. They relate to others on an emotional, intuitive or spiritual level. Being very artistic, creative, innovative and probably into the arts in some form, this element seems to be a little more cultured in some areas than the rest of the traits.

Lastly, add the four mundane or everyday suits (Wands, Pentacles, Swords, and Cups) and interpret the cards by what the figure(s) in the cards are doing, not doing, holding or not holding, etc., and start asking the following questions until you come up with your own questions or personal method in the future. You can use these questions for the general overall interpretation of the year ahead by seeing how many figures in the cards are on a solid foundation, etc., or you can use the following questions for each card.

(You always read the cards from the Reader's (your) point of view as they are set up in front of you).

- Is the foundation solid and grounded or is it water showing a foundation of emotion and sensitivity?
- In which direction is the figure in the card looking (past, present, or future)? If the figure in the card is looking to the left from the Reader's point of view, he is looking backwards or to the *past*, the wrong direction. If the figure in the card is looking directly at the Reader in the middle of the card it is now the *present*. If the figure in the card is looking to the right, it means he is looking ahead to the *future* or in the right direction.
- Are the figures happy and celebrating or do they look sorry for themselves or desperate?

Putting all the associations together gives the Reader a very good indication of the cards' meanings. Readings do become more intuitive each time you practice, but it still amazes me that the meanings seem to be somewhat different or varied each time you use the cards. I find that this happens in my own readings. In this way, it means that you are making progress in the understanding of the cards. No two readings will be identical and you should just let spirit speak through you and have confidence in yourself to actually tell the Querent the information you received. Also, you should reread the chapter on Interpretation of the Cards for a more in-depth question list to help you with your understanding of the cards.

COURT CARDS

The Page

- He represents a youthful child and innocence. It also indicates a new beginning of a journey or adventure in the suit it represents (i.e., Wands – careers, health and education; Pentacles – financial security and abundance; Swords – arguments, conflicts and decisions; and Cups which represent love, happiness, joy and inner peace).
- This card represents the beginning of an experience or event involving that suit or you can say that you have moved about one quarter of the way on this issue. Let us use a pie, for example. If it is one quarter eaten, then there are three quarters left. This is just the beginning so be prepared for more adventure and surprises along the way and do not let my references to pie make you hungry!

The Knight

- He represents a teenager of either sex, youth, action, or daring personality.

- This card continues the journey from the page in the suit that was chosen. You are now half way through the situation or new beginning. Now half of the pie is eaten or gone.

The Queen

- She represents an adult female, family, and mother. The card also indicates that the journey is nearly completed and you should tie up the loose ends quickly because things will be resolved soon. The pie is almost completely gone.
- The journey or adventure in the suit chosen is three quarters completed. You are a pro in your chosen field or in the situation that you were dealt. The Queen represents that you are almost over with all of the issues and troubles that you have had.

The King

- He represents an adult male, father, boss and authority figure. It also indicates the completion of your goal, dream, ambition, aspiration or adventure. So now the pie is one hundred percent eaten. It must be time to get another pie, right?
- The journey or adventure in the suit chosen has reached its conclusion. So now, it is making you ready for your next new beginning with another Page.

How do the Court Cards let me know where my client/student/Querent is in his or her goal or adventure?

Let me state this in an easy fashion, by example. We are talking about the Page, Knight, Queen and King of Cups. Cups represent love, happiness, prosperity, and joy, inner peace, guidance, strength, wisdom, self-confidence, self-esteem and everything else to make you happy. So how do the court cards work in cups?

- The Page may represent when you first meet a romantic significant other or someone new in your life.
- The Knight represents when the couple is dating and getting to know each other. They are falling more deeply in love.

- The Queen is perhaps a discussion of being exclusive with each other or an engagement. They are planning a future together.

- The King represents marriage. Remember, in the early 1900's when this deck was invented, living together was not socially accepted or possibly not even thought of at that time, so the King could represent marriage and/or living together.

Now does this make more sense to you? It works equally well for each suit.

- Wands represent one's health, career and education.
- Pentacles represent finances, financial security, prosperity and abundance.
- Swords represent conflicts, arguments, misunderstandings, obligations, responsibilities, obstacles and issues.
- Cups represent love, happiness, prosperity, and joy, inner peace, guidance, strength, wisdom, self-confidence and everything else you need to be happy, inner peace, guidance, strength, wisdom, knowledge and everything that can make you happy.

Concentrate and do not mix up the Court Cards with the Major Arcana. Court cards have the names of the Page, Knight, Queen or King written on them and always mention a suit such as the wands, pentacles, swords, or cups.

The Major Arcana cards have one or two words on the bottom of the card indicating the main figure or theme of the spiritually guided cards, such as: The Magician, The Hermit, The Empress, The Moon, Temperance, Strength, etc. This can be confusing since in some of the Major Arcana cards, the minor suits are represented in the drawing of the card, but it is never mentioned on the card. However, if you see a representation of one of the suits, but do not see the name of the suit on the card, then it is a Major Arcana or gifts from God and Goddess.

TYPES OF SPREADS

CELTIC CROSS SPREAD

THE TRADITIONAL MEANINGS and placement of the cards are as follows:

FIRST CARD: The Significator, Querent or Sitter

SECOND CARD: A problem or obstacle crossing you.

THIRD CARD: Foundation card.

FOURTH CARD: The past.

FIFTH CARD: Crowning card.

SIXTH CARD: The future.

SEVENTH CARD: Emotions.

EIGHTH CARD: Influences around you.

NINTH CARD: Hopes and dreams.

TENTH CARD: Outcome.

My meanings and placement of the additional cards:

ELEVENTH CARD: Additional insight card.

TWELFTH CARD: Summation of all the cards.

TWELFTH The above interpretation of each card is if you need further clarification of an area of life that is being affected. As a beginner, you should get the feel of the spread and read it as a whole experience for now. If you need to clarify the various parts of the reading, you can always do so at a later time when you feel more comfortable with reading the cards. Read the cards in general. Clarify things even more by using the cards for the months of the year. Start with card #1 as the current month and then continue with the rest of the months in the year. This is very handy when one does not want to do a yes/no spread.

One can look towards the month and answer a particular question with the upright/reverse position, Major/Minor Arcana positions or Intuitive Insight as stated before in the three ways you can read the cards.

I modified this spread since the original Celtic Cross Spread has only ten cards so you cannot do "a reading by month" or get information for one full year with the old method. My method still has the same meanings of the original cards but adds some added insight cards into the year ahead spread.

CELTIC CROSS DIAGRAM

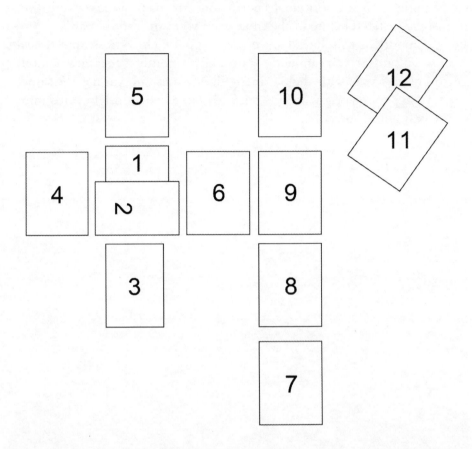

Use twelve cards instead of the traditional ten because if your Querent wants to ask a question about a specific month, it is easier to look at the card representing that particular month than doing a yes/no spread. Remember to start counting with Card #1 as the current month, not with January.

ASTROLOGY SPREAD

THIS IS A wonderful spread for individuals with some knowledge of astrology because the cards are spread out like the natural or natal chart. They represent the sun signs and house meanings, or you can even use the house numbers as the months of the year just as was described in the Celtic Cross Spread. In this respect, you can decide whether you would like to use the 12 houses (listed below) or the 12 months of the year or combine the two and get a really in-depth reading for your Querent.

House 1 - THE INDIVIDUAL, THE EGO and YOUR ENVIRONMENT

The body, health of the native, personality, individuality, one's physical appearance and ability, change of one's location, one's characteristics, one's disposition, outlook on life, mannerisms, temperament, self interests, personal affairs, and attitudes.

House 2 - MONEY and POSSESSIONS

Possessions, money, losses and gains, earning capacity, financial security, giving and receiving, ownership, profit, prices, stocks and bonds, wealth, incomes, debts, budgets, and assets.

House 3 – COMMUNICATION, SIBLINGS and SHORT TRIPS

Communication, brothers and sisters, neighbors and short journeys, commuting, cars, contracts, information, gossip, ideas, lectures or lecturing, memory, news, rumors, speech, writers, and writing.

House 4 - HOME LIFE and MOTHER

Home, beginning and ending of life, one's birthplace, father (or mother), land, buildings, environment later in life, farms, gardens, gardeners, hotels, motels, illness, old age, old people, outcome, real estate, and estates.

House 5 - ROMANTIC LOVE, CHILDREN and CREATIVITY

Creations (children), pleasure (including sexual), artistic endeavors, baths, bets, casinos, cinemas, concerts, courtships, creativity, entertainers, games, love affairs, parenthood, social parties, procreation, recreation, sports, theaters, vacations, gambling, and the laws of chance.

House 6 - HEALTH and YOUR JOB

Employees, work (your actual job), health (maintaining it), small animals, cleaners, clothing, cooks, labor(ers), nutrition, nurses and nursing, physicians, police, servants, tenants, therapists, dogs, and Army or armed forces.

House 7 – MARRIAGE, PARTNERSHIPS AND LAW

The mate, business or marital partnerships, rivals or open enemies, opponents, divorce, contracts, fiancées, fugitives, nephews and nieces, spouse, wife, husband, contests, and alliances.

House 8 - DEATH, OCCULT and YOUR SPOUSE'S MONEY

Death, occult, inheritances, alimony, insurance and insurance companies, legacies, life after death, rebirth, regeneration, reincarnation, bankruptcy, debts, debtors, graveyards, heirs, IRS, taxes, and wills.

House 9 - HIGHER EDUCATION, LONG DISTANCE JOURNEYS, FOREIGNERS, RELIGION and PHILOSOPHIES OF LIFE

Advertising, churches, attorneys, colleges, college students, foreigners and foreign lands, imports/exports, legal affairs, metaphysics, prayer, publications, rituals, ships, spirituality, spiritual happenings, workshops, lectures, and seminars.

House 10 - CAREER and STATUS IN LIFE

Career, father, authority, bosses, dignity, employment, esteem, fame, famous people, popularity, promotions, public standing or appearance, reputation, and vocation.

House 11 - HOPES, DREAMS and WISHES, GROUPS and ASSOCIATIONS

Friends, dreams, hopes, wishes, groups, large crowds or associations, clubs, associates, companions, corporations, parties and memberships.

House 12 - SECRETS OR SELF-UNDOING, SPIRITUALITY and CONFINEMENT

Confinement, institutions (jails, hospitals, nursing homes, rehabs, etc.), self undoing, secret enemies, sorrows, secret love affairs, anxieties, asylums, blackmail, bribes, charity, cheaters, crime, deception, disappointments, fear, fraud, grief, karma, limitations, losses, meditation, affirmations, and poverty.

Of course, these particular meanings that I had chosen are only a fraction of what each house stands for. As a beginner, you can just use the bolded general meanings after the house number. Then later, you can fine tune your readings to add more depth and insight into your interpretations.

My daughter always uses the astrological spread when we do private parties or corporate events. When I asked her why she did this large spread in a venue where our time frame was limited to five or ten minutes, she explained that everything was there. If the Querent had a question about finances, she would look at the card in the second house position which represents money, wealth, finances, etc. If the Querent were interested in health, she would then give an explanation of the card that was in the sixth house position. If the Querent wanted to know if she was going to get married, she would look at the card in the seventh house position and so on. This is an ingenious way to do a reading. You never have to shuffle the cards more than once. Doing a yes/no spread for each question takes time, so you would be able to read much more information if the spread were stationery. All the information the Querent could possibly want is before you.

On the next page is the diagram for the Astrology Spread.

Notice cards #13 and #14; they are called "Added Insight Cards" which are pulled if the last card is a negative looking one, such as The Devil, The Tower, Death, The Three of Swords, The Ten of Swords, the Five of Swords, The Nine of Swords, etc. This gives the reading a positive ending and also gives more insight into the reading that was just done. No, it is not cheating. The Added Insight card gives the conclusion of what will happen if the client takes your advice. Pull as many as you need to get a really positive one and read them over quickly; however, spend time on the positive last card. Never leave anyone upset or confused by the reading.

ASTROLOGY SPREAD DIAGRAM

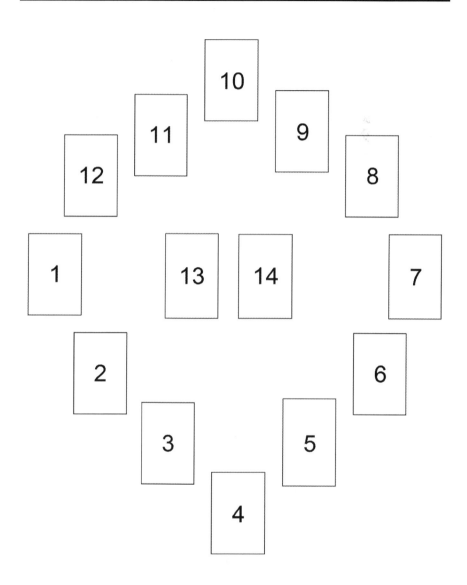

How to be a Tarot Detective

YEAR-AHEAD SPREAD

THIS IS THE easiest of all the spreads for a beginner to learn and understand. You shuffle as usual and then draw at least twelve cards, more if that last card is viewed as negative. They are placed in a simple fashion: three cards across and four rows down. The benefit of this spread is that you may answer questions regarding specific months without doing additional yes/no spreads. This is the spread I frequently use since I invented it (as far as I know) and I love its simplicity as well as its in-depth perceptions.

If you are using the spread to see what will happen to you in each month, start with the first card as the current month and not January and continue through the months until the next year.

As with other spreads, if the last card looks like a negative card, even though you may know it to be a transformation or change card for the better, draw more cards until you get a positive one. These additional cards are called added insight cards. I usually only pull up to 21 cards; however, upon occasion I draw more depending on the client. Always end on a positive card and a positive note. People are getting a reading for guidance and the knowledge that things will get better in the near future. They know how negative their life is already - that is why they came to you for guidance in the first place. Also explain what they can do to counteract each "negative" card so you arm them with options and solutions for upcoming concerns and events.

This spread as with many of the others can be used in substitute of yes/no spreads if they relate to specific months. Count the first card as the current month, even if it is the last day of the month, and continue across to the second, third, etc., card until you get to the month in question.

You can use upright and reversed cards for your answer. Upright means YES and reversed means NO. You can use Major/Minor Arcana as a yes/no as well. Major is YES and Minor is NO. Then there is the one which is a bit trickier and will take lots of practice and patience. It is the one where you would use your own intuitive insight. This should only be done when you have been reading tarot for at least several years. Even if you think you can do this after reading the cards for six months or a year, take my advice. Never put yourself out on a limb by giving information that may be wrong. Use the tried and true methods that I have explained. However, if you use the journal to track your predictions and it works for you, then by all means use the intuitive insight method.

YEAR-AHEAD SPREAD DIAGRAM

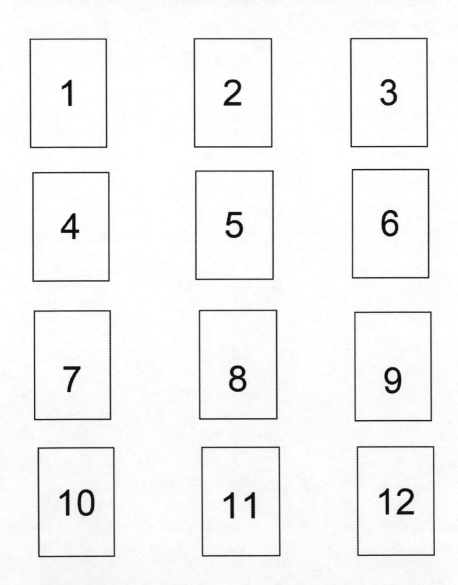

Added insight cards are placed off to the right of the twelve cards or anywhere that makes you feel comfortable. You may draw up to 21 cards in total.

For the four overview steps, remember my friend, Annie Halls' method:

CRUMS: Color, Reversed/Upright, Majors and the Minor Suits.

Do not use the added insight cards for the four overviews. Use the twelve cards for the year-ahead spread for month by month readings or a general year-ahead reading as well. Of course, just like with any other spread, you can use the yes/no method of the cards as well to answer questions without reshuffling.

YOUR OWN SPREAD

YOU CAN DEVISE your own spread. Anything you feel comfortable with is fine. After all, you are working with the universal energies and can decide if you prefer one of your own spreads over the traditional ones. For instance, you may just want to draw one card for a particular issue. Or you may wish to draw 3, 6, or 12 cards. You may wish to only draw four cards, one for each season, or 12 in 4 rows of 3 which I call the Beginner's Year-ahead Spread (previously noted). Whatever you choose is appropriate. Just be consistent.

Remember that you can also shuffle as usual and then spread out the cards in a long line with your left hand across a dining room or coffee table. Let your left hand feel for any variances in temperature (coolness or warmth), your hand may be drawn to a card or you just feel as if this is the card you have to choose. Place three cards on top of the line and yes, please turn them over. You would be surprised at how many times students and clients have asked me that question. I always tell them, "This is not a psychic course, so yes, please turn them over so we know what energies we are dealing with." Sometimes your hand will be drawn downwards towards a certain area of the deck. Do whatever you intuitively feel is the correct way to choose your cards. This simple spread below is started from the bottom, then going up to the next level, you place the first card on the left and then across to the right. Repeat until you have as many rows as you feel comfortable with.

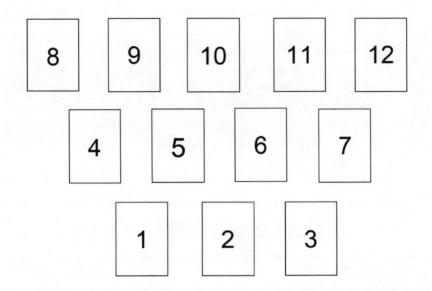

SIMPLE CROSS SPREAD AND DIAGRAM

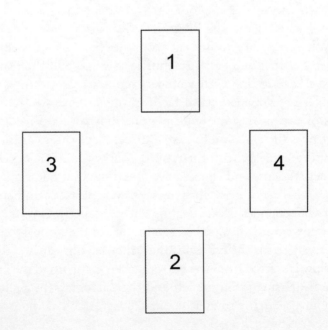

Rev. Vikki Anderson

1. Can be used as a Crowning Card (like an umbrella protecting you for the year) or the Querent.
2. Can be used as the Foundation Card or The Concern. (It can also be used as this card is what you have to deal with your situation).
3. Can be used as the Past or represents The Issue at hand.
4. Can be used as the Future or The Outcome of the issue or circumstance.

If you wish, you can swap the 1 and 2 positions above. See which one works better for you. I have used this spread both ways and it seems that whichever way I use it at the time is the best method for the questions or insight I had needed to help others. The universe works with you, so it is pretty hard to make a serious mistake unless you just are not paying attention.

NAME SPREAD

THIS IS ONE of the easiest spreads you can do and it is a lot of fun. After shuffling the cards, say the alphabet out loud until you come to the first letter in your name. Put those cards underneath the whole deck and continue with the second letter of your name, etc. Once you have all the letters of your name counted out and the cards in front of you in a straight line, you can read the insight available for your particular question or timeframe and get a good idea of what is coming up for you.

For instance, if your name is Victoria, but you usually go by Vikki, then I would use Vikki. If you feel that your full name represents you and prefer others to call you by "your full name," then you would spell out your full name. The cards drawn would be equivalent to the number of letters in a particular name. Decide whether you are going to use just a first name, formal name or complete name with surname.

So, I would pull the cards in order starting with A, B, C, D, E, F, G, H, I, J, K, L, M, N, O, P, Q, R, S, T, U, and then deal V as my first card. You would do this over and over again until the name is spelled out. Remember to put the cards that you have counted through at the bottom of the deck, so that they may be used again otherwise there may not be enough cards for your name to be properly spelled out.

To be more creative, you can spell out the person's full name for an in-depth reading. This will take longer than usual to deal the cards, but the results are worth it.

ONE CARD SPREAD

THIS MAY BE the most simple and yet hardest spread of all. There is one card. What does it mean to you? What is the textbook meaning? Is it reversed or upright? Is it a Major Arcana card meaning this can be a spiritual matter or is it a minor card which refers to a mundane issue: love, money, problems or career? Was this one card spread done for a day, a month, or a year? Was it pulled from a deck on your (or the Querent's) birthday representing an issue that should or must be dealt with during the coming year. Make all the notes you can about this card since it is the only indication you are relying on for advice. Give it your total attention and be a tarot detective. Notice what the card has to say. Better yet, what does the card have to tell you? The backgrounds, figures, symbolisms and colors are extremely important in this one card spread. Use them. Rely on the questions that were previously mentioned to gather more details and insight into the card's meaning.

YES/NO ACE SPREAD

- Shuffle the cards in your usual manner. Then cut them with your left hand into three piles. Shuffle each pile and then put them back into one pile in any order you wish.

- Then count up to twelve (12) in each pile or until you get an Ace. Once you get an Ace or 12 cards, you start a new pile and start counting again.
- Remember, there are only 4 Aces in the deck of seventy-eight cards, so I find this yes/no spread to be exceedingly accurate.
- For instance, your first pile could be 12 cards, the second pile could be 12 cards, but your third could be 3 because your third card was an Ace.
- You can have 3 piles of 12 cards or even three piles of one card each, if all three cards were Aces.
- Aces indicate a "yes" to your question.

Three Aces indicates	=	definite yes or 100%
Two Aces indicates	=	most likely or 60-80%
One Ace indicates	=	slim chance or 25-50%.
No Aces indicates	=	definite no or 0%

SEE NEXT PAGE:

You would draw 12 cards in three piles even if you pulled an Ace. This is not the Ace spread so the Aces do not matter. Deal 12 cards in each pile. Read the top cards. How many are upright? How many are reversed? See next page.

This can also be used for added insight into someone's life for the next year. The top cards would be interpreted which should give insight into your Querent's issues and concerns or insight into the upcoming year.

YES/NO SPREAD
WITH ACES

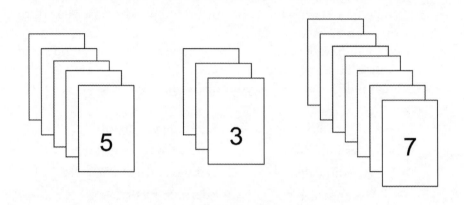

YES/NO SPREAD
REVERSED - UPRIGHT

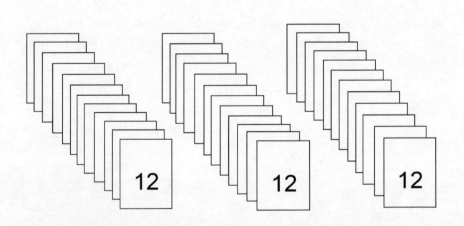

YES/NO
REVERSE-UPRIGHT SPREAD

Shuffle the cards in the usual manner. Then cut them with your left hand into three piles. Shuffle each pile and then put them back into one pile in any order you wish.

Count out 12 cards in each of the three piles no matter whether or not you deal an Ace. This is not the Ace spread, so Aces do not count this time!

After the cards are dealt, read the upright or reversed cards for the yes/no answer.

Three (3) upright means	=	definite yes.
Two (2) upright means	=	most likely.
One (1) upright means	=	slim chance.
No (0) upright means	=	definite no.

YES/NO SPREAD
MAJOR AND MINOR ARCANA

THIS IS A very simple form of Yes/No.

- Simply shuffle your cards as usual until you feel comfortable asking your question as specifically as possible including time frames, names, and your good intent.
- Make three piles with your left hand and shuffle each pile individually.
- With your left hand, put the cards back into one pile.
- If you have a Significator present, then give the cards to her.

- She will shuffle the cards like you or any way she wishes.
- When the Significator gives back the cards, cut the deck into two piles.
- Ask the Significator to put her hand over both piles. Which one does she feel she is supposed to choose?
- Turn over the top card in that pile.

A Major Arcana card = YES

A Minor Arcana card = NO

It does not matter whether the cards are upright or reversed, but rather only if they are a Major or Minor Arcana. Remember, upright cards show that the issue will happen from now throughout the next six months; reversed cards mean the issue will happen from seven to twelve months from now.

Here is a sample question:

Would it be in my best interest (or if in a partnership and it involves you partner) would it be in our best interest to . . . (Fill in the blank)?

(Move, change employment, get into a relationship with Curtis, end my relationship with John McKayla by next month, marry Tyrone by the end of this year, or move to Europe for my work within the next three months? There are so many questions everyone wants to know.) Put a time frame to every question so you know when your "answer" will take place or happen.

- Shuffle as usual.
- You can do the same spread as the yes/no with the two piles listed above.
- With your left hand, feel the vibrations of each pile.
- Choose one pile and flip over the top card of the pile just chosen.
- Whatever the card is, study it and notice the particular issue that is relevant to you during this time. The risk would be to handle that issue in a very positive and confident manner so you could get on with your life and leave negativity, a negative person or situation behind you.

BIRTHDAY SPREAD

A GREAT WAY TO celebrate your birthday is to get guidance for the year-ahead by shuffling your cards and pulling out one single card. This would represent the intricacies of your next year, unless you do something to change the path or choices.

Shuffle as usual. Spread the cards out on a table or large straight surface in a straight line. Let your left hand glide over the cards so that you can feel the energy being emitted by them. You may feel a slight pull towards a particular card, heat or coldness. Everyone reacts differently to the cards so you should practice on family and friends to see how the cards react to you.

Pull out the card from the deck in any way you wish and place it above the line of cards. Is it upright? This would represent a more favorable year in the suit or meaning of the card drawn. Reversed? It may indicate delays in getting the result of the card drawn. Read it exactly the way it was drawn from the deck and that particular card will be your "issue" for your birthday year. A birthday year is from your birthday from this year until your birthday next year. Obviously, you should pull this card as close to your birthday as possible if you cannot actually pull it on your birth date.

THREE CARD SPREAD

S HUFFLE AS USUAL. See Birthday Spread above and copy it; however, this time, remove three cards from the line. You will do this by guiding your left hand over the cards from left to right. You may do this several times if you do not feel the energy in all the three cards you need to pull with one pass over the line of the cards. Stop and pull a card when you feel you should. You may feel cold, heat, a pulling of your hand towards a certain card or just feel as if you should stop and pick the card. You can detail the events or circumstances that will be on your mind for the next year. You can use this as a Yes/No Spread as well. Just decide ahead of time what you are using this particular spread for so the universal energies work with you to give an accurate reading.

When the Yes/No spreads are done and you do not like the answer, many ask, "Can I change the outcome?"

Yes, they can be changed. We all have free will and freedom of choice. A good example is a friend of mine who had a sister who had a nervous breakdown. Her doctor fell madly in love with her, and this was the best thing (in her family's opinion) that could have happened to her. My client (her sister) was worried that the sister would change her mind about her relationship with the doctor because of her confusion and indecision. The cards came out "slim chance," that she would marry this doctor. My friend asked, "What can I do to help this marriage take place?" We know she will be happy if she married him; she's just afraid.

My advice was simple. If you want her to get married and you think you have to make the decision for her, you must get her interested in wedding dresses, look at reception halls, visit caterers, and ask whom she would choose as bridesmaid if she were getting married and the colors she would choose for their dresses. My friend took my advice. Her sister got married after going through all the steps I suggested above and is living happily ever after. You must use good judgment on how to help others. I knew my friend for many years and also knew she had the best of intentions for her sister. I, in turn, was giving my best insight possible to help them in this situation and it worked out well.

If you see something very negative, perhaps about health or death, you should not divulge that particular information. You are not God and Goddess or Go. We cannot upset and scare people (like the charlatans that scare people to remove curses for ridiculous amounts of money) regarding this very serious subject. In fact, if we were wrong, imagine the pain and mental suffering we could put someone through. What I always say is "When was the last time you had a checkup?" Most people get anxious and reply, "Why, what do you see? Am I going to get sick?" I calm them down and say; "I do not really see a major health problem. However, I think that if you have not had a physical exam for some time, now would be a good opportunity to get a clean bill of health. If by chance something is found, it will be remedied quickly and without further complication."

PAST, PRESENT AND FUTURE SPREAD

Past	Present	Future
1	**2**	**3**

EXAMPLE: OUT OF a clear blue sky, my younger sister Rose asked for a tarot reading. I did not like what I had seen regarding her health. I used the same technique as I would have on anyone else and asked her when she saw the doctor last. She replied about 2 or 3 years ago. I suggested she make an appointment. She asked when, and I said tomorrow. That very night, she found a lump in her breast and immediately made an appointment. The lump turned out to be nothing, but many tests were done to see why she was not feeling well. Being an Aquarius, she had not told the family that she was not feeling well for some time. We later found out that the five arteries to her liver were engorged with blood and were ready to burst - she possibly had a week to live if she had not gone to a doctor. The operation followed within a couple of days and was a success (I determined the astrologically beneficial date, of course), but part of her liver had to be removed as well as her gall bladder which was filled with blood. If she had not asked for a reading, or if she had not gone for these medical tests, we may not have been able to plan the family outings and get-togethers with her that we have enjoyed since that time and I would have lost the best friend I ever had! (Aren't I a good sister?).

My advice is to study each card and see what it represents to you. Jot down your feelings and observations. Add or delete your thoughts to the meanings of the cards until they feel correct to you. Eventually, the precise meaning of each card will evolve *FOR YOU*. Be patient and do not try to force the meanings; they will come. As long as you do readings for the good of all involved, with love, compassion and integrity, you are heading in the proper direction toward spirituality and enlightenment.

If you are doing a tarot house party or a corporate event, a great way to make the line move is to shuffle as usual, and then let your Querent shuffle. Make one pile and then fan out the cards in a long line. Let your Querent pick out three cards and read them. This would take approximately five minutes, but if you do not make the five minute quota, then you can ask about their birthday and give them their Karmic Lessons as well.

DAILY CARDS

A VERY PREDICTABLE AND crazy phenomenon in new tarot students is that they pull a card each and every day. It is a good way to learn the cards; however, it is too much information for someone who does not know all the intricacies of the cards to think that you will have a betrayal from a friend today or that you are going to grieve over something that happens or that a new job opportunity is coming today! Use a card a day for 78 days as a learning tool and a way to concentrate on the different energies of the cards and not for predictive purposes. Notice the colors of clothing on the figure in the card. What are they doing? Are there castles in the cards? Water? In which direction is the main figure looking: past, present or future? You know how to do this, so with practice it will become second nature.

Once you are more experienced, you can pull a card each and every day to concentrate on the issues of that particular day. Even though that would be a wonderful mental discipline, it is not necessarily appropriate for "the beginner" since you may not know the exact issue you must handle at this time which is depicted by the card. You may try pulling one card a week or one a month and work with those energies until you feel more comfortable with the cards and their meanings.

A better idea would be for you to pull a card every day after the deck has been shuffled properly and ask for guidance to have a good day with positive opportunities for the good of all involved. I never recommend pulling a card a day. Get your one or two tarot readings per year and that is more than enough information to deal with rather than worrying about what else is going to happen today. It is rare that people pull all the good luck or positive cards, so pulling a card a day may instill more fear, anxiety and negativity than was anticipated.

Then what you could do is write all of the impressions you have gotten from the card including the feelings, meanings and images you have felt after you have chosen the card. Eventually, you will start to know that every time you pick that particular card, these feelings, etc., would accompany you. It is also appropriate to read your notes on your cards when you do a reading for someone or are just looking for a little insight for yourself.

A recent trick I taught students is to get a deck as a class deck. Buy a black Sharpie pen and write some key words on them that represents the card to you. This of course will not be used in regular readings, but you may use this method if you are just starting to read or are a beginner. It gives you clues as to other meanings which will lead to other insights, etc.

When you are ready to read, whether it is for money or not, you will use another new deck without your cheat sheet. By drawing a card and reading your notes, you will be able to gather the information of the cards quicker and easier than before. Why did I just bring this thought up at the end of the book? Well, if I told you to do this at the beginning of the book, would you have read through the rest of the book?

QUICK REFERENCE SECTION
THE MAJOR ARCANA

THE FOOL

THE FOOL IS a card that we use for new adventures, going in different directions and trying to take that leap of faith that you are going on the right path. It is a card about taking a risk and being okay with the risk because you are ready to change your life and move on from the issues that you are currently enduring. Remember to use The Fool as the last card if you are working on numerology.

THE MAGICIAN

You must overcome your giving nature because you are being spread too thinly. You must become assertive and passionate about what you want out of life, and reach for your goals, objectives and dreams. If so, you will have all the love, prosperity, happiness, a wonderful career and a resolution to all of your conflicts. Everything is on the table for you just waiting to become a reality. The scepter is bringing spirituality and enlightenment down from Above through you so that you can help others with your new knowledge and wisdom. The eternity sign over your head shows that you are already a very spiritual person, but will be going further into spirituality, metaphysics, esoteric teachings or religion. You will be helping those in need, but must make sure you are protected from negativity and depression of others. You will attract many despondent and unhappy people along the way and you must make sure that your optimism and altruistic tendencies stay secure.

THE HIGH PRIESTESS

It is as though you are everyone's therapist. Everyone talks to you and dumps all their negativity on you. You have mothering instincts and energy and although you feel comfortable with that, it gets to be overwhelming. Everyone trusts you with their secrets and deepest thoughts and after awhile, it becomes a liability. You listen attentively, but also know that at some point, you must release their negativity. You must limit your help and tend to your own emotional needs and sensitivity. You may not have many people to talk to, but you attract those who need to unburden themselves and you are the lucky winner! Take a day off from stress occasionally so that you can rejuvenate and revitalize yourself. Helping others is a wonderful service; however, if it makes you upset, boundaries must be set.

THE EMPRESS

This is the best mother in the world card, but also this is someone who has learned not to be so giving that she does not fulfill her own needs. She is creative, spiritual, artistic and inventive and tries to help her family and friends develop their creativity. The Empress is remarkable with children and knows how to set boundaries although she does have a super soft spot in her heart for them. She takes control of many situations and thinks she has to protect everyone. Although she is quite intelligent and logical, this is not the case where her children are concerned. She should teach her children all she knows in the arts and in thinking "outside of the box." This is a person who would help anyone with a problem even before thinking about herself and is someone totally dedicated to making her children the upright standing citizens they will become.

THE EMPEROR

This card usually represents a man, but may also represent a woman, who needs to be in control of everything and thinks he knows best in every situation. An Aries card, this person needs to feel important and tells everyone how to run their life. He can't express his feelings very well, but wants the best for those he loves. His beard shows wisdom, so we know he is knowledgeable and intelligence. He just has forgotten how to communicate with normal people including family members and tells people what to do. Perhaps the lesson here is to listen more and get a broader point of view. The message is about showing the ones you care about that you truly love them, not by you telling them what to do so they do not make a mistake; it is about showing physical love, closeness, hugging, and constantly building up other's confidence in themselves.

THE HIEROPHANT

This is someone who puts himself above others or has a better position than those around him. He needs to balance his spiritual and mundane life and listen to those around him. He is a very spiritual person and needs to help those around him with all of their fears, doubts, worries, anxieties and indecision. Others look up to him for guidance and assistance. He may need to stop being a sucker (being too giving, caring, loving, kind, generous, honest and helping everyone who never help him back in return) and become more adamant, strong, assertive, aggressive while using his intelligence and logic to get his points across to the masses and to balance many energies and issues for all. He has stopped at least three times (see the cross's vertical lines) to handle mundane or family issues and now is going back on a spiritual quest.

THE LOVERS

I do not consider this a positive Lover's card and use the Two of Cups for that purpose; however, this represents a couple both naked, which means they are both naive, innocent, vulnerable and innocent and may not understand what the other is doing or how they think. Angels are blessing them and the sun is bringing in positive energy to help them. The mountain connotes a major issue that will always separate them, but with compromise anything will work.

THE CHARIOT

This is the worst procrastination card in the deck. The man is going nowhere fast in his cement chariot and the sphinxes trying to move him forward are waiting around for a decision to be made. They cannot go anywhere because he does not know what he wants to do. With his back towards the castles (indicating home life, love, happiness and joy), he wants to run away from responsibility, but then knows he should deal with his obligations. Thus, this is why it is called the procrastination card. Guilt always plays a part in this card which keeps him from moving forward to a better and less complicated life.

STRENGTH

There is much procrastination in this card. Being you are a big sucker, you let others take advantage of you over and over and do not stand up for yourself. You also trust too many people and use your own standards to judge others. No one is as honest and good as you, so you need to see reality that others may be dishonest or untrustworthy and deal with them accordingly. Do not tell anyone anything that you don't want spread around the world in the next five minutes.

THE HERMIT

You are a spiritual teacher and help others in so many areas but you do not take your own good advice. You shine the light for others, help them, give them advice, and counsel them as you become exhausted. You keep their negativity and worry about their well being while the energy is being drained out of you. Help those who really need it, and spend more time in nurturing yourself. Get rid of that gray cloak you are wearing, move to the future and find your own light.

THE WHEEL OF FORTUNE

This is a great card to get everything that you need in life. If you get more wisdom and knowledge (classes, lectures, seminars, reading, training, or formal education, etc.), if you are more persistent and tolerant, call upon your inner strength and courage and take appropriate risks, you will get everything that you need to survive in this world and be happy.

JUSTICE

This is the only legal card in the deck, so there may be a court case coming up, a speeding ticket or signing of contracts/leases. You may be dealing with a lawyer. The other meaning is that you are too fair and accommodating to others and that it is time to stand up for yourself and get what you want out of life. It is no fun being the one who always has to help others and you are getting tired of it. You feel as if you are not appreciated and you want to change many things around you.

THE HANGED MAN

This card is an interesting one since it asks you to look at things from another perspective. It is showing you are intelligent and logical; however, you need balance now more than ever. You need to be more assertive and let the compassionate, sensitive and emotional self go. Balance in finances is also mentioned. You are actually handling more mundane matters now and not dealing with the spiritual. You must decide what is best for you.

DEATH

Even though too many people use this as a physical death card, I rarely do. I use it as a way of life or a transition card. You are moving from one point in your life to the next step. It is a card which signifies the letting go of others "as if they were dead" because they have taken from you for far too long and have given you nothing in return. You must move forward without them. They are users and takers and you have had enough. You are moving quite slowly on the horse to the future, but you are going in the right direction. The two castles in the future indicate that there will be double the love, happiness, prosperity and joy, etc., which should be significant since the sun is shining between them.

TEMPERANCE

There you go wearing white again so we know the sucker energy is present! You are making matters worse by trying to balance emotions with the cups and water. You are making the water more upsetting by pouring it between the cups. You are causing your own emotional issues and although you are being blessed by angels, you do need to deal with your procrastination issues or you will not move forward.

THE DEVIL

In my opinion, this is the worst card in the deck. It denotes the Querent (person for whom the reading is being done) is chained to a negative person or situation and finds it hard to leave. The couple in this card is wearing self imposed chains so at any time you may take them off, open the door underneath the Devil and escape to a better life. You may try as hard as you can to help this person or change this situation, but in the long run, nothing will change and you will be left with all the negativity. Leave the negative person and finally you will see that (s)he will have to take responsibility for his or her own life and rebuild their lives.

THE TOWER

This is another volatile card; however, I use it as the "go with the flow" card. When you think the worst day of your life has happened, I suggest you "go with the flow" because God and Goddess (or whomever you believe in) wants better for you than you already have. You may think you know what you want, but Spirit knows better than you. You will be surprised at all the blessings you will get from this change once you actually admit that the change was in your best interest.

THE STAR

The vulnerability of the Querent is apparent by her being nude. Her foot in the water denotes she is causing her own emotional problems. The white stars are spiritual knowledge stars showing her that she has to at least make one major decision intellectually and logically. Her emotions are betraying her. Procrastination is an issue. She can't decide. See how she is balanced between the two jugs of water being poured out - water is emotion, so she is confused and unbalanced regarding an issue. If she does not handle the emotional issue now, there are five ponds being made in the future instead of the one now she has to contend with.

THE MOON

This is a great card for creativity and artistic ability. This is a wonderful card for writers because her imagination can run wild. The sun/moon combination suggests that the Querent sees what she wants to see and hears what she wants to hear, but it is not always the truth. She must get out of the water (emotion) and take the path of intelligence before she can get to the mountains in the background to get to her opportunities and blessings from God and Goddess.

THE SUN

This is a vibrant card which shows that the Querent is going towards the future in a new and exciting way. She leaves the past behind the stone wall and those issues will not hurt her ever again. The sunflowers mean that there are many new ventures, journeys, beginnings and new roads ahead. She is starting life like a baby - with high ideals and wonder. The sun is bringing vitality, energy and optimism to this new venture.

JUDGEMENT

The judgment card (spelled incorrectly for our time, but was correct at the time the cards were made) suggests that the person for whom the reading is being done is too much of a giver and needs to learn the lesson of becoming a receiver. You have done as much as you can in the world and now you need to be rewarded for your kindness to others. Say, "Yes, thank you," when someone offers you something so that the angels can also assist you by helping you reach your goals. Your first test is accepting help from humans - then angels will automatically be there for you as well.

THE WORLD

This card is very much like the The Wheel of Fortune. See description above. The only real difference between the two is that after you do everything you are supposed to do, you have everything that you need and want as well. You are becoming more spiritual and are surrounded by prosperity and abundance.

THE MINOR ARCANA

ACES

THESE CARDS ARE gifts from God and Goddess in the suit they represent.

- **Ace of Wands** is a gift from God and Goddess in protecting your job or giving you the opportunity for a better one, help you with your education or training courses, and will bless your health.
- **Ace of Pentacles** is a gift from God and Goddess in your financial security, how you make money, how much money you spend and keep, and possibly means that you may obtain a winning lottery ticket or get an inheritance. (Lottery is a fleeting idea; however, if you were ever going to win, it would be when this card was drawn. If you did not win, then do not waste any more money on buying tickets in the future!)
- **Ace of Swords** is a gift from God and Goddess in resolving your conflicts, problems, obligations, etc. You would also resolve any arguments or fighting you have had with others.
- **Ace of Cups** is a gift from God and Goddess in your love, happiness, prosperity, and joy, inner peace, guidance, strength, wisdom, self-confidence and everything else you need to make you happy. You meet the love of your life or things change so that everything in your life is going in the right direction and you are totally happy. This is the best card in the deck and you will be very blessed in the year it comes out in a spread for you.

How to be a Tarot Detective

WANDS – FIRE

WANDS REPRESENT SEVERAL things, your career, your education and your health.

Court Cards time events in the suit they represent. They have their own meanings, of course, but basically:

- **The Page** represents a new beginning or 1/4 through the venture, so The Page initiates a new job or looking for a new position, health issue or formal education (training, certifications, lectures, seminars or workshops to take or teach).
- **The Knight** continues the action of the new beginning or 1/2 way through the venture. The Knight learns the job and gets all the information she needs to do her job properly. It can also be a learning curve about your health issue (interviewing doctors or surgeons, or going a holistic or nutritional route) or finding your place in your new school, etc.
- **The Queen** is almost at the top of this new venture or 3/4s of the way there. The Queen knows what she is doing and is comfortable at the job and now people come to her for advice.
- **The King** has finished the objective of the job, health or school issue. The King is now in charge of the position or has people working under him. Of course, this can mean that the King is now the owner or Chairman of a company as well. The decision has been made about your health care or you may have already had surgery or whatever the help or support was to be and you are getting healthier as time moves forward. If it relates to school, you have either graduated or will be graduating very shortly with good grades and possibly honors.
- **Ace of Wands** is a gift from God and Goddess in protecting your job or giving you the opportunity for a better one, help you with your education or training courses, and will bless your health.

Two of Wands II

This card represents you looking out into the world to see what your next move might be. You are holding onto a job for security purposes and the paycheck and not because you like it any longer. You are looking to the left (or past) so are not going in the right direction with your job (or education). Your health may also be an issue; however, there is a wand in the future which you do not see yet and the mountains in the future show that you will get your goals once you look outside of the box.

Three of Wands III

This card represents being in the middle of your job, education or health issues and you are standing on a cliff, a very precarious position. You have everything you need to make a good decision and eventually will pick the wand (opportunity) in the future and be happy. You have money and are passionate about your life, but are still looking for more opportunities.

Four of Wands IV

This is a dualistic card meaning love, happiness, prosperity, and joy, inner peace, guidance, strength, wisdom, self-confidence and everything else you need to make you happy, inner peace, guidance, strength, wisdom and knowledge. It also can represent an engagement or relationship going to the next level - sometimes it means marriage. It also represents your career which is on a firm foundation and will become prosperous and abundant. This is the second best card in the deck.

Five of Wands V

This is a competition card. You are vying for a new position and have equal competition. You are on firm ground and will get the position that you really want. The competition cannot compare to you. You have confidence, are the best candidate for the position and your personality shines through to get you the job. Don't be afraid to be a bit assertive during this time.

Six of Wands VI

This is the victory on the job card. You are going in the right direction, are above everyone else (which can mean a promotion or having people report into you) and are seated on green for prosperity. You have the laurel wreath on your head and on your wand indicating your success. This can also be used for a successful education or if your health was not the best, it shows it will improve. It may also represent a successful operation.

Seven of Wands VII

Even though you are quite intelligent and logical, you are trying to keep your balance within work, school or with your health. You are wearing green so money is not the issue. You have the potential to do well, but your fear of failing will keep you "off balance" for some time. Believe in yourself and your abilities and all will work out for your best interest.

Eight of Wands VIII

You have too many tasks or responsibilities now and you are trying to handle them all at once. When suits go "down" in the future, they become more troublesome. Prioritize your goals and objectives, chores and responsibilities to one a day, or one a week, let others help you with your responsibilities or put some on the back burner and return to it another time. This may affect your health because you are too exhausted and just do not have the time to take care of yourself. Rest.

Nine of Wands IX

This is a card which tells the Reader that you have been hurt on the job, probably not physically, but by snide comments, gossips or innuendo. You are holding on to your job for security and are afraid to let go of it while behind you there are many more opportunities that will make your happier and bring you much more prosperity. The green mountains reflect the many choices and opportunities you will have if you take the risk and change your work life for the better.

Ten of Wands X

You are overburdened by your responsibilities; however, you are going into the future, but at what cost. Your feet are not planted firmly on the ground and although you feel that things are going well, you wish that you had more time to enjoy your life and spend time with your family, loved ones or friends. You need to let go of some of these responsibilities for now and only handle the most important ones that will make your life easier now! You are intelligent and logical, but for some reason, you are being a sucker now and have decided you need to handle everything for everyone. That will wear on your health; you need to rest and take care of yourself.

PENTACLES – EARTH

PENTACLES REPRESENT YOUR financial security, your prosperity and abundance, your money, your possessions and your attitude about these issues.

Two of Pentacles II

This is the card that I tell clients not to use their credit cards - they are spending much too much and will get into a financial hole. You are trying your best to balance your finances, but are not doing a good job. There is too much instant gratification going on from your point of view - you need everything now. Buy what you need and not what you want for now so that you can deal with paying off your debt. The lower Pentacle in the future denotes money problems and the water in the background indicates that this time will be like an emotional rollercoaster unless you immediately deal with the issue.

Three of Pentacles III

Try not to be a sucker at work and do much more than you are getting paid to do. It is a cooperation card and suggests that you not stand out at this time because you will be taken advantage of. You are the only one on the bench which means you can fall off and get hurt. Be careful, take your breaks and your lunch and do what you can do within your specific work day and try to limit volunteering to do other projects. They will only make you tired and won't help your career growth.

Four of Pentacles IV

This is someone who is a miser or is so afraid of spending money to get the things he needs because he is afraid that his finances will suffer. The message of this card is that you have all the money for everything that you truly need (rent, mortgage, food, clothing, repairs, car maintenance, and monthly expenses) and if you have to spend your money to get these projects done, you will still have enough leftover to feel secure.

Five of Pentacles V

I call this the "leech card." You are trying to cover up your compassion, empathy, sensitivity, sympathy and emotional self. You want to go into the right direction, but others are pulling you back with their sad stories or need for your help in every aspect of their lives. You need to let go of people who always take from you and give you nothing back in return and find people who will give you reciprocal energy. You are tired, and want to be free of issues that are not your own. You must learn how to receive from others by simply saying, "Thank you," when something is offered.

Six of Pentacles VI

You are the one in blue waiting to be treated fairly by a boss, father or someone who controls your money or financial well being in some way. The trick of this card is others will get more than you or a better promotion, etc., but you have to be a professional and congratulate the person who gets more. You are being watched to see how you react in specific situations; eventually, you will get all that is due you and you will get much more than you originally thought.

Seven of Pentacles VII

This card brings with it fears, doubts, worries and anxieties about your financial future. You think about the past and how your life was better, more fun, more interesting, etc., and when you had MORE. Concentrate on the future or your money and financial security will be reduced. You are trying to become more grounded, centered, secure and stable in finances, but nothing will come of your worry and fear about your financial future.

Eight of Pentacles VIII

This card shows how many jobs you have had in your life and how many different things you can do to make a living. You are concentrating on one job now and do not see the other job behind you that will be in your future. It can be another full time job, part time job or home based business. Your back is towards the castle which means that you are not there as much as you would like, so your family relationships may not be what you wish them to be. Your artistic or creative nature helps you think of many different ways to work smarter and not harder.

Nine of Pentacles IX

This is an intelligent woman who knows how to handle her money; however, this card indicates that she needs to balance her finances more at this time and also needs to take a financial risk. Her money will not be as abundant in the future if she does not change something in the way she deals with her finances. The castle in the future indicates that she will have love, happiness and prosperity and joy and must learn how to keep that state of mind and not worry about her finances.

Ten of Pentacles X

This is someone who has done everything they had planned to do to get to their financial goals. There may be a couple who sees money differently and this is a problem within the relationship. There is fidelity and honesty within this card and the older figure is someone whom you trust who has the money you need if you must borrow for a particular reason. You will be blessed with finances but just know that you may also have to borrow to get your finances in order and then straighten out everything at another time.

Court Cards time events in the suit they represent. They have their own meanings, of course, but basically:

- **The Page** represents a new beginning or 1/4 through the venture, so The Page initiates a new job or looking for new money opportunities.
- **The Knight** continues the action of the new beginning or 1/2 way through the venture; therefore, The Knight contemplates on what he should do with his new found money.
- **The Queen** is almost at the top of this new venture or 3/4s of the way there. The Queen is concerned about her money, but knows there is enough to do what needs to be done.
- **The King** has finished the objective, dream, venture, project, aspiration, journey or goal. The King is doing very well financially and has all the money he could possibly need for financial stability and security.
- **Ace of Pentacles** is a gift from God and Goddess in blessing your financial security, prosperity and abundance in all things.

SWORDS - AIR

SWORDS REPRESENT CONFLICTS, problems, responsibilities, obligations, obstacles, concerns, issues and worries. They can also indicate aggressive attitudes or fighting.

Two of Swords II

This person is wearing white, the sucker color so we know she is being taken advantage of by others. She is too giving, caring, loving, kind, generous, honest, etc., and now feels as if it is better to live in a world where she sees what she wants to see and hears what she wants to hear. Even though the swords are up with means that you can handle anything that comes your way, they are crossing her heart which indicates that she is afraid of getting hurt again. Emotions run deep in the water depicted behind her and even though there are mountains moving off to the future, she does not see the opportunities to change her life, so she does not get them.

Three of Swords III

Occasionally if this card comes up in reference to heart problems, it can indicate that there will be a medical issue. Usually, it means that the person will be betrayed three times in the time period of the reading (usually one year) unless the Querent stands up for herself and confronts the one causing her pain. Once this is done, the other two times never happen. The rain in the background indicates crying and the gray indicates the fears, doubts, worries, anxieties, etc., that the Querent is feeling during this time.

Four of Swords IV

This card has many interesting explanations. One explanation is that you need to pray or meditate more on what you truly want - the stained glass window has the word PAX in the upper left hand corner indicating through prayer or MEDITATION/AFFIRMATION, you will find peace of mind, body and spirit. The other meaning can be that there are many issues over your head that need a decision or need to be handled. You are to deal with only the most important issue (below you) and handle that. Once handled, the other ones will be changed enough so that they are more easily taken care of. It warns once you make an intelligent or logical decision indicated by the yellow, do not change your mind or your choice will be wrong.

Five of Swords V

See the streaking clouds - they mean you are in an argument or dispute now or in the very near future. The man's swords are up saying that he can handle anything that is given to him. He can also win at least two of the issues and the one he is holding is undecided at this time. The water indicates that these are emotional issues. The message of this card is to be a gracious winner or he will lose everything he has gained.

Six of Swords VI

The people are going to a new life - leaving the turbulent emotions to a much calmer and better new beginning. Family and friends help to get the Querent there. Usually, the person inside the boat is the Querent. She is covering herself with a very grounded, focused, and stable cloak as she wishes that all of her problems would just go away. Many times, children go with her. (This could be a single mother starting over as well). She will now take all of her issues with her but can handle them one at a time until her life is the way she wants it to be.

Seven of Swords VII

The first color on the man is white underneath his tunic, which means he is a sucker. He is headed into the past (the wrong direction) with many swords. These can be thought of as family and friend issues and problems and he is trying to handle them all. He keeps looking to the right of the card (the future) at the two swords which are the projects and perhaps the life he would like to have but he can't do anything with his dreams or goals since he is so busy dealing with everyone else's. He may be able to juggle many things in life, but at this point, he is overwhelmed and should concentrate on accomplishing only a few things at a time.

Eight of Swords VIII

This is a self made prison card. She is afraid to make any type of move because she feels her life will be worse. She is already standing in water causing her to be her own worst enemy; her hair is black so we know she is thinking in a negative fashion and her heart is bound which indicates she is afraid to love or trust again. The gray sky brings in all that negativity of fear and doubt, etc., but what she needs to know is that if she handles one issue on the right of her and perhaps one on her left, the other swords (problems) will be resolved or concluded. The lovely castle in her future, bringing love, happiness, prosperity, and joy, inner peace, guidance, strength, wisdom, self-confidence and everything else you need to make you happy, etc., is there for her if she tries to look past her fears.

Nine of Swords IX

This is basically the "insomnia" card and usually it is not because of an illness. It is because the person is thinking of all the issues and worries above her (swords) and her mind keeps racing so she can't sleep. Her hair and clothing are white (the sucker color) so she even thinks in a way that keeps her at a disadvantage. She cannot face all of her issues any longer, but continually tries to be helpful to everyone in her life. The black background is negativity, the weight of the world on her shoulders and obsession with these problems. She needs to be strong and start weaning people away from her or to simply be strong enough to say "no."

Ten of Swords X

When my daughter was three, she called this the Swiss cheese card. Even though it looks ominous, it has a good meaning. It shows that the worst is over and you are starting a fresh life. Your head is facing the future new energy and opportunities will come into your life. The water is calm now so emotions are grounded and the mountains across the back of the card indicate that there are so many wonderful opportunities for you to have, but you have to grab them or they will pass you by. You are using your intelligence like the dawn to push the negativity away from you.

You can time events with Court Cards. They have their own meanings, of course, but basically:

- **The Page** represents a new beginning or 1/4 through the venture or The Page initiates or protects himself from a new conflict, obligation, responsibility or argument.
- **The Knight** continues the action of the new beginning or 1/2 way through the venture as The Knight charges backward without looking where he is going and will probably make a mistake, but he is in the mess so does not know what else to do.

- **The Queen** is almost at the top of this new venture or 3/4s of the way there. The Queen is looking forward to the future and although she can defend herself, she would like to be friendly towards everyone and have peace.
- **The King** has finished the objective of the venture, journey or project. The King is balancing the energy of all the conflicts and resolutions and keeps negativity in check. He is compassionate, but not afraid to use his intelligence to get his way or win the battle.
- **Ace of Swords** is a gift from God and Goddess in resolving your conflicts, problems, obligations, etc. You would also resolve any arguments or fighting you have had with others.

CUPS - WATER

CUPS ARE FILLED with love, happiness, prosperity, and joy, inner peace, guidance, strength, wisdom, self-confidence and everything else you need to make you happy. If the cup is on its side, it means you have lost these things or are mourning for their loss.

Two of Cups II

I use this card as "The Lovers" card, much better than The Lovers in the Minor Arcana. This couple is looking at each other which mean that there are no lies, deceit, secrets or dishonesty between them. There is total love from the cups. Cups show love, happiness, prosperity, and joy, inner peace, guidance, strength, wisdom, self-confidence and everything else you need to make you happy, etc., and they are both suckers for each other, so one of them is not being taken advantage of - they are both happy to help the other. The wings mean that angels are blessing them and the Caduceus which shows that it is a healthy relationship. Notice the green mountains in the background showing financial security and the home meaning more love, inner peace, guidance, strength, happiness, etc.

Three of Cups III

This is the celebration card. It can be looked at in two ways. One is that she is celebrating with friends or family about a certain event (sometimes the birth of a child or engagement). There is fruitfulness around you (meaning prosperity) so it can represent a new job, promotion, new venture, etc., where you will be more financially stable. The second way to look at this card is that she is getting financially secure now and has turned from a sucker (giving, caring, loving, kind, etc., person) in the past in to a person who is taking control of her destiny wearing the very assertive and grounding colors of red and orange in the present. In the future, she is covering up the white color with yellow or gold explaining she will deal with issues in a very logical or spiritual way. She no longer will have the door mat syndrome in her life. She is more in control than in the past.

Four of Cups IV

This man is contemplating his life and does not want to accept a gift from God and Goddess (the universe, or whomever that person believes in) because his life is going well and he does not want to upset the apple cart. His money will keep growing in the future. All the cups are upright showing love, happiness, prosperity, and joy, inner peace, guidance, strength, wisdom, self-confidence and everything else you need to make you happy, inner peace, guidance, strength, wisdom and knowledge and everything that could make him happy. His first instinct was to say no to the gift, but once he thought about it, he accepts it and his life gets even better.

Five of Cups V

This is sometimes called the widow or widower card as it sometimes means that someone has passed and he is mourning the loss. It could be the loss of a pet as many families consider pets just like children. Mainly, this is a man who is stuck in negativity and is looking towards the past where many issues and concerns have hurt him. He does not see the positive future because he is stuck in the past. He also is covering himself with black, one of the worst negative colors, so it will take some time before he gets over this depression, negativity or feelings of despair. The water makes his emotions turbulent and even though there is a castle in the cards, he is not looking at it which would bring him all that love, happiness, prosperity, and joy, inner peace, guidance, strength, wisdom, self-confidence and everything else you need to make you happy, etc.

Six of Cups VI

This card represents someone who is gullible, innocent, naive and vulnerable who thinks everyone is as honest and trusting as himself. The woman is two faced (notice the extra face in her hair) and wears a glove which signifies there are hidden truths that are not being told to him at this time. The man is giving a cup of love, happiness, prosperity, etc., and will be disappointed. See the last victim in the left of the card walking away after being the target of this woman in the past. He is the next victim. He must use his intelligence to overcome any deceit or dishonesty. The message is to not tell anyone new in his life anything that can be used as gossip or hurt him in any way until he absolutely trusts the person.

Seven of Cups VII

The man is all black because he is attracting negativity because he has not been able to make a decision. He has many decisions to make, but he is procrastinating and not moving forward. If he continues to be overwhelmed with his choices, he will continue to stay in the same negative environment with life getting worse. Only like energies attract, so if he makes at least one major decision, he can be placed into a positive energy field where like energy will help push him into a bright future.

Eight of Cups VIII

This is normally considered the divorce card. If the Querent is not married, it could be a breakup of a relationship or that he is bored with the way things are. He's going to the future to experience life, have fun, do new things, take a few chances and have a grand adventure. His life is boring in his eyes and wants a different life for the time being. It can sometimes mean that he goes off to find another woman to have fun with, and realizes that what he really wants is home with his wife and children. However, by this time, it's too late and he will be going through a divorce. The large black mountain in the future is not positive and the sun/moon combination represents living in fantasy land (mid life crisis) and never really sees the truth.

Nine of Cups IX

This is the "I'm satisfied with everything I have," card. Yes, he still is wearing white; however, he has a red hat and is crossing his chest (heart) so he will be a sucker only up to a point and then will set boundaries. The yellow and blue indicates a better balance between his emotions and intellect so in essence, he can make better decisions. He has the cups behind him filled with love, happiness, prosperity, and joy, inner peace, guidance, strength, wisdom, self-confidence and everything else you need to make you happy, etc., which he is protecting. Everything runs smoothly, all are happy and blessed at this time.

Ten of Cups X

This is the Happily Ever After card. The couple is facing the house giving them everything they need to be happy, the children are healthy and happy as well and life is good. Emotions are calm and rational and life goes in a very positive direction. Happily ever after is different for everyone. Usually if someone asks how many children they will have, this indicates at least two. Someone else may want a vacation home, an expensive car or a world-wide cruise. It all depends on what the Querent considers happily ever after. This card indicates that within the year, they will have the option to live their dream, if they wish.

The Court Cards time events in the suit they represent. They have their own meanings, of course, but basically:

- **The Page** represents a new beginning or 1/4 through the venture. So, The Page gets involved with a new romantic significant other or partner and is looking forward to the whole "love" situation unfolding before his eyes.
- **The Knight** continues the action of the new beginning or 1/2 way through the venture so The Knight indicates that the

couple will get to know each other by dating, spending time together, learning about each other's interests, likes and dislikes and what makes their partner tick.

- **The Queen** is almost at the top of this new venture or 3/4s of the way there. The Queen looks forward to their future together whether there is a possibility of moving in together or getting engaged.
- **The King** has finished the objective of the venture, journey or project. The King indicates that there will be a forthcoming marriage (you will at least be asked or will be doing the asking, but it does not necessarily mean that the person will automatically accept.) Living together in tarot is also considered a marriage since living together was not even considered when this deck was invented in 1908. At its best, this card is about planning the rest of your lives together.
- **Ace of Cups** is a gift from God and Goddess in your love, happiness, prosperity, and joy, inner peace, guidance, strength, wisdom, self-confidence and everything else you need to make you happy. You meet the love of your life or things change so that everything in your life is going in the right direction. This is the best card in the deck and you will be very blessed in the year it comes out in a spread for you.

ASTROLOGICAL HOUSE INTERPRETATIONS

1. Yourself, the personality you show to the world and your environment growing up.
2. Your money, possessions and how you deal with finances throughout life.
3. Siblings, short distance travel, communication, computers and family in general.
4. Home life, home life environment, and your relationship with your mother.
5. Fun, gambling, speculation, children and romantic love.

6. Service to others, health, exercise, diet, health in general and your work ethics.
7. Marriage, partnerships (both business and personal), living together, law, lawyers, speeding tickets, court cases, leases, contracts, and relationships in general.
8. Occult, death, IRS, inheritances, your spouse (or significant other's) money.
9. Higher education, long distance travel over oceans, foreigners, philosophy and religion.
10. Career, your status in life and the relationship with your Father.
11. Fun, groups, associations, hopes, dreams and wishes.
12. Secrets, secret enemies, secret love affairs, any place of incarceration (hospitals, nursing homes, jails, rehabs, etc.), metaphysics, esoterica and spirituality.

ASTROLOGICAL SUN SIGNS

Aries 3/21–4/19
Suit: Wands
Element: Fire
Quality: Cardinal
Symbol: The Ram
Ruling Planet: Mars

KEYWORDS: BABIES OF the Zodiac, initiators, doers, need to be in the limelight, educated, out spoken, aggressive and can be loud and sometimes tactless. They are usually "A" type personalities and want everything done yesterday. They have little patience for stupidity and can usually do things better themselves than waiting for others to do something for them.

Taurus 4/20–5/20
Suit: Pentacles
Element: Earth
Quality: Fixed
Symbol: The Bull
Ruling Planet: Venus

Keywords: Stubborn, persistent, works behind the scenes, likes organization and making lists, loyalty and fidelity towards family and friends. Can tend to be lazy if she is not interested in whatever she is doing. These are very nurturing people, if you are on their good side. Otherwise, they can be your worst nightmare. They are unforgiving or if they do forgive you, they will never forget what you had done to them and your friendship or relationship will never be the same.

Gemini 5/21–6/21
Suit: Swords
Element: Air
Quality: Mutable
Symbol: The Twins
Ruling Planet: Mercury

Keywords: Spontaneous, go with the flow, versatile, artistic, creative, quick thinkers, can change their minds frequently and very eclectic. These are the scattered, action oriented, talkers of the zodiac. They need personal interaction and would rather be in a people oriented job than being an accountant or person who works alone in a warehouse or at a desk with little or no contact with others.

Cancer 6/22–7/22
Suit: Cups
Element: Water
Quality: Cardinal
Symbol: The Crab
Ruling Planet: Moon

Keywords: Family oriented, security minded, nurturing, great mothers, extremely sensitive, shy at first, and one of the nicest people of the zodiac. They are called the "Mothers of the Zodiac," and not just because they are good mothers to their own children. They very often take the place of a mother to others when giving out their sage advice or listening to others' tales of woe.

Leo 7/23–8/22
Suit: Wands
Element: Fire
Symbol: The Lion
Ruling Planet: Sun

Keywords: Robust, likes to talk and be the center of attention, very dramatic, not too forgiving, will give you the shirt off of their back, helps everyone unless someone tells them what to do (and then you will be ignored). These people love you or dislike you and no matter what you do, it is hard for them to change their minds. They are one of the most generous of all the signs and will help you with anything that you need unless you tell them that they have to do something – and then it will be on the bottom of the list of their priorities. Don't cross this sign – you will be very sorry that you did.

Virgo 8/23–9/22
Suit: Pentacles
Element: Earth
Quality: Mutable
Symbol: The Virgin
Ruling Planet: Mercury

Keywords: Intellectual, analytical, organized, everything done in the proper order, follows policies, can be a bit too critical and nagging, need to always be right and backs it up with facts, would rather do jobs in the background such as accountant or organizer, and is always ready to tell you what you did wrong! They tend to be a bit of know-it-alls at times, but do have a thirst for knowledge and not only in their field. They love to learn and may even be perpetual students.

Libra 9/23–10/22
Suit: Swords
Element: Air
Quality: Cardinal
Symbol: The Scales
Ruling Planet: Venus

Keywords: Too giving, caring, loving, kind, generous and honest and have a hard time saying no, even when they want to. This sign in particular has a very difficult time with decisions and procrastinates a lot. They do not wish to rock the boat, so many times do not do what they really want to do, but rather they do what they think is expected of them. I call these people the suckers of the zodiac because their whole life is a combination of what others want and trying to balance their needs as well, which never goes over well. The mature Libran can set boundaries and limitations, but some actually get physically ill if they have to say no to someone.

Scorpio 10/23–11/21
Suit: Cups
Element: Water
Quality: Fixed
Symbol: The Scorpion, Phoenix or Eagle
Ruling Planet: Pluto

Keywords: Secretive, non-sharing, family oriented, nurturing, aloof, you'll never know everything about this person, they do not like to chit chat, do not waste time, everything is calculated for the best outcome or benefit for him or his family. Money as security in the bank for the family is of paramount importance. This is one sign that you will never know fully and they like it that way. It's like pulling teeth when you need to know something. So never ask them a question that can be answered with a simple yes or no because that's all you'll get.

Sagittarius 11/22–12/21
Suit: Wands
Element: Fire
Quality: Mutable
Symbol: The Centaur/Archer
Ruling Planet: Jupiter

Keywords: Fun-loving, traveler, helpful, artistic, creative, clowns of the zodiac, explorers, insightful, optimistic and freedom-loving. These people love to be able to leave for an unknown or unplanned destination at the drop of a hat. They love their independence and the men of this sign many times love their friends more than their family. Always ready to help others, this sign is friendly, helpful and considerate unless they speak before their mind kicks in and then there may be some trouble.

Capricorn 12/22–1/19
Suit: Pentacles
Element: Earth
Quality: Cardinal
Symbol: The Goat or Sea Goat
Ruling Planet: Saturn

Keywords: Conscientious, wise, reliable, patient, ambitious, career oriented, career builder, needs to be in charge (especially at work) because control of a situation is very important. Good organizer and manager. This sign is great at helping projects move from the beginning to end, but may have some problem delegating and empowering others because he is afraid if there is a mistake, others will think that this was his responsibility.

Aquarius 1/20–2/18
Suit: Swords
Element: Air
Quality: Fixed

Symbol: The Water Bearer

Ruling Planet: Uranus

Keywords: Friendly, people oriented, altruistic (to a degree), humanitarian, has tons of friends, loves to blend in with friends, family usually comes second (especially with the men of this sign). Some Aquarians do not know how to do manual labor around the house or yard, but can talk your ear off about things he read on the web today. You may find yourself bored listening to the endless drone of the upcoming weather or news reports that may not be of interest to you. The women of this sign are nurturers, helpful, can take on many responsibilities around the house, with family the yard and at work. They are the true Aquarian ideal.

Pisces 2/19–3/20

Suit: Cups

Element: Water

Quality: Mutable

Symbol: The Fish

Ruling Planet: Neptune

Keywords: Intellectual, rebellious, independent, altruistic, unconventional, scattered, chatty, spiritual or religious, have an insatiable desire to know things that are of interest to them. Many are artistic whether it is in the arts, acting, singing, dancing, music, etc. They bring beauty to the world and oftentimes teach the arts to share their love of creativity, beauty and artistic ability. Fun to talk to and once you get them on track, you will learn a lot from this sign about compassion, empathy and love.

Remember, there are horoscope general dates for each sun sign and every year there may be different ones. Because we have 365.25 days in a year, the sun signs may go back or forward a day or two in any given year. Even if the current year has different dates for your sun sign, you are always the sun sign you were born.

PLANETS

THE PLANETS ARE listed in order. The luminaries or lights (sun and moon) are always listed first.

Sun
This luminary rules Leo, the lion.

28 days in each sign

Keywords: The person, the ego, the individual, vitality, power, dignity, confidence, arrogance, conceit and egotism.

Some other keywords for the sun are the desire for achievement, ambition, bragging, celebrities, children, creativity, entertainment, father, famous people, fame, gambling, gold, husbands, leaders, the principles of life, oxygen, things of pleasure, politics, politicians, speculation, the stage, and Sunday.

Using the sun as the center of the universe in a natal chart is called a heliocentric chart or sun based chart.

Moon
This luminary rules Cancer or Moon Child.

Time in orbit: 29 ½ days
2 ½ days in each sign

The feminine power of the moon represents emotions, thoughts, illusion, delusion and mother energy. It is a creative energy force which also controls your subconscious mind. The moon is sensitive, very compassionate, empathetic and sympathetic. It represents the God and Goddess energy, nurturing, caring, love and intuitive insight.

Keywords: rules the subconscious, responses, domestic matters, emotions, moods, inconsistency, oversensitivity and introversion.

Some other keywords for the moon are beaches, averages, boats, breasts, childhood environment, crowds, emotions, evening, females, fish, fluids, glassware, insomnia, mother, navigation, the public, sea, sensitivity, silver, sleep, water, wife, and women.

Mercury
This planet rules two sun signs: Gemini,
the twins and Virgo, the virgin.

Time in orbit: 88 days
7 days in each sign.

Keywords: The conscious mind, communication, intellectual and education matters, expression, criticism, restlessness, indecisiveness, nervousness and tension.

Some other keywords for Mercury are accounting, accuracy, advertising, advice, agreements, air travel, amnesia, animals, architects, asthma, authors, brothers and sisters, charts, computers, conferences, conversations, cousins, critics, dictionaries, diet, doctors, employees, hygiene, insomnia, journalists, languages, letters, libraries, magazines, mentors, neighbors, nerves, pencils, pens, pneumonia, printers, publishers, readings, schools, telephones, textbooks and travel.

Venus
This planet rules two sun signs: Taurus, the bull and Libra, the scales.

Time in orbit: 224.7 days
19 days in each sign

Keywords: Love, harmony, artistic, pursuits, beauty, gentleness, indolence, laziness and weakness.

Some other keywords for Venus are actors, affection, alimony, artists, ballet, beauty, bedrooms, blood, brides and bridegrooms, candy, dancing, desires, drama, engagements for marriage, flowers, gems, genitals, guests, harmony, hobbies, holidays, innocence, interior decorators, love affairs, lovers, money, music, ornaments, painting, pleasures, sculpture, skin, social functions, society, treasurers, venereal diseases and women.

Earth

Most modern charts are called geocentric which means that they are based as if earth was the center of the universe.

Time in orbit around the sun: 365 days

The Earth circles the sun in approximately 364.25 days, so you need to check a current calendar each year to see if one or more of the sun signs' dates have shifted. Also, it seems to change the Spring Solstice and the Vernal Equinox by a day on either side of the traditional date. You can erect a chart that uses the sun as the center of the universe. Most astrologers use geocentric charts which mean that the Earth is the center of the universe instead of the sun.

There are no true attributes given to Earth in astrology. It is the center of our universe for a natal chart. It is also a great place to live!

Mars

This planet rules Aries, the ram.

Time in orbit: 687 days
60 days in each sign

Keywords: Energy, heat, mechanical ability, activity, aggressiveness, recklessness, accident and irritability.

Some other keywords for Mars are accidents, activity, adrenalin, adventures, arguments, armed forces, assertiveness, battles, bladder, blemishes, boxers, bravery, brutality, burglars, burns, carpenters, challenges, chemistry, cooks, courage, crimes, dentists, druggists, exercise, fire, firemen, friction, garnets, genitals, gun, head, headaches, heroes, impatience, inflammation, injuries, sharp instruments, iron, lust, machinery, males, military, murder, passion, patriotism, pornography, and rage, ted, sports, temper, tobacco, torture, violence, wars and weapons.

Jupiter
This planet rules Sagittarius, the centaur.

Time in orbit: 11.86 years
1 year in each sign

Keywords: Abundance, benevolence, optimism, happiness, development, excess, extravagance and extremism.

Some other keywords for Jupiter are abscesses, acquisition, adrenal glands, advantages, altars, attorneys, banks, Bible, blessings, blood, carelessness, censors, ceremonies, churches, clergymen, colleges and university, students, courts, customers, doctors, embezzlement, ethics, exaggeration, excellence, expensive, fat, fines, fortune, gratitude, hospitality, inheritances, judges, juries, law, lawyers, passports, peace, philosophy and philosophers, physician, races, religion, teachers, textbooks, travel, trust, truth and voyages.

Saturn
This planet rules Capricorn, the sea goat or goat.

Time in orbit: 29.5 years
2 ½ years in each sign

Keywords: Patience, coolness, caution, organization, aspiration, limitation, coldness, pessimism, loss and depression.

Some other keywords for Saturn are aches, agriculture, anxieties, apprehension, bankruptcy, bereavement, burdens, chiropractors, conservatives, crystals, darkness, debts, deceit, elderly people, envy, farms, fatigue, fear, foundations, frost, funerals, grief, grudges, handicaps, integrity, invalids, knees, lead, leather goods, martyrs, mines, misery, mountains, old age, orderliness, organization, politics, real estate, relics, secrets, senility, seriousness, underground, unhappiness, workers.

Uranus
This planet rules Aquarius, the Water Bearer.

Time in orbit: 84.02 years
7 years in each sign

Keywords: Change, originality, individuality, inventiveness, eccentricity, rebellion, disruption, and willfulness.

Some other keywords for Uranus are abnormalities, accidents, air, airplanes, airports, astrology, automation, bicycles, bombs, broadcasting, cinema, crises, deviation, discovery, disorganization, earthquakes, electricity, emancipation, eviction, expeditions, explorations, explosives, fanatics, freaks, freelancing, fugitives, healing, homosexuals, inventions, machinery, miracles, miscarriages, psychiatrists, radio, suicides, television, tornadoes, the unusual, wires and x-rays/x-ray technicians.

Neptune
This planet rules Pisces, the two fish swimming in
opposite directions tied by a golden cord.

Time in orbit: 164.8 years
14 ½ years in each sign

Keywords: Idealism, intuition, imagination, creativity, inspiration, vagueness, impracticality, deception and dreaminess.

Some other keywords for Neptune are abstract, actors, alcohol, assassins, astral plane, aviators, baths, bottles, cameras, chemistry, cinemas, caffeine, coffee, con men, counterfeit, dancers, drama, dreamers, drugs, ESP, fish, floods, forgery, gas, gasoline, glass, hypnotism, illusions, imagination, intoxication, intuition, liquids, narcotics, occult, oceans, oil, photography, prison, private investigators, psychics, seamen, secrets, sleep, sorrows, spies, steam, water, witches, witchcraft, and yoga.

Pluto
This dwarf planet rules Scorpio, the Scorpion, Phoenix or Eagle
and is co-ruler with Mars.

Time in orbit: 248.4 years
20 years in each sign

Keywords: Regeneration, elimination, the masses, cooperation, compulsion, crime and subversion.

Some other keywords for Pluto archeology, atomic energy, calamities, coercion, corpses, cremation, crime, corpses, death, demolition, dictators, executions, filth, force, gangsters, groups, hell, horror, kidnappers, legacies, lust, mausoleums, monsters, murder, plutonium, pollution, pornography, reincarnation, rejuvenation, reproduction, reptiles, sewers, spoilage, toilets, underworld, universal welfare, venereal diseases, volcanoes, and that which is wasted.

POSITIVE AND NEGATIVE SIGNS

POSITIVE AND NEGATIVE signs do not mean that half of the zodiac is positive and half of them are negative. This refers to their polarity – masculine or feminine or positive or negative. Positive signs are masculine signs and Negative signs are considered feminine signs.

POSITIVE SIGNS

Aries, Gemini, Leo, Libra, Sagittarius and Aquarius. - Masculine

Positive signs are outgoing, friendly, talkative, interested in learning, always seeking adventure, fun, like meeting new people, travel and like to remain constantly busy and like to be center of attention.

NEGATIVE SIGNS

Taurus, Cancer, Virgo, Scorpio, Capricorn and Pisces - Feminine

Negative signs are the best parents and nurturers of family and friends. They are grounded, interested in security for the family, protection, keeping people in their lives safe, happy and financially secure. They like to remain in the background and are outstanding in research, as a support system or team member.

GLOSSARY

Air Signs

G EMINI, LIBRA AND Aquarius. Air signs are the intellectual signs, and the communicators of the zodiac. Air signs also get along with Fire signs.

Astrology Spread

This is a wonderful spread for individuals with knowledge of astrology because the cards are spread out like the natural or natal chart. They represent the signs and house meanings, or you can even use the house numbers as the months of the year.

Astrological Natal House Meanings

1. Yourself, the personality you show to the world and your childhood environment.
2. Your money, possessions and how you deal with finances throughout life.
3. Siblings, short distance travel, communication, computers and family in general.
4. Home life, home life environment, and your relationship with your mother.
5. Fun, gambling, speculation, children and romantic love.
6. Service to others, health, exercise, diet, health in general and your work ethics.
7. Marriage, partnerships (both business and personal), living together, law, lawyers, court cases, leases, contracts, and relationships in general.
8. Occult, death, IRS, inheritances, your spouse (or significant other's) money.
9. Higher education, long distance travel over oceans, foreigners, philosophy and religion.
10. Career, your status in life and the relationship with your Father.

11. Fun, groups, associations, hopes, dreams and wishes.
12. Secrets, secret enemies, secret love affairs, any place of incarceration (hospitals, nursing homes, jails, rehabs, etc.), metaphysics, esoterica and spirituality.

Candle Magick

Candle Magick is a form of magick which brings candles into a spell or wish. It is a very mild and easy way of getting better energy, more positive results or answers to your dreams and wishes in a very unobtrusive way. With candle magick, remember never to blow out your candle. You must use a snuffer or a lid that may have come with your candle. Never leave a candle unattended for any length of time. However, you should snuff it out it out if you are leaving the house or store for a period of time and then you may relight it and continue with your prayers and wish when you return. Always be safe.

- You must divide the candle into thirds so that you can burn the one candle three nights in a row. Write a spell or affirmation about whatever it is you are looking for and then put the paper underneath the candle that you are burning.
- Prosperity spells should start on a Thursday plus the two additional nights and a love spell would start on a Sunday plus the two additional nights.
- Remember, to collect the residue and bury it in your yard or a planter so it can be grounded and stay within your property to help you. However, if it is a black candle (to get rid of negativity, challenges and problems around you), then you may wish to get rid of it by throwing it in a flowing stream or river which is moving away from you (your home or place of business) so that the water will carry away all the negativity you were trying to release. In this way only positive energy will come to you.
- Use the color interpretations for the actual color of your candle and its meaning.

Celtic Cross Spread

The traditional 10 card spread to read the cards for the year ahead. Vikki uses 12 cards in order to also represent the months of the year.

Charlatans

Psychic Readers who use fear tactics to get you to come back over and over again because they tell you that there is a curse on you or your family, and they need to burn candles and say prayers for you at a cost. Stay away from these people as they will only cost you a lot of money and do nothing for you in return.

Council of Nicaea

This was a council of Christian bishops convened in Nicaea in Bithynia (present-day İznik, Turkey) by the Roman Constantine I in 325 AD. This first ecumenical council was the first effort to attain a consensus in the Church through an assembly representing all of Christendom. Its main accomplishments were settlement of the Trinitarian issue of the nature of The Son and his relationship to God and Goddess the Father, the construction of the first part of the Creed of Nicaea, settling the calculation of the date of Easter, and promulgation of early canon law.

Court Cards

Each of the Minor Arcana suits (wands, pentacles, swords and cups) have a Page, Knight, Queen and King which are referred to as the Court cards.

Cups

This suit is easy to identify because they look like chalices or cups. This suit is ruled by Water and represents love, happiness, prosperity, and joy, inner peace, guidance, strength, wisdom, self-confidence and everything else you need to make you happy. Inner peace, guidance, strength, wisdom, knowledge and everything you need to make you happy.

Earth Signs

Taurus, Virgo and Capricorn. They are the stable, secure, no-nonsense, always right people and may also be procrastinators. Earth signs also get along with Water signs.

Fire Signs

Aries, Leo and Sagittarius. They are the quick thinkers, always have to be the center of attention and may speak without thinking. Fire signs also get along with Air signs.

Major Arcana

There are twenty-two (22) cards starting with 0 The Fool and ending with XXI, The World. These are the spiritually guided cards which hold karmic lessons for you to learn in this lifetime. However, when figuring out numerology numbers, we use The Fool as the last card in the deck or number XXII because 0 cannot be used as a number.

Minor Arcana

There are 56 cards which are divided into Wands, Pentacles, Swords and Cups. These cards number from Ace through X, and then have a Page, Knight, Queen and King in each of the suits as well. Typically when using them, we normally start with the number II and place the Ace after the Court Cards.

Pentacles

The suit that looks like coins or money. This suit is ruled by Earth signs and represents prosperity, wealth and financial security in general. Pentacles have to do with finances, possessions and your attitude towards them.

Positive and Negative Signs

Positive and negative signs do not mean that half of the zodiac is positive and half of them are negative. This refers to their polarity – masculine or feminine or positive or negative.

- Positive signs are masculine signs and Negative signs are considered feminine signs. Positive signs are: Aries, Gemini, Leo, Libra, Sagittarius and Aquarius.
- Negative signs are: Taurus, Cancer, Virgo, Scorpio, Capricorn and Pisces.

Preponderance

If you have an abundance of one element or one suit in a chart or tarot reading, this is called a preponderance. This preponderance weighs the odds for or against you by the number of elements or qualities. Usually this is at least 4 planets and cards in the same sign or element.

Querent

This is the person with the questions or queries. This is the person for whom you are doing the reading. The client, friend, family member, etc., is also called the Significator. See explanation in the next paragraph.

Reversed Cards

These cards are no longer read as the opposite of an upright card nor does it mean that something bad is going to happen to you. It is an outdated notion and Readers get more positive information from reversed cards now than they did back in the 1970s.

Significator

The Significator is the person for whom you are doing a reading. This is the most significant person in the reading. Significator and Querent are interchangeable. It is your choice.

HOW TO BE A TAROT DETECTIVE

Simple Cross

Four cards are used to tell your fortune for the next year.

Swords

This is the suit that represents conflicts, problems, responsibilities and obligations and is the easiest to resolve. You handle the most important issue and the others take care of themselves.

Upright and Reversed Cards

Depending upon whether the card drawn is upright or reversed, gives us an indication of when that card's energy will come to pass. If it is an upright card, the time frame is 0-6 months. If it is a reversed card, the time frame is 7-12 months from now.

Wands

This is the suit that looks like branches of a tree. This suit is ruled by Fire signs and represents career choices, school and health. If you volunteer, are retired or a housewife, then that is still your job so you would read them as governing your job in some way.

Water Signs

Cancer, Scorpio and Pisces. They are the sensitive, caring, giving, artistic and creative of all the signs. Water signs also get along with Earth signs.

Reader

The professional who interprets the cards for someone who wants their cards read. Be sure that it is an ethical Reader or you can be taken for a lot of money with talk of curses on you and your family, and needing prayers or other devices to make you save.

Reading

The act of interpreting the cards for a client, customer, Querent or Significator, such as reading the year-ahead spread or pulling cards for answers to specific questions. Cards may also be read for any time frame you are interested in.

Symbology

The actual symbols within the pictures of the card which help delineate the meaning of a particular card.

Year-Ahead Spread

A year-ahead spread is the laying down of cards in a certain order or design pattern which foretells the most likely choices, decisions and circumstances that will happen within the next year.

LAST THOUGHTS

ENJOY THE TAROT. I am sure it will bring many happy hours and new opportunities to your life, so embrace them!

The recurring themes of procrastination, betrayal, being too caring, giving, loving, honest and not being able to say no, trying to balance a mundane and spiritual side, and all the health issue cards try to give you an understanding of what you need to do to make your life better in some way. It is up to you whether or not you heed the information. You do have free will; however, if the universe is trying to help you move in the right direction, why would you resist?

Have fun with it. Do not take it so seriously at first as your interpretations may not be precise. Give yourself enough time to learn the true meanings of the cards. I have given you enough clues to follow that it should be easy to learn. Do one clue at a time. Look at the mountains for one day in many of the cards. Another day, look in which direction the figure is facing and its meaning. Look at the color of the figure's clothing, hat, shoes, etc. You will get the concept in no time at all.

Remember, the tarot is not a game nor should it be taken lightly. It is not for children; please read this small article I wrote after having an altercation with an irate parent because I was hesitant to give her seven year old daughter a reading.

Approximately five years ago, I was hired by Nordstrom where I gave tarot readings to its clientele as part of a promotion. On the average, these types of events are fun; I give five minute tarot readings so the client can usually ask three questions or so, get answers, and then be on their way.

The event, as was the other ones for that whole week, was quite successful and I had two minutes left before I was to leave, go down to the shore and do another presentation, so my timing was critical. A very rich and snobbish woman came up to me and threw her seven year old daughter into the chair in front of me and demanded, *"She could have a tarot reading."* I looked at my watch and explained that I had to leave in a few minutes, but would be happy to answer a few of her questions. The young child had no idea what I was talking about, so I asked, "Do you want to know about school or do you want to know about any of your friends, teachers or boys?" to give her a clue about what to ask. She had a blank stare on her face (not the brilliant child I was blessed with), looked at her mother who said, "Just do it for fun." I looked at the mom and said, "Well, do you have any questions that you would like to ask for your daughter?" She then went in a tirade that her daughter was only seven and what questions could she have? My point exactly.

She pulled her daughter out of the seat and yelled, "You are rude! This is Nordstroms not K-Mart!" I was stunned. Her behavior was not appropriate to the venue or to me. I was amazed that anyone could be so clueless and not understand that tarot is not for children and it is not for fun. It is a serious modality to help people make positive choices about their futures. She stormed off, so I made sure I talked to the manager before leaving to tell her about this unfortunate incident and to my relief, she apologized for the customer's obnoxious behavior.

It actually surprised me that this parent was so totally unaware that tarot is a serious modality that should be used for older teenagers and adults and definitely not for small children. My concern was what happened if the Death card had come out, or 3 of Swords (which has three swords in a heart) or the Ten of Swords (ten swords in a dead man's back); did she want her child to see that? How could I satisfactorily explain them away when she could have seen the pictures?

It got me to thinking that maybe, if I am ever in that situation again, I could make a small deck of fake tarot cards that say cute things like FUN, VACATION, FAMILY, BROTHERS, SISTERS, BEST FRIEND, SCHOOL WORK, SPORTS, etc. to give me something to work with. Another thought would be for me to invent a child's tarot deck (unless there is one out there that I have not discovered yet). I know I could use a fairy deck, angel deck, animal deck, etc., but I am truly interested in learning if there are decks specifically created for a young child. My rule of thumb is that the person has to be at least eighteen years old. These are young adults who know what to ask. They have questions about relationships, careers, college majors, etc., and are seriously interested in the answers.

The next day when I did the promotion in a neighboring state at the same store chain, I had placed a tent card saying TAROT READINGS FOR 18 YR. OLD AND UP. There was no problem and fortunately for me, there were no rude parents and I had an enjoyable time.

You would think that customers of upscale stores would be intelligent enough to understand or acknowledge that the services that are offered by these stores are usually top notch and many times they are for adults. I am exceedingly qualified in my field and felt I knew what would be best, especially for this seven year old girl, to determine which way I should handle a reading. I am glad I had made my decision to ask for the child's questions. When doing that, the universe actually kept me from doing a reading for her whom I thought was a mistake in the first place. Always trust the universal energy to help you in any situation, as I did and will continue to do.

AUTHOR'S BIOGRAPHY

REV. VIKKI ANDERSON has been teaching metaphysics and parapsychology internationally and on cruises for forty-three years. She is a special person who has enriched the lives of many with her love, her guidance, her writings and her generosity. Throughout her life, she has been an eclectic learner of all things esoteric and metaphysical.

Her love of helping others pushed her on a path of learning as much as possible about predictive modalities and received the proper certifications to teach and practice each one. Now she certifies people in a number of modalities including tarot and astrology. Vikki teaches a variety of subjects including crystal therapy, palmistry, numerology, tarot, astrology, oracle cards, I Ching, graphology, candle magick, chakras, Feng Shui, meditation, past life regression, angels, Bible history, karmic lessons through tarot and numerology and pendulums.

In addition, she writes the monthly horoscopes column for "Inner Realm" since its inception eighteen years ago and has written many articles appearing in that magazine, on the web, as well as in newspapers and magazines. She has written an astrology column for a northern college newsletter entitled, "The Rave", and had fairytales and an astrology column in Modern Collage magazine. She also wrote the astrological comparison column for FIND YOUR TRUE LOVE, a newsletter dedicated to "personals." Vikki had published her own "It's Fairy Obvious Newsletter" in 1996, dedicated to spreading light and love about esoteric and metaphysical subjects, including fairies and angels. Many of her articles are now on both of her websites and her blogs for your enjoyment.

Vikki was a Board Member of the Metaphysical Center of New Jersey, where she was Sunshine Chairman for seven years and was the Publicity Chairperson, Website Coordinator, Newsletter Proof-Reader and Psychic Coordinator for Psychic Fairs and MCNJ Conferences for over ten years. She was also a MCNJ certified teacher of tarot, astrology and numerology. She had resigned from her MCNJ responsibilities to pursue other interests, finishing her books and handling her expanded classes. She had been involved in some capacity with MCNJ for over 30 years under Jean Munzer, Director of MCNJ for over 25 years.

Her other memberships include: The International Feng Shui Guild, The American Dowsing Association, The National Guild of Hypnotists, The Sanctuary of the Beloved and The Order of Melchizedek. She is also a Silva Mind International graduate.

She has developed a new, easy to learn tarot method that anyone can use almost immediately. In the good old days, Vikki learned tarot the old fashioned way with upright cards' meanings being positive and reversed cards being negative. With the help of her angel's guidance, she has changed most of the negative meanings as well as the additional seventy eight reversed meanings into opportunities to change one's life and start on a more rewarding path. Vikki will show you that the few cards that still display some negativity also give you answers of how to reverse its effects. In fact, each card has a special message on how to change the circumstance that is challenging you.

There was one particular pet peeve that Rev. Anderson had with many of her original teachers when she was a teenager. When she asked her metaphysical teachers why a particular card had a specific meaning, the answer she always received was, "Because it always meant that." Being very logical and able to see all sides of every situation, Vikki did not like that answer. There had to be a logical reason that anyone could figure out, she thought. She saw patterns in foundations, directions, colors and numbers, the amount of water in a card, the directions of mountains and castles, etc. This is how she teaches tarot today.

Total disconnected or robotic memorization of each card is no longer necessary in her method, but remembering what the symbolism means helps you to interpret any card instantaneously. The title of the book was chosen because, "You can be *like a tarot detective,*" by looking at the clues in each card to come up with a viable description of the person seated before you, know what is going on in his or her life and how to guide them in a positive manner so that they can make good choices for their future.

Rev. Anderson lays out the cards in a very easy format so that anyone can learn. She taught her daughter metaphysics, especially tarot and astrology, when she was only three and a half years old, so she is confident that anyone who is interested in reading the cards will learn easily. Her method is different than traditional ones, so you must let go of all of your preconceived notions about the cards. They are helpful and informative as well as give guidance and insight into your future.

The cards are not negative or evil and they are not the work of the Devil, as some people suggest (These, of course, are the Fundamentalists or Born Again Christians who take the Bible literally). If it is the work of the Devil, he must have switched careers and is working on Heaven's team as it is one of the most helpful and positive modalities we have today to help those who are troubled, confused and overwhelmed to make sense of their lives and move on in a very positive manner. The cards are also not as mysterious as many Readers or teachers want you to believe. The author of this book takes the mystery out of the cards and uses them as a divination tool to help others in a practical way.

Common quotes she receives about The Totally Tarot Method are: "Where were you twenty years ago when I was learning this?" or "If I knew it was this easy, I would have studied tarot a long time ago."

Vikki asks that you read this book and learn tarot with an open mind, caring spirit and ethical and moral intentions towards others. Tarot is not to be used to spy on people or to learn things about your family or neighbors that are none of your business. She does believe in karmic payback, so make sure you do this with a genuinely loving heart or the consequences to you may be quite nasty and unsettling.

Please enjoy this book and the information Vikki has acquired from Spirit. It has helped thousands of her students and clients resolve many of their issues and will continue to help many others. They will then find their road to positive conclusions, happy outcomes, and logical decisions to make life the one that they had always hoped and dreamed about.

Vikki can be reached for an appointment for tarot, astrology or Feng Shui or for setting up group and private classes, corporate events, private parties, lectures, workshops and seminars by visiting her websites at:

www.vikkianderson.net

www.fengshuimoon.com

REFERENCES

Rider tarot and the Waite tarot reproduced by permission of U. S. Games Systems, Inc., Stamford, CT 06902 USA. Copyright© 1971 by U. S. Games Systems, Inc. Further reproduction prohibited. The Rider-Waite Deck® is a registered trademark of U. S. Games Systems, Inc.

Printed in the United States
By Bookmasters